how2become

Psychometric Tests

www.How2Become.com

As part of this product you have also received **FREE** access to online tests that will help you to pass the Psychometric Tests.

To gain access, simply go to:

www.PsychometricTestsOnline.co.uk

Get more products for passing any test or interview at:

www.how2become.com

Orders: Please contact How2become Ltd, Suite 2, 50 Churchill Square Business Centre, Kings Hill, Kent ME19 4YU.

You can order through Amazon.co.uk under ISBN 978-1-910602-22-5, via the website www.How2Become.com or through Gardners.com.

ISBN: 978-1-910602-22-5

First published in 2015 by How2become Ltd.

Typeset for How2become Ltd by Anton Pshinka.

Disclaimer

CONTENTS

INTRODUCTION

INTRODUCTION TO YOUR NEW GUIDE

Welcome to your new guide, *Psychometric Tests*. This guide is a comprehensive testing book which provides hundreds of sample test questions that are appropriate for anyone who is preparing to sit a psychometric test.

Psychometric tests have become a prominent feature within job selection processes. Psychometric testing assesses a number of attributes including numerical reasoning, verbal reasoning, diagrammatic reasoning and intellectual ability. These types of tests are primarily used in order for recruiters to gain a better overall evaluation of a candidate's ability, by determining specific skills and abilities that are required for a particular job role.

Within this professional guide, we have provided you with different testing sections that form different areas of psychometric testing. It is not uncommon to be asked by recruiters to undertake more than one type of assessment. The areas that are most likely to be assessed are as follows:

- Numerical Reasoning
- Verbal Reasoning
- Non-Verbal Reasoning
- Concentration Tests
- Mechanical Comprehension
- Checking Tests

Good luck and we wish you the best with all your future endeavours.

The how2become team

The How2Become Team

ABOUT
PSYCHOMETRIC
TESTS

WHAT ARE PSYCHOMETRIC TESTS?

If you break up the word 'psychometric'; you get 'psycho' *(which refers to the mind)*, and 'metric' *(which is a type of measurement)*. Thus, psychometric tests are foremost, a test that measures the mind. Unlike facets such as education, experience, skills, appearance or punctuality, psychometric tests are used to provide a more objective overview of candidates. These tests allow candidates to be assessed on their personality, behaviour, strengths, weaknesses, working style, performance and other important factors that are imperative to the job role for which they are applying.

Moreover, psychometric testing can be defined as a process of measuring a candidates 'suitability'. Not only does the candidate need to show high levels of suitability to the job role, but also, the job position needs to be tailored to a certain type of person, and thus it is important to match up the correct job with the correct person.

WHEN DO I TAKE A PSYCHOMETRIC TEST?

An ever increasing number of jobs now require you to sit some form of psychometric assessment, in order to identify certain aptitudes, personality and abilities. If a job requires you to sit a psychometric test; it is crucial that you do your utmost to ensure you gain the best results possible.

Most psychometric tests are performed online, although different jobs use different means of formats. Tests are often used as a preliminary screening process in order to filter out the strong candidates from those deemed less desirable. You may be required to sit a psychometric test before or after an interview; you may be asked to sit these tests before an interview is even offered; or you may be asked to attend an Assessment Centre, whereby you will be assessed alongside other candidates.

TYPES OF PSYCHOMETRIC TESTS

A psychometric test is based around key skills and attributes required for the specific job role for which you are applying. The most common types of psychometric tests include:

- **Numerical Reasoning** – mental arithmetic, data interpretation, quantitative reasoning, speed / distance / time, charts and graphs.
- **Verbal Ability** – spelling, punctuation, grammar, reading and comprehension.
- **Non-Verbal Reasoning** – spatial, abstract and inductive reasoning.
- **Concentration** – work rates, numerical visual comparison, and dots concentration tests.
- **Mechanical Comprehension** – pulleys, weights, levers and circuits.
- **Checking Tests** – dials and switches.

Although each type of psychometric test assesses different key skills and qualities, practising more than one type of psychometric test will almost guarantee to improve your overall ability to succeed.

If you know what kind of test you will be sitting, you can practice those types of questions thoroughly. However, we suggest that you work through a number of different tests in order to better your chances. For example, you may be asked to complete a numerical reasoning test. It makes sense to practise mostly questions regarding numerical data, however, psychometric tests like concentration tests can also help to improve your speed and accuracy and thus improve your overall performance.

HOW DO I PREPARE FOR A PSYCHOMETRIC TEST?

The only way to prepare for a psychometric test is to practice. Ultimately, the more you practice, the more likely you are to achieve higher marks, and thus better your chances at securing a job.

We have deliberately supplied you with lots of sample questions to assist you through your preparation. It is crucial that when you get a question wrong, you take the time to find out why you got it wrong. Understanding the question is very important!

It is important that, prior to your assessment, you find out as much information as possible about your test and what will be involved. There are many forms of psychometric testing, so you need to fully prepare for the test by understanding what is expected.

If you can, try to find out the type of psychometric test you will be sitting, i.e. is it a numerical test, a verbal ability test, a concentration test etc. It will also help if you find out if your test is going to be taken under any time limits. If your test is under timed conditions, it is imperative that you practice some tests under the same timed conditions. This will allow you to not only practice the test itself, but also improve on your timing skills.

STRUCTURE OF THE BOOK

This book follows a very simple structure in order for you to make the most out of the guide.

We have provided you with an array of question styles that are guaranteed to help you through the preparation stages, and ultimately better your chances of success. This book contains six different testing sections, each with a variety of questions and levels of difficulty for you to work through. Work through each chapter, and then check your answers to make sure you understand how to reach the correct answer!

This comprehensive 'Psychometric Tests' guide follows the structure as formulated below:

- Introduction – introducing your new guide
- About Psychometric Tests
- Tips for Passing Psychometric Tests
- Numerical Reasoning
- Verbal Ability
- Non-Verbal Reasoning
- Concentration
- Mechanical Comprehension
- Checking Tests
- A Few Final Words…

TIPS FOR PASSING
PSYCHOMETRIC
TESTS

TIPS FOR PASSING PSYCHOMETRIC TESTS

The most effective way in which you can prepare for psychometric tests, is to carry out lots of sample test questions.

Here are a few general tips for any psychometric test:

- It is important that before you sit your test, you find out what type(s) of test you will be required to undertake. You should also take steps to find out if the tests will be timed, and also whether or not they will be 'multiple-choice' based questions.

- Even if you are only required to sit one type of test, we highly recommend that you attempt a variety of different testing questions. This will undoubtedly improve your overall ability to pass the test that you are required to undertake.

- Confidence is an important part of the preparation stages. Have you ever sat a timed test and your mind goes blank? This is because your mind is focused on negative thoughts and your belief that you will fail. If you practice plenty of test questions under timed conditions, then your confidence will grow. If your confidence is at its peak at the commencement of the test, then there is no doubt that you will actually look forward to sitting it, as opposed to being fearful of the outcome.

- Do not spend too much time on one particular question. You may find some questions easier than others. You may struggle at a certain 'type' of question and so it is important not to ponder about questions you are unsure of. Move on, and then come back to those questions at the end.

- If you are unsure about the answers, make sure you use our detailed answers and explanations to understand how to reach the correct answer. Knowing where you went wrong is just as important as getting the questions correct.

- Make sure that you get a good nights sleep the night before your assessment. Research has shown that people who have regular 'good' sleep are far more likely to concentrate better during psychometric tests.

- If you have any special needs that need to be catered for, make sure you inform the Assessment Centre or recruitment team prior to the day of your assessment. You will not be treated negatively; in fact the exact opposite. They will give you extra time in the tests, which can only work in your favour.

- The online practice tests should be practiced with little distraction around. You want to fully concentrate on these tests, which will ultimately make you feel more positive when it comes to taking your real assessment.

Tips for Numerical Reasoning:

- Make sure you practice your mathematical skills. You will find the numerical reasoning test difficult if you are not great at maths. Practice your adding, subtracting, multiplying and dividing. Also practice mathematics including fractions, percentages and ratios.

- Try practising numerical test questions in your head, without writing down your workings out. This is very difficult to accomplish, but it is excellent practice for the real test. Also, practice numerical reasoning tests without a calculator. This will guarantee to better your mathematical ability. You do not want to rely on the use of a calculator.

- If you are permitted to use a calculator, make sure you know how to use one!

- Questions will often require you to identify what mathematical formulae is being used (division, percentage, ratio etc). Before you answer the question, carefully read what the question is asking you! Be sure to understand what you need to work out, before attempting to answer the question.

- Practice is key. The more you practice your mental arithmetic and other mathematical formulae; the easier it becomes. This is why we have provided you with lots of sample questions for you to work through. The more you practice these tests, the more likely you are to feel comfortable and confident with the questions. Remember, practice makes perfect!

- Make sure you pay attention to detail. Recognising units, and measurements and other important mathematical formulas is crucial when it comes to your answer. If a question asks you to write your answer in centimetres, and you write your answer using millimetres, this is a careless mistake that is going to cost you easy marks!

Tips for Verbal Ability:

- Practice is key. The more you practice your Verbal Reasoning skills, the better chance you have at successfully completing the test.

- Find out how many minutes you have to complete the test. Usually, Verbal Reasoning tests are conducted under strict time limits, and so it is important to work on your timing skills, in order to enhance your overall performance.

- Find out as much as possible prior to your assessment day. That way, you should be able to make the most out of your preparation time.

- Brush up on your vocabulary, grammar and punctuation. Verbal Reasoning tests assesses strong eye for detail, and it is important that you are able to show high levels of literary ability.

Tips for Non-Verbal Reasoning:

- Try and visualise the questions.

- **The Cube Questions** – why not make yourself a cube net as you try to work out the questions. This will help you to visualise where the shapes on the cube will be once you have folded the cube together.

- Non-Verbal Reasoning tests are designed to test people under strict time limits. Most people find it difficult to finish all the questions. Therefore these tests are designed to measure people's level of accuracy whilst working in speedy conditions.

- Drawing or writing out your answers is a useful way to see what is going on. Drawing out the answers of what you think it may look like, will help you to visualise the answers.

- Using highlighters are a useful way to distinguish your answers. Highlighting is helpful if you are counting lots of shapes or working out numbers of angles etc.

- **The Complete Grid Questions** – to make sure you have got the correct answer, you can always work backwards. By working backwards, you would have to do the opposite to what is being asked, but it is a useful way to check if you have the correct answer.

- Pay attention to everything! If you are unsure about what the differences are or what is happening in the sequence, pay attention to everything you see. Count all the sides, angles, colours, shading, line types, sizing, rotations, reflections etc. That way you can eliminate what is the same, and what is different about the sequence.

Tips for Concentration Tests:

- The main tip for this type of test is to simply practice. The more you practice and work on your concentration skills, the better chance you have at improving your performance.

- Accuracy is key, but also keep an eye on the time! Not only will you be assessed on your accurate scores, but also on how well you perform under severe time limits.

- Make sure that you practice these questions under timed conditions. Not only do you have to work on getting the answers correct, but the time limit is extremely restrictive, and thus you want to work on your timing skills in order to stand a better chance at passing.

- Whether you are required to sit a Visual Comparison Test based on numbers or alpha-numbers; both styles of tests assess the same thing. So, in order to become more proficient at these tests, it is best to revise both styles to increase your chances of success.

- Don't guess answers! It is better to have answered 50 questions and got them all right, as opposed to answering 80 questions and getting 30 wrong. Never sacrifice quality for quantity.

Tips for Mechanical Comprehension:

- Make sure that you have knowledge regarding the following areas (these areas are typical of Mechanical Comprehension tests):

    o Operating systems
    o Pulley systems
    o Mechanical advantage
    o Circuits
    o Levers

- Many tests are designed so that you are unable to finish them. Once again, simply work as fast as you can but also aim for accuracy.

- Make sure that if you do not reach the correct answer, you take the time to work out how to reach the correct answer.

- The majority of employers will assess you on your speed and accuracy. Therefore, you are advised against random 'guessing'. In order to prevent estimations, practice more and more. Test administrators will deduct marks for incorrect answers. Therefore, during your preparation for your assessment, we recommend you simply practice lots of test questions and understand how the answer is reached.

- If you come up against a difficult question during your Mechanical Comprehension test, move on, but remember to leave a gap on the answer sheet. If you fail to leave a gap, you may fill in the following questions in the wrong order, and therefore the answers will be wrong.

- In the build-up to the test, if you feel like you are struggling with basic mechanical concepts, then we recommend you study a car manual such as Haynes. This will give you an idea of how mechanical concepts work. You can obtain a Haynes manual at www.haynes.co.uk.

Tips for Checking Tests:

- Checking tests require great levels of concentration. You can improve your scores for checking tests by practising other psychometric tests such as concentration ability tests.

- Accuracy and speed are very important during this type of test. Be sure to work not only on sample questions, but your timing skills as well. You need to better your overall performance to ensure higher scores.

- Pay attention to everything!

- Make sure you focus on each diagram/image very carefully. You do not want to miss important information.

Finally, we have also provided you with some additional free online psychometric tests which will help to further improve your competence in an array of testing areas.

To gain access, simply go to:

www.PsychometricTestsOnline.co.uk

Good luck and best wishes,

The how2become team

The How2become team

NUMERICAL
REASONING
TESTS

WHAT IS NUMERICAL REASONING?

A Numerical Reasoning test is designed to assess mathematical knowledge through number-related assessments. These assessments will consist of different difficulty levels, and will all vary depending on who you are sitting the test for. Be sure to find out what type of Numerical Reasoning test you will be sitting, to ensure you make the most out of your preparation time.

WHY ARE NUMERICAL REASONING TESTS USED?

Numerical Reasoning is one of the most common forms of psychometric testing which enables employers to filter out strong candidates from those less desirable. Most recruitment processes now contain a form of psychometric and aptitude testing; so it is important that you are 100% prepared!

The majority of Numerical Reasoning tests are administered to candidates who are applying for managerial, graduate and professional positions; any job that deals with making inferences in relation to statistical, financial or numerical data. However, some employers may use these tests as a way of determining important job-related skills such as time management and problem solving efficiency.

WHICH SKILLS ARE MEASURED?

Numerical Reasoning tests can be used to assess the following:

- Basic Mental Arithmetic

- Critical Reasoning

- General Intelligence

- Estimations

- Speed and Concentration

- Financial Reasoning

- Data Analysis

WHAT DO NUMERICAL REASONING TESTS COVER?

Numerical Reasoning tests cover a wide range of mathematical formulae. It is imperative to comprehend the skills and knowledge required to work out the mathematics involved. Most Numerical Reasoning tests contain questions in relation to:

Adding	Subtracting	Dividing	Multiplying
Fractions	Percentages	Decimals	Ratios
Charts and Graphs	Mean, Mode, Median, Range	Areas and Perimeters	Number Sequences
Time	Conversions	Measurements	Money
Proportions	Formulae	Data Interpretation	Quantitative Data

WHAT TO EXPECT

During the Numerical Reasoning test, you will have a specific amount of time to answer each question. It is important that you do not spend too much time on one particular question. Remember, the clock is ticking, so if you are stuck on a question, move on and come back to it at the end if you have time.

Adding Fractions

$$\frac{5}{7} + \frac{3}{5}$$

$$\frac{5}{7} \times \frac{3}{5} = \frac{25 + 21}{35} = \frac{46}{35} = 1\frac{11}{35}$$

Crossbow Method:

The CROSS looks like a multiplication sign and it tells you which numbers to multiply together.

One arm is saying 'multiply the 5 by the 5', and the other arm is saying 'multiply the 7 by the 3'.

The BOW says 'multiply the 2 numbers I am pointing at'. That is 7 times 5.

The answer is 35 and it goes **underneath** the line in the answer.

Subtracting Fractions

$$\frac{4}{7} - \frac{2}{5}$$

$$\frac{4}{7} \times \frac{2}{5} = \frac{20 - 14}{35} = \frac{6}{35}$$

To subtract fractions, the method is exactly the same. The only difference is, you minus the two numbers forming the top of the fraction, as opposed to adding them.

Multiplying Fractions

$$\frac{2}{3} \times \frac{4}{7}$$

$$\frac{2}{3} \times \frac{4}{7} = \frac{8}{21}$$

Arrow Method:

Multiplying fractions is easy. Draw two arrows through the two top numbers and the two bottom numbers (like shown above) and then multiply – simple!

Sometimes the fraction can be simplified, but in the above example, the answer is already in its simplest form.

Dividing Fractions

$$\frac{3}{7} \div \frac{1}{3}$$

$$\frac{3}{7} \div \frac{3}{1} = \frac{3}{7} \times \frac{3}{1} = \frac{9}{7} = 1\frac{2}{7}$$

Most people think that dividing fractions is difficult. But, it's not! Actually, it's relatively simple if you have mastered multiplying fractions.

Mathematicians realised that if you turned the second fraction upside down (like in the above example), and then change the 'divide' sum to a 'multiply', you will get the correct answer – every time!

Percentages

What is 45% of 500?

How to work it out?

- To work out percentages, divide the whole number by 100 and then multiply the percentage you want to find.

- **For example:**

  o 500 ÷ 100 x 45 = 225

  o So, 225 is 45% of 500.

Fractions / Decimals / Percentages

$$\frac{1}{10} = 0.1 = 10\%$$

How to work out fractions into decimals into percentages.

- 0.1 into a percent, you would move the decimal point two places to the right, so it becomes 10%.

- To convert 1/10 into a decimal, you would divide both numbers. For example, 1 ÷ 10 = 0.1.

- To convert 10% into a decimal, you move the decimal point two places to the left. For example, to convert 10% into a decimal, the decimal point moves two spaces to the left to become 0.1.

Volume

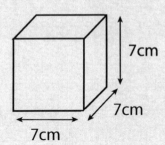

Volume

Length x base x height

- **7 x 7 x 7 = 343**

Areas / Perimeters

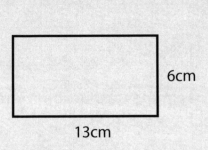

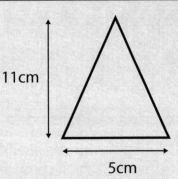

Area of squares / rectangles

Base x height

- $13 \times 6 = 78$ cm²

Area of triangles

½ base x height

- $11 \times 5 \div 2 = 27.5$

Perimeter

Add all the sizes of each side.

- $6 + 6 + 13 + 13 = 38$

NUMERICAL REASONING – MENTAL ARITHMETIC

Question 1

Calculate 4.99 + 19.09

A	B	C	D	E
24.02	28.04	22.08	24.08	22.04

Question 2

Calculate 6.47 – 3.29

A	B	C	D	E
3.12	3.15	4.14	4.16	3.18

Question 3

Multiply 6 by 7 and then divide by 3.

A	B	C	D	E
14	16	12	8	42

Question 4

Divide 120 by 4 and then multiply it by 5.

A	B	C	D	E
200	150	100	50	65

Question 5

What is 9/11 of 88?

A	B	C	D	E
64	42	48	72	78

Question 6

Calculate 4.8 x 3.0.

A	B	C	D	E
13.6	13.2	14.4	14.8	15.0

Question 7

Calculate 2.2 x 22.2

A	B	C	D	E
84.84	48.48	88.44	48.84	44.88

Question 8

Convert 0.8 to a fraction. In its simplest form.

A	B	C	D	E
8⁄10	1⁄2	3⁄4	4⁄5	5⁄8

Question 9

What is 0.9 as a percentage?

A	B	C	D	E
0.009%	0.9%	9%	90%	19%

Question 10

Using BIDMAS work out 23.7 – 2.5 x 8.

A	B	C	D	E
37	2.7	169.6	3.7	3.2

Question 11

In the following question, what is the value of x?

$$\frac{3x - 6}{5} = 9$$

A	B	C	D	E
13	16	17	19	21

Question 12

Convert 7/10 to a decimal.

A	B	C	D	E
0.7	7.0	0.07	0.007	7.7

Question 13

If you count from 1 to 100, how many numbers containing the number '4', will you pass on the way?

A	B	C	D	E
21	20	19	11	10

Question 14

Calculate 144 ÷ 6.

A	B	C	D	E
21	20	24	26	30

Question 15

What is 75% of 3,200?

A	B	C	D	E
2,600	3,000	3,250	2,400	2,750

Question 16

What is 48% of 900?

A	B	C	D	E
412	432	462	400	480

Question 17

What is 1888 ÷ 4?

A	B	C	D	E
514	364	394	457	472

Question 18

What is 8 x 4.9?

A	B	C	D	E
33.2	37.2	39.2	31.2	38.2

Question 19

41 x 9 = 738 ÷ ?

A	B	C	D	E
5	4	7	2	3

Question 20

A function is represented by the following machine.

9 is put into the machine. The output of the machine is 126. What is the missing function in the second part of the machine sequence?

A	B	C	D	E
x 12	÷ 12	x 6	÷ 6	- 8

Question 21

Subtract 3/8 of 104 from 5/7 of 98.

A	B	C	D	E
22	28	39	31	37

Question 22

Here is a spinner. Circle the chance of the spinner landing on an odd number.

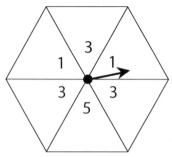

A	B	C	D
6/6 or 1	4/6	1/2	1/3

Question 23

What two numbers come next in the sequence?

2,   4,   8,   16,   32,   64, ...

A	B	C	D
126 and 215	128 and 256	128 and 265	182 and 265

Question 24

Simplify x + 8x − 3x.

A	B	C	D
5x	6x	7x	12x

Question 25

There are 20 buttons in a bag. 12 are red, 5 are green and the rest are white. A button is chosen at random. Work out the probability that the button will be white.

A	B	C	D
3/20	1/5	3/10	9/20

Question 26

On a school trip at least 1 teacher is needed for every 8 students. Work out the minimum number of teachers needed for 138 students.

A	B	C	D
17	14	16	18

Question 27

The sterling to US dollar rate is 1:1.60. How many dollars would you receive if you changed up £450?

A	B	C	D
$490	$720	$780	$650

Question 28

Linda is hiking. Using a compass, she discovers that she is facing west. If she turns 8 right angles clockwise, what way will she be facing?

A	B	C	D
South	North	West	East

Question 29

A family of 4 split the cost of all the household bills equally. The water bill was £80.40, the gas bill was £35.00 and the electric bill was £40.00. The rent for the month was £490. How much does each member of the family put towards covering all the bill costs?

A	B	C	D
£161.25	£191.35	£161.35	£161.50

Question 30

What is 560 ÷ 7?

A	B	C	D
60	90	85	80

ANSWERS TO NUMERICAL REASONING – MENTAL ARITHMETIC

Q1. D = 24.08

EXPLANATION = 4.99 + 19.09 = 24.08

Q2. E = 3.18

EXPLANATION = 6.47 – 3.29 = 3.18

Q3. A = 14

EXPLANATION = 6 x 7 = 42 ÷ 3 = 14

Q4. B = 150

EXPLANATION = 120 ÷ 4 = 30 x 5 = 150

Q5. D = 72

EXPLANATION = 88 ÷ 11 x 9 = 72

Q6. C = 14.4

EXPLANATION = to multiply decimals, it is best to take out the decimal points, do the calculation, and then add them back in after. So, 48 x 3 = 144. Remember, there is one number after the decimal point in the question, so one number needs to be after the decimal point in the answer. So, 144 will become 14.4

Q7. D = 48.84

EXPLANATION = to multiply decimals, it is best to take out the decimal points, do the calculation, and then add them back in after. So, 22 x 222 = 4884. Remember, there are two numbers after the decimal point (one in 2.2 and one in 22.2), so two numbers need to come after the decimal point in the answer. So, 4884 will become 48.84.

Q8. D = 4/5
EXPLANATION = to convert a decimal into a fraction, it is best to make it a percentage, and then work out the fraction. So, 0.8 x 100 = 80%. As a decimal 80% is equivalent to 80/100. This can be simplified to 4/5. Although answer option A is correct, the question specifically asks for the answer in its simplest form, so answer option D would be correct.

Q9. D = 90%
EXPLANATION = 0.9 x 100 = 90%.

Q10. D = 3.7
Following the rules of BIDMAS, you will need to work out the multiplication first. So, 2.5 x 8 = 20.

You can then do the subtraction. So, 23.7 - 20 = 3.7

Q11. C = 17
EXPLANATION = in order to work out the value of x:

9 x 5 = 45 + 6 = 51 ÷ 3 = 17. The important thing to remember is that when you take the number from the top row, you have to do the opposite to what it is saying. so, '-6' becomes '+6'.

Q12. A = 0.7
EXPLANATION 7 ÷ 10 = 0.7

Q13. C = 19
EXPLANATION = from 1 to 100, you would encounter 19 numbers that contain the number 4.

4, 14, 24, 34, 40, 41, 42, 43, 44, 45, 46, 47, 48, 49, 54, 64, 74, 84, 94.

Q14. C = 24
EXPLANATION = 144 ÷ 6 = 24

Q15. D = 2,400
EXPLANATION = 3,200 ÷ 100 x 75 = 2,400

Q16. B = 432

EXPLANATION = 900 ÷ 100 x 48 = 432

Q17. E = 472

EXPLANATION = 1888 ÷ 4 = 472

Q18. C = 39.2

EXPLANATION = to multiply decimals, it is best to take out the decimal points, do the calculation, and then add them back in after. So, 8 x 49 = 392. Remember, there is one number after the decimal point in the question, so there needs to be one number after the decimal point in the answer. So, 392 will become 39.2.

Q19. D = 2

EXPLANATION = 41 x 9 = 369 which is the same as 738 ÷ 2 = 369.

Q20. C = x 6

EXPLANATION = 9 + 12 = 21. 126 ÷ 21 = 6. Therefore if you put (x6) into the equation (because you divided 126 by 6, you would put the opposite into the equation). Therefore, 9 + 12 x 6 = 126.

Q21. D = 31

EXPLANATION = 104 ÷ 8 x 3 = 39.   98 ÷ 7 x 5 = 70.   So, 70 – 39 = 31.

Q22. A = 6/6 or 1.

EXPLANATION = the spinner contains only odd numbers. So no matter what number it lands on, you will always spin an odd number.

Q23. B = 128 and 256

EXPLANATION = the sequence follows the pattern of multiplying by 2 each time. So, 64 x 2 = 128 and 128 x 2 = 256.

Q24. B = 6x

EXPLANATION = x + 8x = 9x.   So, 9x – 3x = 6x.

Q25. A = 3/20

EXPLANATION = 20 – 12 – 5 = 3. So your chance of picking a white button is 3 out of a possible 20.

Q26. D = 18

EXPLANATION = 138 ÷ 8 = 17.25. You need one teacher for every 8 students, therefore you would need 18 members of staff in order to cater for 138 students.

Q27. B = $720

EXPLANATION = £1 = 1.60 US dollars. £450 = 450 x 1.60 = $720

Q28. C = West

EXPLANATION = she is facing west, she turns eight right angles clockwise. 1 turn = north, 2 turns = east, 3 turns = south. After eight rotations of 90°, Linda will be facing West.

Q29. C = £161.35

EXPLANATION = 80.4 + 35 + 40 + 490 = 645.40.   645.40 ÷ 4 = 161.35

Q30. D = 80

EXPLANATION = 560 ÷ 7 = 80.

NUMERICAL REASONING – DATA INTERPRETATION

*Based on 100 students. Marks in English,
Maths and Science examinations.*

MARKS OUT OF 40				
Subject	30 and above	20 and above	10 and above	0 and above
English	19	52	91	100
Maths	13	36	90	100
Science	11	42	87	100
AVERAGE	11	43	89	100

Question 1

If at least 50% in their examination is needed to go on to higher education, how many students in Maths can go on to higher education?

A	B	C	D	E
49	13	36	19	27

Question 2

What is the percentage of students who achieved marks of 20 or above in their English exam?

A	B	C	D	E
36%	41%	56%	52%	48%

Question 3

What is the difference between the number of students who achieved 30 or above in English, and the number of students who achieved 20 and above in Science?

A	B	C	D	E
23	25	27	31	19

Question 4

Using the box labelled 'average', work out the number of students who scored less than 50%.

A	B	C	D	E
43	57	21	17	53

Question 5

What subject had the highest number of students who scored below 10?

A	B	C	D	E
English	Maths	Science	All the same	English and Maths

Employees in departments of a company

Department	January	February	March	April	May	June
Marketing	21	24	17	15	23	27
Admin	18	11	15	13	13	18
Sales	21	22	29	31	28	24
IT	19	13	17	18	22	25

Question 6

How many employees are there in May?

A	B	C	D	E
71	78	83	86	89

Question 7

What was the average number of employees for February?

A	B	C	D	E
9.75	17.5	11.5	13	19.75

Question 8

What was the average number of Admin employees over the 6 month period? To the nearest whole number.

A	B	C	D	E
11	17	15	21	24

Question 9

What was the largest number of people employed at one given time? (I.e. in any month, in any department).

A	B	C	D	E
29	31	27	35	26

Question 10

What is the difference between the total number of employees in Marketing, and the total number of employees in Sales, across the six month period?

A	B	C	D	E
21	26	31	28	35

A pie chart representing the number of crimes in a one month period.

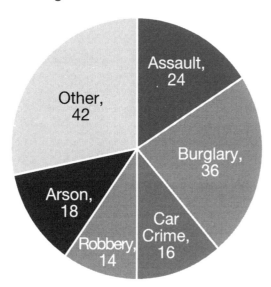

Question 11

What percentage of the total number of crimes were assault-related?

A	B	C	D	E
9%	36%	16%	6%	13%

Question 12

How many crimes are there in total?

A	B	C	D	E
95	100	125	150	175

Question 13

What was the average number of total crimes?

A	B	C	D	E
25	50	15	20	45

Question 14

Work out the difference between the lowest occurring type of crime, and the highest occurring type of crime.

A	B	C	D	E
21	28	32	16	26

Question 15

What percentage of the total number of crimes were burglary and arson-related?

A	B	C	D	E
21%	55%	61%	42%	36%

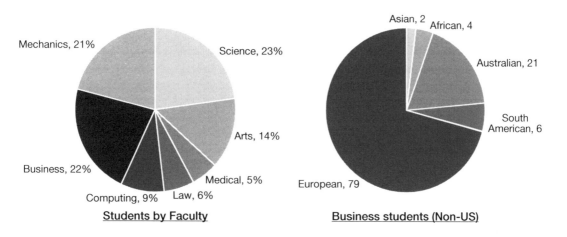

Students by Faculty   Business students (Non-US)

The pie chart above shows the percentage of students in each faculty at Grove University, and the number of Non-US students in the Business faculty. These percentages have been rounded to the nearest whole number. There are a total of 1247 students in the Business faculty. Use this information to answer the following questions.

Question 16

What percentage of students in the Business faculty are non-US students?

A	B	C	D	E
11%	13%	9%	7%	8%

Question 17

How many students are there at the university?

A	B	C	D	E
5558	5668	5685	5585	5686

Question 18

How many students are there in the Law faculty?

A	B	C	D	E
310	290	380	340	270

Question 19

If 7 per cent of Mechanical students are Australian, how many Australian students are there studying Mechanics?

A	B	C	D	E
71	76	55	89	83

Question 20

There are 32 Arts students who are South American. What percentage of the faculty does this represent?

A	B	C	D	E
14%	18%	4%	8%	15%

Study the following chart before answering the questions.

BMW sales

Country	Jan	Feb	Mar	April	May	June	Total
UK	21	28	15	35	31	20	150
Germany	45	48	52	36	41	40	262
France	32	36	33	28	20	31	180
Brazil	42	41	37	32	35	28	215
Spain	22	26	17	30	24	22	141
Italy	33	35	38	28	29	38	201
Total	195	214	192	189	180	179	1149

The above table shows the sales across 6 countries for the model BMW for a 6 month period. The BMW's are imported to each country from a main dealer. Use the information provided to answer the following questions.

Question 21

What percentage of the overall total was sold in April?

A	B	C	D	E
17.8%	17.2%	18.9%	16.4%	21.6%

Question 22

What percentage of the overall total sales were BMW's sold to the French importer?

A	B	C	D	E
15.6%	18.2%	18.9%	25.6%	24.5%

Question 23

What percentage of total imports is accounted for by the two smallest importers?

A	B	C	D	E
35.6%	25.3%	22.6%	28.1%	29.1%

Question 24

What is the average number of units per month imported to Brazil over the first 4 months of the year?

A	B	C	D	E
28	24	32	38	40

Question 25

What month saw the biggest increase in total sales from the previous month?

A	B	C	D	E
January	February	March	April	May

Annual percent change in Dollar amount of sales
at five retail stores from 2005 to 2007

STORE	PERCENT CHANGE FROM 2005 TO 2006	PERCENT CHANGE FROM 2006 TO 2007
P	-20	8
Q	-10	10
R	6	10
S	-9	-14
T	16	-6

Question 26

If the dollar amount of sales at store Q was $600,000 for 2005, what was the dollar amount of sales at the store in 2007?

A	B	C	D	E
$625,000	$594,000	$660,000	$315,000	$543,000

Question 27

At store T, the dollar amount of sales for 2006 was what percent of the dollar amount of sales for 2007? Give your answer to the nearest 0.1 percent.

A	B	C	D	E
36.4%	102.3%	106.4%	110.4%	64.6%

Question 28

The dollar amount of sales at store S for 2007 was more than 21 percent less than that for 2005. True or False?

A	B
True	False

Question 29

The dollar amount of sales at store R for 2007 was more than 16 percent greater than that for 2005. True or False?

A	B
True	False

Question 30

If the dollar amount of sales at store S was $325,000 for 2005, what was the dollar amount of sales at the store in 2006?

A	B	C	D	E
$215,250	$265,500	$285,750	$225,500	$295,750

ANSWERS TO NUMERICAL REASONING – DATA INTERPRETATION

Q1. C = 36
EXPLANATION = 50% of 40 = 20. Number of students who scored 20 and above in Maths = 36.

Q2. D = 52%
EXPLANATION = 100 students, 52 students achieved marks of 20 or above = 52%.

Q3. A = 23
EXPLANATION = Number of students with 30 or above in English = 19. Students with 20 or above in Science = 42. So 42 -19 = 23.

Q4. B = 57
EXPLANATION = 50% of 40 = 20. Number of students who scored 20 marks or above for average = 43. So, 100 – 43 = 57.

Q5. C = Science
EXPLANATION = scores of 10 or below = English = 9, Maths = 10, Science = 13.

Q6. D = 86
EXPLANATION = 23 + 13 + 28 + 22 = 86.

Q7. B = 17.5
EXPLANATION = 24 + 11 + 22 + 13 = 70 ÷ 4 = 17.5.

Q8. C = 15
EXPLANATION = 18 + 11 + 15 + 13 + 13 + 18 = 88 ÷ 6 = 14.6. To the nearest whole number = 15.

Q9. B = 31
EXPLANATION = the largest number of people employed at any given time occurred in April, and that was for the department of Sales.

Q10. D = 28
EXPLANATION = Marketing 21 + 24 + 17 + 15 + 23 + 27 = 127. Sales 21 + 22 + 29 + 31 + 28 + 24 = 155.   155 – 127 = 28.

Q11. C = 16%
EXPLANATION = 24 ÷ 150 x 100 = 16%.

Q12. D = 150
EXPLANATION = 42 + 18 + 14 + 16 + 36 + 24 = 150.

Q13. A = 25
EXPLANATION = 150 ÷ 6 = 25.

Q14. B = 28
EXPLANATION = 42 – 14 = 28.

Q15. E = 36%
EXPLANATION = 36 + 18 = 54 ÷ 150 x 100 = 36%.

Q16. C = 9%
EXPLANATION: 112 ÷ 1247 x 100 = 8.98. Rounded up to the nearest whole number = 9%.

Q17. B = 5668
EXPLANATION: 1247 x 100 ÷ 22 = 5668.

Q18. D = 340
EXPLANATION: 5668 ÷ 100 x 6 = 340.

Q19. E = 83
EXPLANATION: 5668 ÷ 100 x 21 = 1190.   1190 ÷ 100 x 7 = 83.

Q20. C = 4%
EXPLANATION: 32 ÷ 794 x 100 = 4.03%. Rounded to the nearest whole number = 4%.

Q21. D = 16.4%

EXPLANATION: to work out the percentage overall total that was sold in April, divide how many BMW's were sold in April (189) by the total (1149) and then multiply it by 100. (189 ÷ 1149 x 100 = 16.4%).

Q22. A = 15.6%

EXPLANATION: to work out the percentage overall total that was sold to France, divide how many BMW's were sold to France (180) by the total (1149) and then multiply it by 100. (180 ÷ 1149 x 100 = 15.6%).

Q23. B = 25.3%

EXPLANATION: to work out the percentage overall for imports accounted by the two smallest importers, divide the total (1149) by how many BMW's were sold from the two smallest importers (UK and France = 150 + 141 = 291) and then multiply it by 100. (291 ÷ 1149 x 100 = 25.3%).

Q24. D = 38

EXPLANATION: to work out the average number of units per month imported to Brazil over the first 4 months of the year, you add up the first 4 amounts (Jan-April) and then divide it by how many numbers there are (4). So, (42 + 41 + 37 + 32 = 152 ÷ 4 = 38).

Q25. B = February

EXPLANATION: to work out the biggest increase in total sales from the previous month, you work out the difference between the totals for each of the month. Between January and February, there was an increase by 19. None of the other months have a bigger increase and therefore February is the correct answer.

Q26. B = $594,000

EXPLANATION = if the dollar amount of sales at Store Q was $600,000 for 2005, then it was 10% greater for 2006. So, this accounts to 110% of that amount (110% of $600,000 = $660,000). For 2007, the amount of sales was 90% of 2006. To work out the sales for 2007: 90% of $660,000 = $594,000.

Q27. C = 106.4%

EXPLANATION = If A represents the dollar amount of sales at store T, from 2006 to 2007 there was a decrease by -6. 6 divided by 100 = 0.06, which means 0.94 is the dollar amount for 2007. Therefore, you need to divide A by 0.94. So 1 divided by 0.94 = 1.06382... To work out the percentage, multiply this by 100 to give you 106.38. To 1 decimal place and thus, the correct answer is 106.4%.

Q28. A = true

EXPLANATION = if B is the dollar amount of sales at store S for 2005, then the dollar amount for 2006 is 0.91 % of B: (100 – 9 = .91). The dollar amount for 2007 would be (100 – 14 = .86). So, 0.91 x 0.86 = 0.7826, as a percent = 78.26. So, this represents a percent decrease of 100 – 78.26 = 21.74%, which is more than 21% so the statement must be true.

Q29. A = true

EXPLANATION = For Choice C, if C is the dollar amount of sales at store R for 2005, then the dollar amount for 2006 is given by 1.06C and the dollar amount for 2007 is given by 1.10. So, 1.10 x 1.06 = 1.166. Note this represents a 16.6% increase, which is greater than 16%, so Choice C must be true.

Q30. E = $295,750

EXPLANATION = if the dollar amount of sales at Store S was $325,000 for 2005, then it was -9% decrease for 2006, this accounts for 91%. So, 325,000 ÷ 100 x 91 = $295,750.

NUMERICAL REASONING – SPEED, DISTANCE AND TIME

Question 1

A train travels 60 miles in 3 hours. What is the train's speed?

A	B	C	D
10 mph	20 mph	30 mph	40 mph

Question 2

You are travelling at a speed of 30 mph for 75 minutes. How far do you travel?

A	B	C	D
35 miles	28 miles	37.5 miles	22.5 miles

Question 3

You are travelling at 75 mph for 1 and a half hours. How far do you travel?

A	B	C	D
110 miles	95 miles	97.5 miles	112.5 miles

Question 4

You travel 140 miles at a constant speed of 35 mph. How long are you travelling for?

A	B	C	D
3 hours	3 hours and 30 minutes	4 hours	4 hours and 10 minutes

Question 5

You drive at an average speed of 45 mph on a journey of 135 miles. How long does the journey take?

A	B	C	D
3 hours	2 hours	5 hours	1 hour

Question 6

You travel a total of 351 miles. In the first 4 hours, you travel 216 miles. What is your average speed for the first part of your drive?

A	B	C	D
62 mph	50 mph	54 mph	60 mph

Question 7

You walk at a speed of 4 mph for 2 and a half hours. How far do you walk?

A	B	C	D
8 miles	10 miles	12 miles	6 miles

Question 8

You cycle at an average speed of 8 mph. If you cycle for 7 hours and 30 minutes, how far will you travel?

A	B	C	D
80 miles	110 miles	120 miles	60 miles

Question 9

You travel 140 miles in 2 hours. What speed are you travelling at?

A	B	C	D
70 mph	80 mph	60 mph	25 mph

Question 10

You are travelling at 32 mph for a quarter of an hour. How far do you travel?

A	B	C	D
12 miles	12.25 miles	15.5 miles	8 miles

Question 11

You are travelling at 35 mph for half an hour. How far do you travel?

A	B	C	D
20 miles	12.5 miles	17.5 miles	22 miles

Question 12

At 3mph, how long does it take to travel 3 miles?

A	B	C	D
30 minutes	1 hour	1 hour and 30 minutes	2 hours

Question 13

At 36 mph, how long does it take to travel 72 miles?

A	B	C	D
1 hour	1 hour and 30 minutes	30 minutes	2 hours

Question 14

At 20 mph, how far do you travel in 24 minutes?

A	B	C	D
10 miles	8 miles	4 miles	12 miles

Question 15

What speed covers 6 miles in 4 minutes?

A	B	C	D
80 mph	70 mph	90 mph	55 mph

Question 16

What speed covers 30 miles in 2 hours and 30 minutes?

A	B	C	D
12 mph	18 mph	25 mph	30 mph

Question 17

An aircraft flying from London to Madrid is cruising at a speed of 534 mph. The distance from departure is 500 miles and the time remaining to reach Madrid is 1 hour and 10 minutes. What is the distance, in miles, from London to Madrid?

A	B	C	D
1,123 miles	623 miles,	1,234 miles	1,325 miles

Question 18

On a flight from London to Rome, the following is shown on the information screen in the passenger cabin.

Current speed: 822 km/hr

Distance from departure: 1222 km

Time to destination: 22 minutes.

What is the distance, in kilometres, from London to Rome?

A	B	C	D
1,523.4 km	1,423.4 km	1,624.5 km	1,724.5 km

Question 19

The speed of sound in air is 340 m/s. If you can hear a clash of thunder 3 seconds after you see the lightning, how far away was the lightning from where you heard the thunder?

A	B	C	D
1,100 metres away	1,020 metres away	1,200 metres away	1,500 metres away

Question 20

At 4 mph, how long does it take to travel 1 mile?

A	B	C	D
30 minutes	1 hour	15 minutes	45 minutes

Question 21

At 13 mph, how long does it take to travel 13 miles?

A	B	C	D
13 hours	30 minutes	1 hour	3 hours

Question 22

At 165 mph, how long does it take to travel 132 miles?

A	B	C	D
48 minutes	1 hour	1 hour and 48 minutes	3 hours

Question 23

You have to travel a total of 520 miles. You travel the first 300 miles in 4 hours. Calculate your average speed for the first part of the journey.

A	B	C	D
75 mph	56 mph	58 mph	60 mph

Question 24

Elliott can type 960 words in 20 minutes. Calculate his typing speed in words per minute (wpm).

A	B	C	D
40 wpm	42 wpm	48 wpm	50 wpm

Question 25

Rebecca cycles 20 miles on her bike for 2 hours and 30 minutes. Calculate her average speed in mph.

A	B	C	D
5 mph	12 mph	7 mph	8 mph

Question 26

Sally has to travel a total of 351 miles. She travels the first 216 miles in 4 hours. If her average speed remains the same, calculate the total time for the complete journey.

A	B	C	D
5 hours	6.5 hours	8 hours	7.5 hours

Question 27

Julie can type 50 words in 2 minutes. Debbie can type 300 words in 15 minutes. Calculate Julie's typing speed in words per hour.

A	B	C	D
1,500 words per hour	1,000 words per hour	2,000 words per hour	1,700 words per hour

Question 28

You are travelling at 65 mph for 1 hour and 10 minutes. How far do you travel? Rounded to the nearest whole number.

A	B	C	D
50 miles	68 miles	76 miles	71 miles

Question 29

Melissa travelled the first 2 hours of her journey at 40 mph and the last 3 hours of her journey at 80 mph. What is the average speed of her travel for the entire journey?

A	B	C	D
58 mph	72 mph	64 mph	60 mph

Question 30

Mark travels the first 3 hours of his journey at 60 mph and the remaining 5 hours at 24 mph. What is Mark's average speed for the whole journey?

A	B	C	D
40 mph	37.5 mph	33.25 mph	35.75 mph

ANSWERS TO NUMERICAL REASONING – SPEED, DISTANCE AND TIME

Q1. B = 20 mph
EXPLANATION = 60 ÷ 3 = 20 mph.

Q2. C = 37.5 miles
EXPLANATION = 30 mph = 0.5 miles per minute (30 ÷ 60)

So, 0.5 x 75 (minutes) = 37.5 miles.

Q3. D = 112.5 miles
EXPLANATION = 75 mph = 1.25 miles per minute (75 ÷ 60)

So, 1.25 x 90 (minutes) = 112.5 miles.

Q4. C = 4 hours
EXPLANATION = 140 ÷ 35 = 4 hours.

Q5. A = 3 hours
EXPLANATION = 135 ÷ 45 = 3 hours.

Q6. C = 54 mph
EXPLANATION = 216 ÷ 4 = 54 mph.

Q7. B = 10 miles
EXPLANATION = 4 x 2.5 = 10 miles.

Q8. D = 60 miles
EXPLANATION = 8 x 7.5 = 60 miles.

Q9. A = 70 mph
EXPLANATION = 140 ÷ 2 = 70 mph.

Q10. D = 8 miles
EXPLANATION = ¼ of 32 miles=8 miles.

Q11. C = 17.5 miles

EXPLANATION = ½ of 35 miles=17.5 miles.

Q12. B = 1 hour

EXPLANATION = this question is very simple. You are already told that travelling 3 miles will take one hour (3 miles per hour), so the answer is 1 hour.

Q13. D = 2 hours

EXPLANATION = 72 ÷ 36 = 2 hours.

Q14. B = 8 miles

EXPLANATION = 20 mph = 0.333... miles per minute (20 ÷ 60)

So, 0.333... x 24 (minutes) = 8 miles.

Q15. C = 90 mph

EXPLANATION = 6 ÷ 4 = 1.5.   1.5 x 6 = 9 x 10 = 90 mph.

Q16. A = 12 mph

EXPLANATION = 2 hours and 30 minutes is equivalent to 150 minutes. So, 30/150 is the same as 1/5. 60 (minutes) ÷ 5 = 12 mph.

Q17. A = 1,123 miles

EXPLANATION = 500 miles have already been covered by the aircraft, the speed is 534 mph and the time of flight remaining is 1 hour and 10 minutes = 70 minutes = 70 ÷60).

So, distance remaining = speed x time remaining

= 534 x (70÷60).

= 623 miles. So, 623 + 500 miles = 1,123 miles.

Q18. A = 1,523.4 kilometres

EXPLANATION = 1222 km has already been covered. So, distance remaining = speed x time remaining

Speed = 822 km/hr, Time = 22m = 22 ÷ 60 hours

Remaining distance = 822 x (22 ÷ 60) km = 301.4 km. So, 301.4 + 1222 = 1,523.4 km.

Q19. B = 1,020 metres away

EXPLANATION = sound travels at 340 m/s from the source of the thunder. If you hear it 3 seconds later, distance = speed x time.

Distance = speed x time

= 340 x 3

= 1,020 metres away.

Q20. C = 15 minutes

EXPLANATION = if it takes 1 hour to travel 4 miles, then it will only take 15 minutes to travel 1 mile. (60 ÷ 4 = 15 minutes).

Q21. C = 1 hour

EXPLANATION = it takes 1 hour to travel 13 miles. (13 miles per hour).

Q22. A = 48 minutes

EXPLANATION = 60 ÷ 165 = 0.3636…

So, 0.3636… x 132 = 48 minutes.

Q23. A = 75 mph

EXPLANATION = average speed = distance ÷ time = 300 ÷ 4 = 75 mph.

Q24. C = 48 wpm

EXPLANATION = typing speed = 960 ÷ 20 = 48 words per minute.

Q25. D = 8 mph

EXPLANATION = average speed = 20 miles ÷ 2.5 hours = 8 mph.

Q26. B = 6.5 hours

EXPLANATION = first you need to work out Sally's average speed. Average speed = distance ÷ time = 216 ÷ 4 = 54 mph. So to work out the complete journey, if her average speed remains the same = time = distance ÷ speed = 351 ÷ 54 = 6.5 hours.

Q27. A = 1,500 words per hour

EXPLANATION = average speed = 50 words ÷ 0.0333 hours = 1,500 words per hour.

Q28. C = 76 miles

EXPLANATION = 65 ÷ 60 = 1.0833...

So, 1.0833... x 70 (minutes) = 75.833. To the nearest whole number = 76 miles.

Q29. C = 64 mph

EXPLANATION = average speed of travel = total distance travelled ÷ total time taken.

Distance covered in first 2 hours = speed x time = 40 x 2 = 80 miles.

Distance covered in last 3 hours = speed x time = 80 x 3 = 240 miles.

So, 240 + 80 = 320 over 5 hours in total.

320 ÷ 5 = 64 mph.

Q30. B = 37.5 mph

EXPLANATION = average speed of travel = total distance travelled ÷ total time taken.

Distance covered in first 3 hours = 3 x 60 = 180 miles.

Distance covered in the next 5 hours = 5 x 24 = 120 miles.

So, 120 + 180 = 300 miles across 8 hours = 300 ÷ 8 = 37.5 mph.

VERBAL ABILITY
TESTS

WHAT ARE VERBAL ABILITY TESTS?

Verbal Reasoning or Verbal Ability tests are specifically designed to assess a candidate's ability to reason with words, language or comprehension, and demonstrate a solid understanding of written information within the English language.

The ability to spell words correctly, use correct grammar and punctuation, understand word meanings, and interpret written information, is an imperative skill that is required in a range of situations and job roles. Thus, it is important that you are able to demonstrate these skills to a high standard and perform to the best of your ability.

WHY IS VERBAL ABILITY ASSESSED?

Most employers who use psychometric tests in job selection processes will include a Verbal Reasoning or Verbal Ability test of some form. This is because there are very few graduate careers which don't require the ability to understand, analyse and interpret written information, often of a complex or specialised nature.

Therefore, it is important that recruiters hire a candidate who show strong levels of verbal and literary ability, in order to be competent and able within the job role.

WHO TAKES A VERBAL TEST?

Verbal Ability tests have become increasingly popular for a whole range of career selection processes. Doctors, dentists, police officers, even pupils who wish to undertake the 11+ test, are all required to sit a Verbal test.

WHAT DOES A VERBAL TEST CONSIST OF?

Verbal Reasoning tests come in different formats. Be sure to find out what type of test it is you are going to be sitting. This will help you to practice the questions to the best of your ability. Even if you are required to sit a particular test i.e a Verbal Comprehension test, it is best to practice a range of Verbal tests to ensure that you are ready for anything that might be used in your actual assessment.

Typical formats of the Verbal test include:

- Verbal Logical Reasoning
- Verbal Reasoning
- Verbal Comprehension
- Vocabulary test
- Spelling and Grammar test
- Word Meanings test
- Word Relations test

In order for you to gain the best knowledge and practice, the following testing sections will include a variety of question types to ensure you are fully prepared for any Verbal Ability test that you may be required to sit.

EXAMPLES OF VERBAL REASONING

Reading and Comprehension

Passage

Many organisations find it useful to employ students over the summer period. A lot of permanent staff like to take their holidays over this period, especially if they have children. Summer is normally a peak period in terms of business, and therefore companies need to maintain a solid workforce to cope with the high levels of demand. Giving students the opportunity for part time work over the summer could result in a more permanent position after their education. Unlike permanent staff, students working on a part time basis are not eligible for holiday pay or bonus incentives.

Statement

Some companies need to recruit part time staff over the summer, because they have more work to do.

True, False, or Impossible to say?

How to work it out

The statement already mentions that 'some' companies experience their 'peak' times over the summer, therefore the statement would be true.

Answer

True

Correct Sentences

Question

A. Graduates are finding it more difficult to get a job that is relevant to there studies.

B. Graduates our finding it more difficult to get a job that its releveant to their studies.

C. Graduates are finding it more difficult to get a job that is relevant to their studies.

D. Graduate's are finding it more difficult to get a job that is relevant to their studies.

How to work it out

A – Uses the wrong 'there' so therefore is incorrect.

B – Uses the wrong 'our' and 'relevant' is spelt incorrectly.

C – Provides the most logical sentence structure, with correct grammar and punctuation.

D – 'Graduate's' should not have an apostrophe and is therefore incorrect.

Answer

C

Correct Words

Question

Hearing music can be a result of listening to loud loss.

How to work it out

- If you read the sentence out loud, you will notice that it does not make sense.
- Hearing **music** can be a result of listening to loud **loss**.
- If you swap the **highlighted** words around, the sentence makes sense.

Answer

Music and loss, 'Hearing loss can be a result of listening to loud music'.

Missing Words

Question

It was _____ choice where they went to college. _____ are some great colleges to choose from.

How to work it out

- Their = is the possessive form. In other words it indicates something belonging to someone.
- There = is a place. I.e. not here. Also used when saying there 'is' or there 'are'.

Answer

Their / there

Correct Letters

Question

The same letter must be able to fit into both sets of brackets [?] in order to complete the word in front of the bracket, and begin the word after the bracket.

Question

Happ [?] ellow

Wh   [?] awn

How to work it out

A	B	C	D
W	H	Y	N

- The only letter that could fit inside the bracket in order to make 4 words is = Y.
- Happy, yellow, why, yawn

Answer

C = Y

Odd One Out

Identify which word is the odd one out.

Question

A – Desk
B – Shelf
C – Cupboard
D – Chair
E – Wood

How to work it out

- The odd one out is wood.
- All of the other words are objects rather than an actual material.

Answer

E – Wood

Word Jumble

*In the sentence, the word outside the brackets will only go with three of the words inside the brackets in order to make a longer word. Which ONE word will it **NOT** go with?*

Question

	A	B	C	D
Un	(adaptable	able	appropriate	afraid)

How to work it out

- Unadaptable
- Unable
- Unafraid
- **Unappropriate** is not a word. The correct term would be **inappropriate**.

Answer

C – Appropriate

VERBAL ABILITY – GENERAL APTITUDE – (TEST 1)

Question 1

Which word does not have a similar meaning to – imaginary?

A	B	C	D
Apocryphal	Fictional	Illusory	Inconsistent

Question 2

Which word does not have a similar meaning to – important?

A	B	C	D
Miniature	Significant	Imperative	Of substance

Question 3

Which word does not have a similar meaning to – belittle?

A	B	C	D
Trivialise	Denigrate	Overrate	Malign

Question 4

Which word does not have a similar meaning to – conclusion?

A	B	C	D
Outcome	Upshot	Denouement	Cause

Question 5

Which word is the odd one out?

A	B	C	D	E
Beef	Mutton	Cow	Pork	Ham

Question 6

Which word is the odd one out?

A	B	C	D	E
London	Paris	Lisbon	Prague	Nuremberg

Question 7

Which word is the odd one out?

A	B	C	D	E
Rose	Lily	Daisy	Petal	Sunflowers

Question 8

Which word is the odd one out?

A	B	C	D	E
Hungry	Ravenous	Famished	Esurient	Stuffed

Question 9

Which word is the odd one out?

A	B	C	D	E
Ostrich	Parrots	Penguins	Dodo	Owls

Question 10

Find two words, one from each group, that are the closest in meaning.

Group A

Abysmal, placid, exhausted

Group B

Energetic, docile, wonderful

A	B	C	D
Exhausted and docile	Placid and docile	Abysmal and docile	Placid and wonderful

Question 11

Find two words, one from each group, that are the closest in meaning.

Group A

Confused, enraged, terrified

Group B

Calm, trance, incensed

A	B	C	D
Enraged and incensed	Confused and calm	Confused and trance	Terrified and trance

Question 12

Find two words, one from each group, that are the closest in meaning.

Group A

Determined, frightened, informal

Group B

Normal, resolute, unravelling

A	B	C	D
Determined and resolute	Determined and unravelling	Frightened and unravelling	Informal and normal

Question 13

Find two words, one from each group, that are the closest in meaning.

Group A

Gratitude, shy, courageous

Group B

Bold, audacious, friendly

A	B	C	D
Shy and friendly	Gratitude and friendly	Courageous and audacious	Gratitude and bold

Question 14

Which 3 of the 8 three-letter 'bits' can be combined to create a word meaning "having been deserted or left"?

> *aba, del, tru, ndo, mne, ned, fli, ing*

Answer [   ]

Question 15

Which 3 of the 8 three-letter 'bits' can be combined to create a word meaning "the use of icons to represent something", or "something can be referred to in linguistic terms"?

> *bet, bol, bal, ism, pre, ing, sym, rai*

Answer [   ]

Question 16

Which 3 of the 8 three-letter 'bits' can be combined to create a word meaning "incorrectly positioned or temporarily lost?"

> *ten, pla, tra, mis, als, ing, ced, den*

Answer [   ]

Question 17

Which 3 of the 8 three-letter 'bits' can be combined to create a word meaning "part of the body that contains all the structures between the chest and the pelvis?"

> *Tre, ple, omi, art, abd, wre, ing, nal*

Answer [   ]

Question 18

In the line below, the word outside of the brackets will only go with three of the words inside the brackets to make longer words. Which one word will it not go with?

	B	C	D	E
Un	(alike)	(adjusted)	(capable)	(affected)

Question 19

In the line below, the word outside of the brackets will only go with three of the words inside the brackets to make longer words. Which one word will it not go with?

	B	C	D	E
In	(appropriate)	(justice)	(ethical)	(animate)

Question 20

In the line below, the word outside of the brackets will only go with three of the words inside the brackets to make longer words. Which one word will it not go with?

	B	C	D	E
Down	(out)	(size)	(ward)	(load)

Question 21

In the line below, the word outside of the brackets will only go with three of the words inside the brackets to make longer words. Which one word will it not go with?

	B	C	D	E
In	(decisive)	(reference)	(destructible)	(convenience)

Question 22

Rubbish is to bin as bread is to..?

A	B	C	D
Breadbin	Knife	Buy	Wheat

Question 23

In each question, there are two pairs of words. Only one of the answers will go equally well with both these pairs.

(Tree   Stem)   (Growl   woof)

A	B	C	D
Cover	Branch	Bark	Dog

Question 24

Peter won an award for outstanding achievement. He _____ the award _____ .

A	B	C	D
excepted / grascious	accepted / graciously	expected / gracily	eccepted / graciously

Question 25

The evidence _____ the jury to reach a unanimous _____ .

A	B	C	D
led / decisive	lead / decision	led / decision	leed / decishion

Question 26

The _____ of the school enforced many _____ to ensure an effective code of conduct.

A	B	C	D
principal / principles	principles / principal	princepal / principals	principle / principles

Question 27

She _____ the piano every day. _____ makes perfect.

A	B	C	D
practices / practices	practices / practices	practises / practice	practises/ practisce

Question 28

Which sentence is written correctly?

A – We will be in contact with you shortly.
B – We will be in contact with you shortley.
C – We will in contact be with you shortly.
D – Shortly will we be in contact with you.

Answer

Question 29

Which sentence is written correctly?

A – Yours sincerity
B – Your's sincerely
C – Yours sincerely
D – You're sincerely

Answer

Question 30

Which sentence is written correctly?

A – I regret to inform you that you did not get chosen for the internship.
B – I inform to regret you that you did not get chosen for the internship.
C – I regret to inform you, that, you did not get chose for the internship.
D – I regret to inform your that you did not get chosen for the internship.

Answer

ANSWERS TO VERBAL ABILITY – GENERAL APTITUDE (TEST 1)

Q1. D = inconsistent

EXPLANATION = the term 'imaginary' can be defined as "existing only in the imagination". The words apocryphal, fictional and illusory, all carry the same connotations as 'imaginary'. Inconsistent is a term used to describe something that "does not stay the same throughout".

Q2. A = miniature

EXPLANATION = the term 'important' can be defined as "being of great significance". The words significant, imperative and crucial, all carry the same connotations as 'significant'. Miniature is a term used to describe something "on a smaller scale".

Q3. C = overrate

EXPLANATION = the term 'belittle' can be defined as "dismissing someone or something as unimportant". The words trivialise, denigrate, and malign, all carry the same connotations as 'belittle'. Overrate is a term used to describe "a higher opinion of something or someone than is deserved".

Q4. D = cause

EXPLANATION = the term 'conclusion' can be defined as "the end or finish or reaching a final decision". The words outcome, upshot, and denouement, all carry the same connotations as 'conclusion'. Cause is a term used to describe something that has "been made to happen; causing it to occur".

Q5. C = cow

EXPLANATION = 'cow' is the odd one out because all of the other words refer to a type of meat. A cow is the animal in which beef comes from.

Q6. E = Nuremberg

EXPLANATION = 'Nuremberg' is the odd one out because all of the other words are capital cities, whereas Nuremberg is not a capital city.

Q7. D = petal

EXPLANATION = 'petal' is the odd one out because all of the other words refer to a type of flower, whereas petal is part of a flower.

Q8. E = stuffed

EXPLANATION = 'stuffed' is the odd one out because all of the other words are synonyms for being hungry, whereas stuffed is the opposite of being hungry.

Q9. D = dodo

EXPLANATION = 'dodo' is the odd one out because all of the other types of birds, are birds that are still alive today, whereas a dodo bird is extinct.

Q10. B = placid and docile

EXPLANATION = placid and docile are the closest in meaning. Both these words refer to calm, peace and submissiveness; with little movement or activity.

Q11. A = enraged and incensed

EXPLANATION = enraged and incensed are the closest in meaning. Both words refer to being very angry and furious.

Q12. A = determined and resolute

EXPLANATION = determined and resolute are the closest in meaning. Both words refer to being determined and unwavering.

Q13. C = courageous and audacious

EXPLANATION = courageous and audacious are the closest in meaning. Both words refer to willingness to take bold risks; they carry connotations of being bold and daring.

Q14. Abandoned

EXPLANATION = the word that can be created in order to demonstrate something being deserted or left, is abandoned.

Q15. Symbolism

EXPLANATION = the word that can be created in order to represent something through icons, and can be referred to in linguistic terms, is symbolism.

Q16. Misplaced

EXPLANATION = the word that can be created in order to demonstrate something being placed in the incorrect position, or temporarily lost, is misplaced.

Q17. Abdominal

EXPLANATION = the word that can be created in order to demonstrate part of the body that contains all the structures between the chest and the pelvis, is abdominal.

Q18. C = capable

EXPLANATION = unalike, unadjusted, unaffected. Therefore the word that (un) does not go with is capable. (Instead it would be incapable).

Q19. C = ethical

EXPLANATION = inappropriate, injustice, inanimate. Therefore the word that (in) does not go with is ethical. (Instead it would be unethical).

Q20. A = out

EXPLANATION = downsize, downward, download. Therefore the word that (down) does not go with is out. This does not make a word and makes no sense.

Q21. B = reference

EXPLANATION = indecisive, indestructible, inconvenience. Therefore the word that (in) does not go with is reference. Instead this would need to be two separate words i.e. in reference to…

Q22. A = Breadbin

EXPLANATION = rubbish is stored in the bin as bread is stored in the breadbin

Q23. C = bark

EXPLANATION = bark can mean part of a tree, or the bark (woof) sound of a dog.

Q24. B = accepted / graciously

EXPLANATION = accepted and graciously are the correct words in order to fit in with the sentence structure.

Q25. C = led / decision

EXPLANATION = led and decision are the correct words in order to fit in with the sentence structure.

Q26. A = principal / principles

EXPLANATION = principal and principles are the correct words in order to fit in with the sentence structure.

Q27. C = practises / practice

EXPLANATION = practises and practice are the correct words in order to fit in with the sentence structure.

Q28. A = 'We will be in contact with you shortly'.

EXPLANATION = sentence A is the only sentence that is written correctly.

Q29. C = 'Yours sincerely'

EXPLANATION = sentence C is the only sentence that is written correctly.

Q30. A = 'I regret to inform you that you did not get chosen for the internship'.

EXPLANATION = sentence A is the only sentence that is written correctly.

VERBAL ABILITY – GENERAL APTITUDE – (TEST 2)

Question 1

Which of the following is **not** an anagram for 'types of food'?

A	B	C	D	E
Past eight	Can I roam	Boar win	Can peak	Cool cheat

Question 2

Which of the following is **not** an anagram for 'a country'?

A	B	C	D	E
Plane	Chain	Serial	Enemy	Slow

Question 3

Which of the following is **not** an anagram for 'a type of sport'?

A	B	C	D	E
Loop	Petals	Kiss	Swelter	Lovely

Question 4

Which of the following is **not** an anagram for 'a colour'?

A	B	C	D	E
Genre	Sore	Voile	Cheap	Hatred

Question 5

Which of the following is **not** an anagram of 'a type of tree'?

A	B	C	D	E
Hat sere	Koak cor	Boules	Mace roys	Cut coon

Question 6

Start at one of the corner letters and move clockwise around the square finishing in the centre to create a nine-letter word.

A	B	S
T		
C		R

Answer

Question 7

Start at one of the corner letters and move clockwise around the square finishing in the centre to create a nine-letter word.

	M	I
D	S	
	C	A

Answer

Question 8

Start at one of the corner letters and move clockwise around the square finishing in the centre to create a nine-letter word.

U	E	
	S	E
B		L

Answer [   ]

Question 9

Start at one of the corner letters and move clockwise around the square finishing in the centre to create a nine-letter word.

S		B
	D	O
G	A	

Answer [   ]

Question 10

Which two words need to be swapped around in order for the sentence to read correctly?

Having an operation will restrict in a loss of muscle strength and will possibly result movement.

Answer

Question 11

Which two words need to be swapped around in order for the sentence to read correctly?

The elderly like to memories about their past to not only make conversation, but keep their reminisce alive.

Answer

Question 12

Which two words need to be swapped around in order for the sentence to read correctly?

Minimum benefits has now been raised to over £5.00 in 2014, which wage employees aged 18 to 20.

Answer

Question 13

Which two words need to be swapped around in order for the sentence to read correctly?

Doctors recommended us to eat the advise amount of fruit and vegetables to ensure a healthier lifestyle.

Answer

Question 14

My family decided to take a long road trip down a small remote and _____ route. It was _____ having to sit in the car with my brothers for hours.

A	B	C	D
torturous / tortureous	torturous / tortuous	tortoise / tortuous	tortuous / torturous

Question 15

It is important to get _____ in case anything happens. It is fundamentally important to _____ my family are well looked after.

A	B	C	D
ensured / insured	insured / ensure	insure / insurance	onshore / ensure

Question 16

A business cannot afford to be _____ about security. They need to demonstrate high levels of safety and security _____ .

A	B	C	D
complaisant / procedures	complacent / proceedures	complaisant / prosedures	complacent / procedures

Question 17

The police are working on a _____ that teaches them how to _____ a potentially dangerous situation.

A	B	C	D
scheam / defuse	scheme / defuse	sceme / diffuse	scheme / diffuse

Question 18

Which of the following words is closest to the word - tentative?

A	B	C	D	E
Caring	Desire	Watching	Hesitant	Scared

Question 19

'Bona fide' means the same as..?

A	B	C	D	E
Correct	Genuine	Guessing	Caring	Wanting

Question 20

Which of the following words is the odd one out?

A	B	C	D	E
Pink	Salt	Ball	Red	Grey

Question 21

Fill in the brackets [?] with a letter that completes all the words.

Distan [?] rouble
Fac   [?] ense

A	B	C	D
e	b	d	t

Question 22

Fill in the brackets [?] with a letter that completes all the words.

Attac [?] ose
Arc   [?] and

A	B	C	D
k	h	m	e

Question 23

Fill in the brackets [?] with a letter that completes all the words.

Bas   [?] agle
Flam [?] ar

A	B	C	D
e	h	y	b

Question 24

Fill in the brackets [?] with a letter that completes all the words.

Rea [?] ight
Bal [?] ead

A	B	C	D
m	n	e	l

Question 25

In each question, there are two pairs of words. Only one of the answers will go equally well with both these pairs.

(Animal   quack)   (Down   dip)

A	B	C	D
Species	Duck	Bend	Lower

Question 26

In each question, there are two pairs of words. Only one of the answers will go equally well with both these pairs.

(Sway   shake)   (Stone   boulder)

A	B	C	D
Body	Movement	Rock	Cliff

Question 27

In each question, there are two pairs of words. Only one of the answers will go equally well with both these pairs.

(Variety   type)   (Arrange   organise)

A	B	C	D
Sort	Tidy	Style	Move

Question 28

In each question, there are two pairs of words. Only one of the answers will go equally well with both these pairs.

(Insect   wings)   (Hover   Levitate)

A	B	C	D
Bug	Fall	Air	Fly

Question 29

Chose the word that offers the closest in meaning to the word in CAPITALS.

While he is recovering from his operation, the doctors have suggested to keep him on a LIGHT diet.

A	B	C	D
Fair	Lamp	Simple	Huge

Question 30

Using the words in the brackets, complete the sentence in order for it to make sense.

Start is to (end   today   begin) as end is to (start   finish   less)

A	B	C	D
Begin / Finish	End / Start	Today / Less	Begin / Less

ANSWERS TO VERBAL ABILITY – GENERAL APTITUDE (TEST 2)

Q1. C = (boar win = rainbow)

EXPLANATION = (past eight = spaghetti), (can I roam = macaroni), (can peak = pancake), (cool cheat = chocolate).

Q2. E = (slow = owls)

EXPLANATION = (plane = Nepal), (chain = China), (serial = Israel), (enemy = Yemen).

Q3. B = (petals = pastels)

EXPLANATION = (loop = polo), (kiss = skis), (swelter = wrestle), (lovely = volley).

Q4. E = (hatred = thread)

EXPLANATION = (genre = green), (sore = rose), (voile = olive), (cheap = peach).

Q5. C = (boules = blouse)

EXPLANATION = (hat sere = ash tree), (koak cor = cork oak), (mace roys = sycamore), (cut coon = coconut).

Q6. Abstracts

EXPLANATION = starting in the top left corner, and moving clockwise around the edge and ending up in the middle, you can make the word abstracts.

Q7. Academics

EXPLANATION = starting in the bottom right corner, and moving clockwise around the edge and ending up in the middle, you can make the word academics.

Q8. Bluebells

EXPLANATION = starting in the bottom left corner, and moving clockwise around the edge and ending up in the middle, you can make the word bluebells.

Q9. Sabotaged

EXPLANATION = starting in the top left corner, and moving clockwise around the edge and ending up in the middle, you can make the word sabotaged.

Q10. restrict / result

EXPLANATION = "Having an operation will result in a loss of muscle strength and will possibly restrict movement".

Q11. memories / reminisce

EXPLANATION = "The elderly like to reminisce about their past to not only make conversation, but keep their memories alive".

Q12. benefits / wage

EXPLANATION = "Minimum wage has now been raised to over £5.00 in 2014, which benefits employees aged 18 to 20".

Q13. recommended / advise

EXPLANATION = "Doctors advise us to eat the recommended amount of fruit and vegetables to ensure a healthier lifestyle".

Q14. D = tortuous / torturous

EXPLANATION = "My family decided to take a long road trip down a small remote and tortuous route. It was torturous having to sit in the car with my brothers for hours".

Q15. B = insured / ensure

EXPLANATION = "It is important to get insured in case anything happens. It is fundamentally important to ensure that my family are well looked after".

Q16. D = complacent / procedures

EXPLANATION = "A business cannot afford to be complacent about security. They need to demonstrate high levels of safety and security procedures".

Q17. B = scheme / defuse

EXPLANATION = "The police are working on a scheme that teaches them how to defuse a potentially dangerous situation".

Q18. D = hesitant

EXPLANATION = the term tentative can be used to describe something "that is done without confidence" i.e. being hesitant.

Q19. B = genuine

EXPLANATION = the term bono fide can be used to describe something that is "real and genuine".

Q20. D = red

EXPLANATION = red is the odd one out because all of the other words contain four letters, red only contains three.

Q21. D = t

EXPLANATION = distant, trouble, fact, tense.

Q22. B = h

EXPLANATION = attach, hose, arch, hand.

Q23. A = e

EXPLANATION = base, eagle, flame, ear.

Q24. D = l

EXPLANATION = real, light, ball, lead.

Q25. B = duck

EXPLANATION = duck can either mean an animal, or it can refer to dipping and 'ducking' out of the way.

Q26. C = rock

EXPLANATION = rock can either mean a person to rock or sway back and forth, or a stone and type of rock.

Q27. A = sort

EXPLANATION = sort can mean a 'type of' or 'variety' of something i.e. a type of tree. Or it can mean to sort things, to arrange and organise.

Q28. D = fly

EXPLANATION = fly can refer to the insect or to actually fly somewhere (an aeroplane for example).

Q29. C = simple

EXPLANATION = the closest word in meaning to light in the context of the sentence is simple.

Q30. A = begin / finish

EXPLANATION = "start is to begin as end is to finish". This makes the most sense and is grammatically correct.

VERBAL ABILITY – READING AND COMPREHENSION

For this section, you need to read the passage carefully and answer the questions that follow. For each question/statement, you need to determine whether it is true, false or impossible to say.

An accident occurred on the M6 motorway between junctions 8 and 9 southbound at 3pm. The driver of a Ford Fiesta was seen to pull into the middle lane without indicating, forcing another car to veer into the central reservation. One person suffered a broken arm and was taken to hospital before the police arrived.

A = TRUE   **B** = FALSE   **C** = IMPOSSIBLE TO SAY

Question 1

The accident was on the M6 motorway on the carriageway that leads to Scotland.

Question 2

The driver of the Ford Fiesta was injured in the crash.

Question 3

The central reservation was responsible for the accident.

Question 4

The police did not give first aid at the scene.

Question 5

The accident happened at 1500 hours.

Following a bank robbery in a town centre, 6 masked gunmen were seen speeding away from the scene in a black van. The incident, which happened in broad daylight in front of hundreds of shoppers, was picked up by CCTV footage. Police are appealing for witnesses. The local newspaper has offered a £5,000 reward for any information leading to the arrest of all the people involved.

A = TRUE   **B** = FALSE   **C** = IMPOSSIBLE TO SAY

Question 6

The vehicle in which the gunmen drove off was a black van.

Question 7

Someone must have seen something.

Question 8

The incident was picked up by CCTV cameras.

Question 9

The newspaper will pay £5,000 for information leading to the arrest of all the men involved.

Question 10

Police are not appealing to members of the public for help.

At 1800 hours today, police issued a statement in relation to the crime scene on Armstrong Road. Police have been examining the scene all day and reports suggest that it may be murder. Forensic officers have been visiting the incident and inform us that the whole street has been cordoned off and nobody will be allowed through. Police say that the street involved will be closed for another 18 hours and no access will be available to anyone during this time.

A = TRUE   **B** = FALSE   **C** = IMPOSSIBLE TO SAY

Question 11

Police have confirmed the incident is murder.

Question 12

Forensic officers have now left the scene.

Question 13

The road will be open at 12 noon the following day.

Question 14

Although the street has been cordoned off, taxis and buses will be given access.

Question 15

Forensic officers will be at the scene all night.

During the summer, Mrs Olds called Neslington Country Council on 12 occasions reporting anti-social behaviour. Twenty-five-per-cent of the calls were about local drunk Andy Young loitering and discarding empty beer cans in her garden. Half of all the calls were because local teenagers were causing a nuisance around her semi-detached house, including disturbing behaviour and criminal damage. Mrs Olds reported that she felt scared in her own home.

The only facts known at this stage are:

- Local teenagers have been stopped by police and found with alcohol near Mrs Olds property.
- Two calls were because next door neighbours were playing music too loud.
- The Ford family live next door to Mr and Mrs Olds.
- Mrs Old's husband is retired.
- Mrs Olds lives next to a park where teenagers frequent.
- A neighbour, Mr Cook, has been warned about playing music too loud.

A = TRUE   **B** = FALSE   **C** = IMPOSSIBLE TO SAY

Question 16

Mrs Olds called the council three times about Andy Young.

Question 17

Mrs Olds is retired.

Question 18

Mrs Olds reported Mr Cook twice for playing his music too loud.

Question 19

The park is possibly a reason the anti-social behaviour occurs.

Question 20

Alcohol is the main cause of the anti-social behaviour.

This morning at 6am, Shepham Police raided a property with a warrant to search it for drugs. They found a selection of items commonly used to grow cannabis and a number of small cannabis plants. Police are still searching the property.

The latest reported facts are:

- The house is owned by Amanda Holder.
- She lives in the property with her partner, Michael Smith and his son, James Smith.
- Amanda and James do not get along.
- Michael works on an oil rig and has been away from home for two months.
- The drug growing equipment was found in James' room.
- All three have previous convictions for possessing drugs.

A = TRUE   B = FALSE   C = IMPOSSIBLE TO SAY

Question 21

Amanda Holder has been convicted of producing drugs before.

Question 22

The door of the house was damaged in the drug raid.

Question 23

Michael may not be aware of the drugs.

Question 24

James may have been growing the drugs to spite Amanda.

Question 25

Michael may have planted the cannabis plants a month ago.

A young child disappeared from a local food shop in Kinston after her mother became distracted at the counter. The mother asked the shop assistant to ring Kinston Police when she discovered her child had disappeared. The police arrived 10-minutes after they were called. Another shopper reported the child being walked away from the shop by a male who was approximately 6ft tall, with brown hair.

The only facts known at this stage are:

- The mother Miss Jenkins has red hair.
- Police were called at 10:25am on Saturday morning.
- Miss Jenkins had spoken to her child's father 10-minutes prior to her disappearance.
- The child's name is Molly.
- Molly's father has brown hair and is approximately 5ft 11.
- Tony Woods has a child with Miss Jenkins.

A = TRUE   B = FALSE   C = IMPOSSIBLE TO SAY

Question 26

The police arrived at the scene at 10:25am Saturday morning.

Question 27

Tony Woods is Molly's father.

Question 28

Molly's father may have taken her.

Question 29

Molly disappeared from a food shop in Kinston.

Question 30

Molly must have red or brown hair.

ANSWERS TO VERBAL ABILITY – READING AND COMPREHENSION

Q1. C = Impossible to say

Q2. C = Impossible to say

Q3. B = False

Q4. A = True

Q5. A = True

Q6. A = True

Q7. C = Impossible to say

Q8. A = True

Q9. A = True

Q10. B = False

Q11. B = False

Q12. C = Impossible to say

Q13. A = True

Q14. B = False

Q15. C = Impossible to say

Q16. A = True

Q17. C = Impossible to say

Q18. C = Impossible to say

Q19. A = True

Q20. C = Impossible to say

Q21. C = Impossible to say

Q22. C = Impossible to say

Q23. A = True

Q24. A = True

Q25. B = False

Q26. B = False

Q27. C = Impossible to say

Q28. A = True

Q29. A = True

Q30. B = False

NON- VERBAL
REASONING
TESTS

WHAT IS NON-VERBAL REASONING?

Non-Verbal Reasoning tests are often used to assess a person's ability to recognise shapes and patterns in regards to formations. The questions appear in diagrammatic and pictorial form, and can be broken up into 3 categories: Abstract, Spatial or Inductive Reasoning.

The importance of Non-Verbal Reasoning tests is to determine how well you can understand and visualise information to solve problems. You need to be able to recognise and identify patterns amongst abstract shapes and images.

Non-Verbal Reasoning tests have become a popular tool for job selection processes, so it is imperative that you get to grips with each question type and know how to answer them.

For psychometric testing, you need to aim for speed as well as accuracy. It is important to be able to undergo these tests with the utmost confidence and composure, in order to work swiftly and effectively throughout the test.

WHO TAKES A NON-VERBAL REASONING TEST?

For jobs and careers that involve a practical element, you may be required to sit a Non-Verbal Reasoning test. Non-Verbal Reasoning is also used in school tests, including the 11+ test.

Types of jobs that may require a Non-Verbal Reasoning test are as follows:

- Graduate positions
- Managerial roles
- Technical posts
- Pupils undertaking the 11+ examination.

WHAT DO THE QUESTIONS LOOK LIKE?

The types of questions that you will face in the Non-Verbal Reasoning test will vary depending on the type of test you will be sitting. This chapter provides you with a variety of sample questions and explanations, in order to give you a clearer understanding of what to expect.

Such tests may include:

- Determining identical shapes

- Rotating shapes

- Reflections of shapes

- Finding the odd shape

- Finding the missing shape

- 3D shapes

- Coding

- Shading and colours

- Number sequences

Please note, Spatial Reasoning and Abstract Reasoning are very similar tests, but are different. Thus, it is important to know which type of Non-Verbal Reasoning test you will be sitting. However, practising all types of questions can only work in your favour and better your chances at gaining a higher score.

Abstract (or Diagrammatic) – are tests to measure general intelligence. These tests require you to evaluate the rules surrounding the diagrams.

Spatial Reasoning – are tests which work with detailed and complex plans. Often, they rely on mental rotations of shapes.

EXAMPLES OF VERBAL REASONING

Sequences

Work out which figure comes next in the sequence.

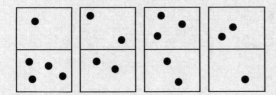

How to work it out

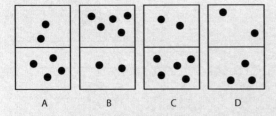

- The answer would be A. Starting from the first diagram in the top box, as it moves along the sequence it follows the pattern of 1, 2, 3, ... swapping from top to bottom box.

- Starting with the bottom part of the diagram, swapping from bottom to top box it follows the pattern 4, 2, 2, 2 ...

Answer

A

Odd One Out

Find the odd one out.

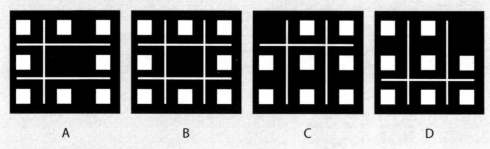

| A | B | C | D |

How to work it out

- Pay attention to everything that is going on: colours, patterns, position, shapes etc.

- You should notice that figures A, C and D all contain three lines, whereas figure B contains 4 lines and therefore makes it the odd one out.

Answer

B

Complete the Series

Question

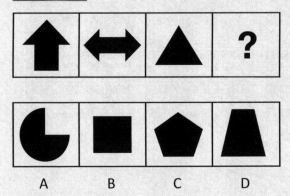

A   B   C   D

How to work it out

- Pay attention to symmetry, shades, shapes, size, patterns etc.
- You should notice that the first shape has one line of symmetry, the second has two, and the third has three.
- So you need a shape with four lines of symmetry to complete the series. Figure B (the square) has 4 lines of symmetry, therefore this would be the correct answer.

Answer

B

Rotating Shapes

Which answer option, if rotated, would look like the question figure?

Question

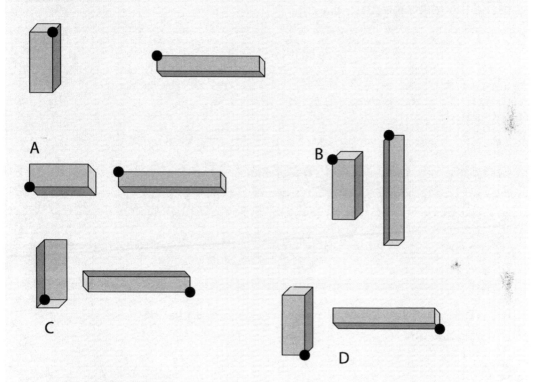

How to work it out

- To get from the figure shown to option C you would rotate both objects 180 degrees clockwise or anticlockwise.

- REMEMBER = both shapes need to be rotated exactly the same number of times, in the exact same direction.

Answer

C

NON-VERBAL REASONING – SPATIAL REASONING

Question 1

Join all of the shapes together with the corresponding letters to make the following shape.

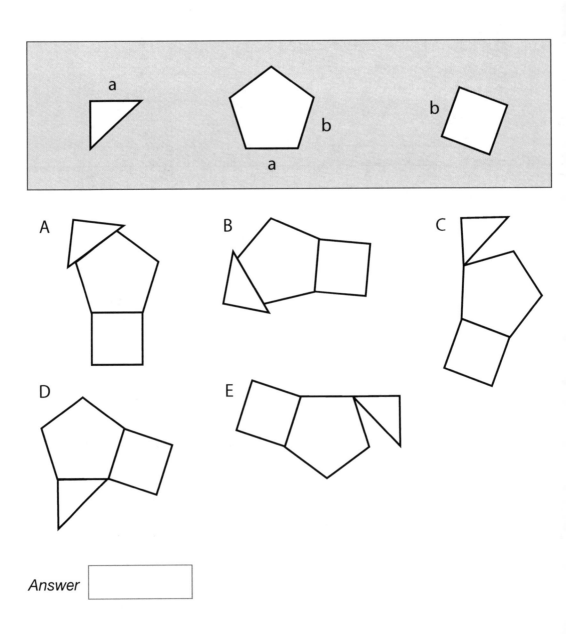

Answer

Question 2

Join all of the shapes together with the corresponding letters to make the following shape.

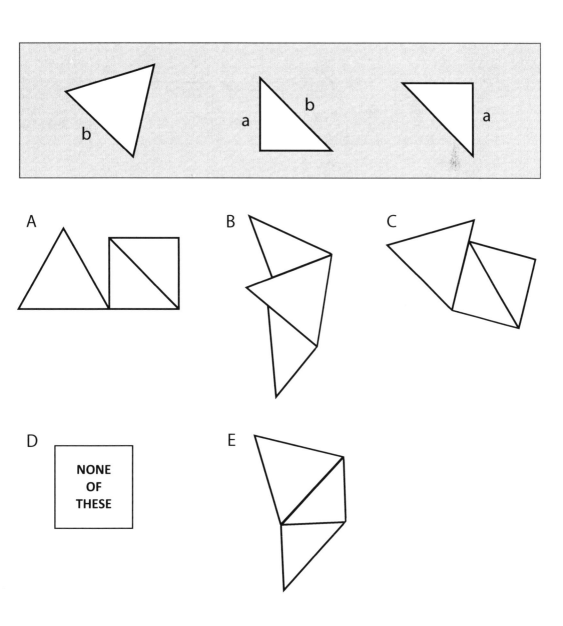

Answer

Question 3

Join all of the shapes together with the corresponding letters to make the following shape.

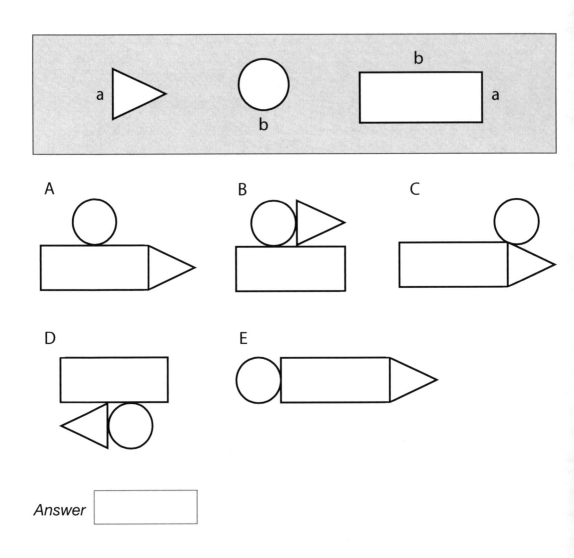

A

B

C

D

E

Answer

Question 4

Join all of the shapes together with the corresponding letters
to make the following shape.

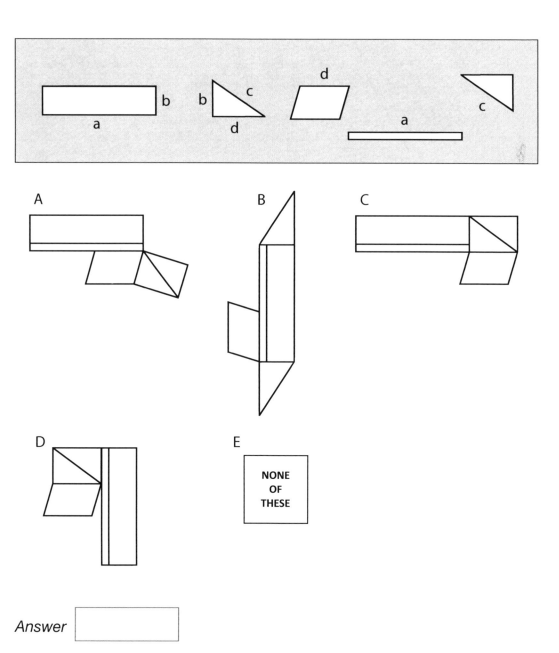

Answer [   ]

Question 5

Join all of the shapes together with the corresponding letters to make the following shape.

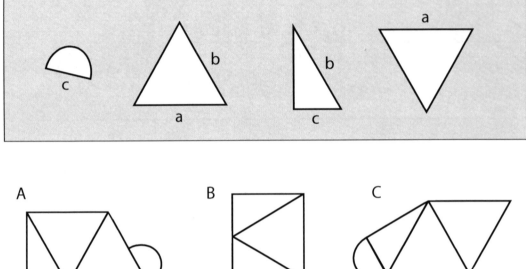

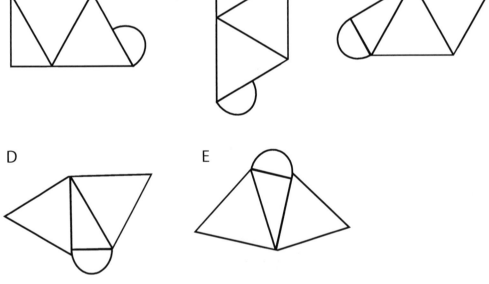

Answer

Question 6

Join all of the shapes together with the corresponding letters
to make the following shape.

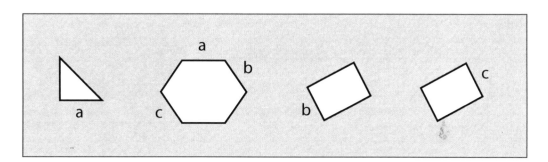

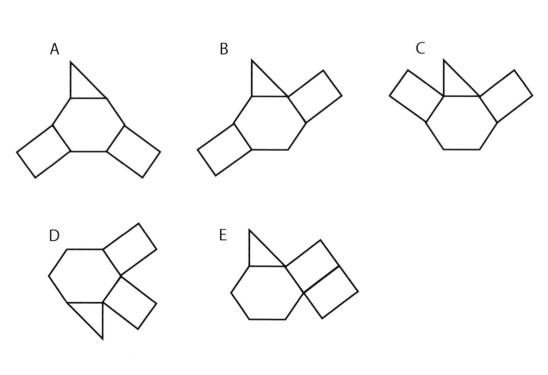

Answer

Question 7

Join all of the shapes together with the corresponding letters
to make the following shape.

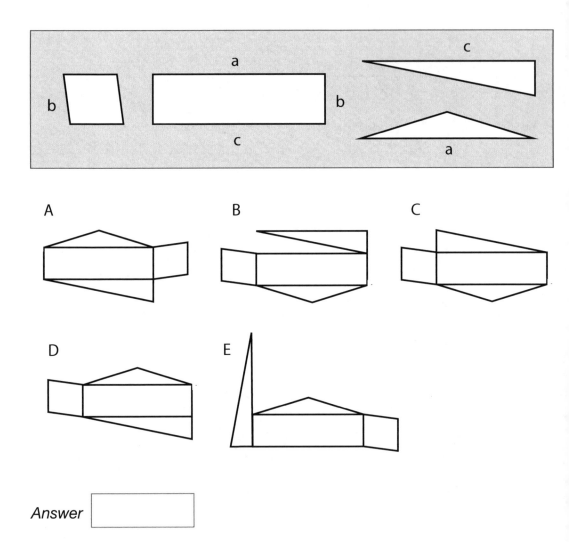

Answer

Question 8

Join all of the shapes together with the corresponding letters to make the following shape.

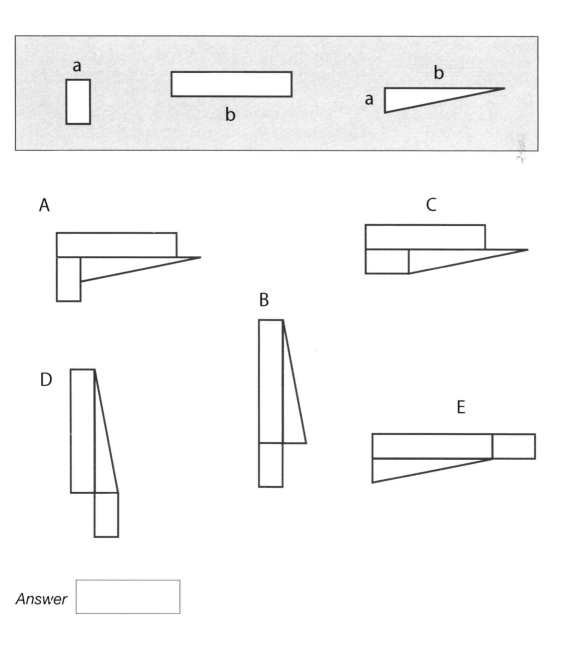

Answer

Question 9

Join all of the shapes together with the corresponding letters to make the following shape.

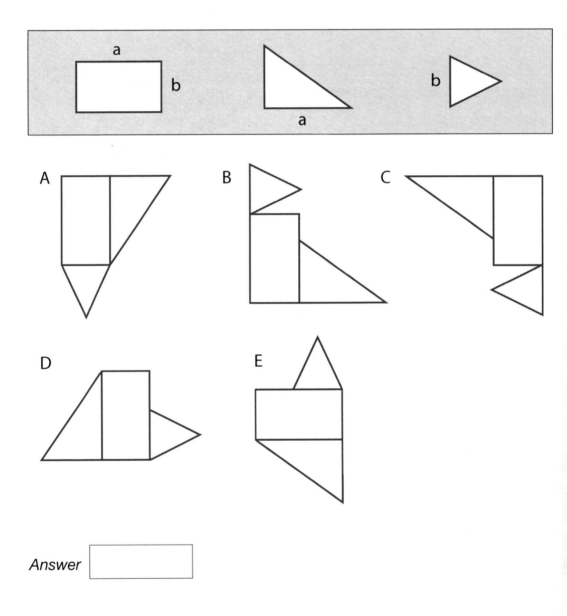

Answer

Question 10

Join all of the shapes together with the corresponding letters to make the following shape.

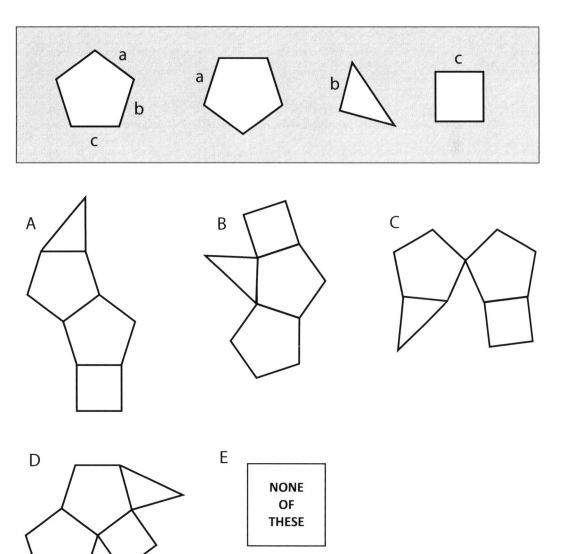

A

B

C

D

E

NONE
OF
THESE

Answer

Question 11

Join all of the shapes together with the corresponding letters to make the following shape.

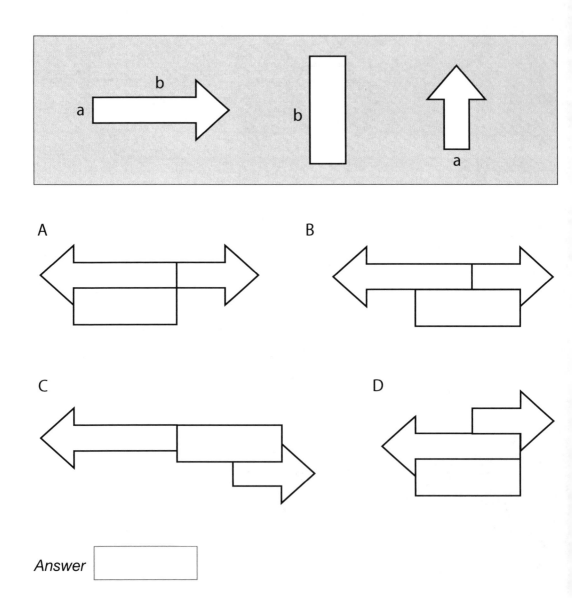

A

B

C

D

Answer

Question 12

Join all of the shapes together with the corresponding letters to make the following shape.

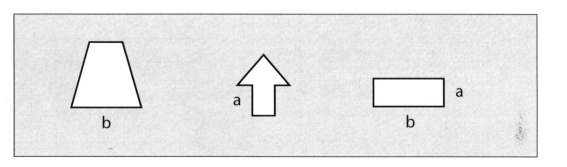

A

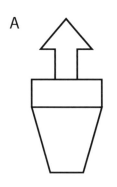

B

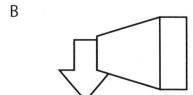

C

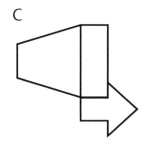

D

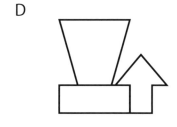

Answer

Question 13

Join all of the shapes together with the corresponding letters to make the following shape.

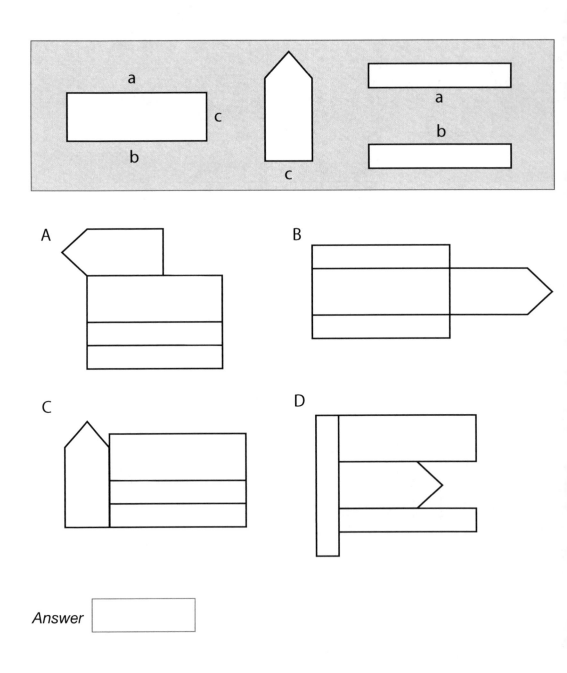

Answer

Question 14

Join all of the shapes together with the corresponding letters
to make the following shape.

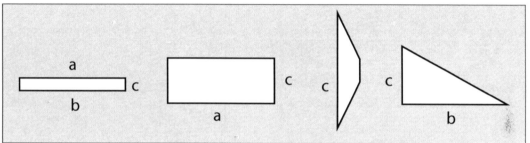

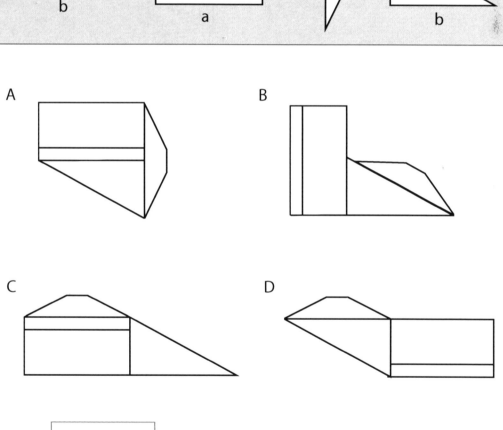

Answer

Question 15

Join all of the shapes together with the corresponding letters to make the following shape.

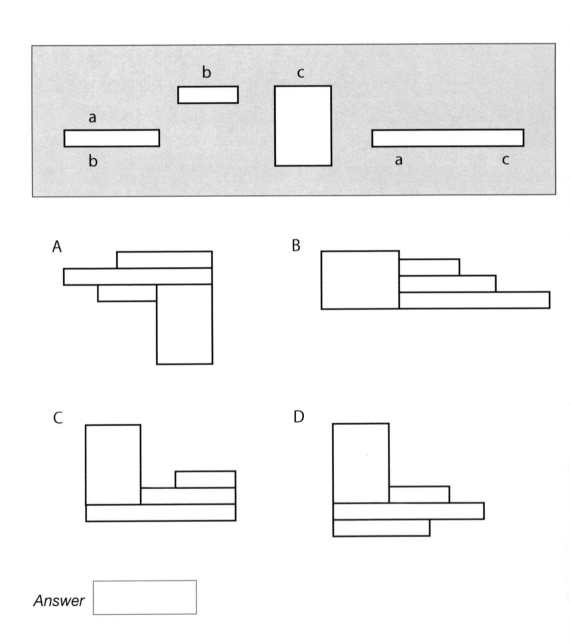

Answer

Question 16

Join all of the shapes together with the corresponding letters
to make the following shape.

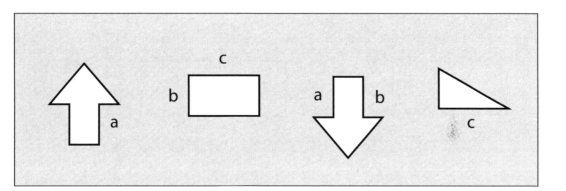

A

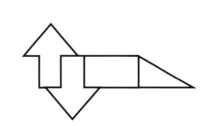

B

C

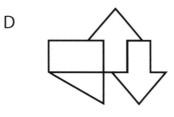

D

Answer _____

Question 17

Join all of the shapes together with the corresponding letters to make the following shape.

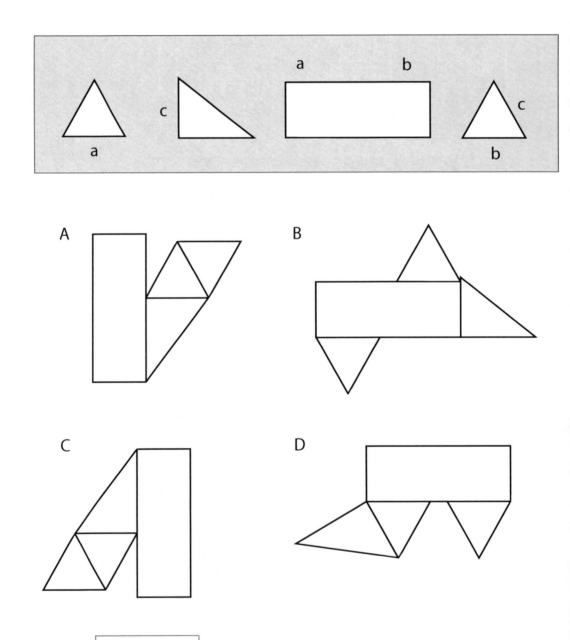

Answer

Question 18

Join all of the shapes together with the corresponding letters to make the following shape.

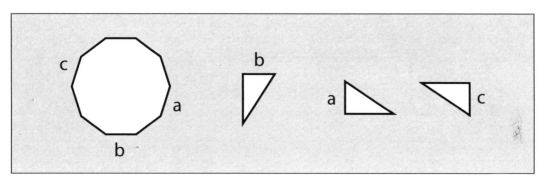

A

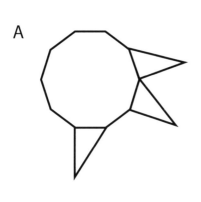

B

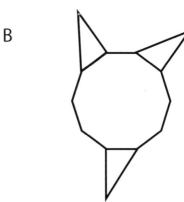

C

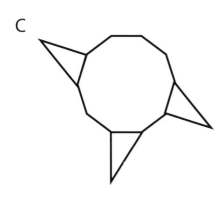

D

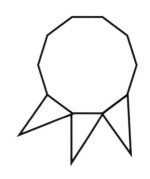

Answer

Question 19

Join all of the shapes together with the corresponding letters to make the following shape.

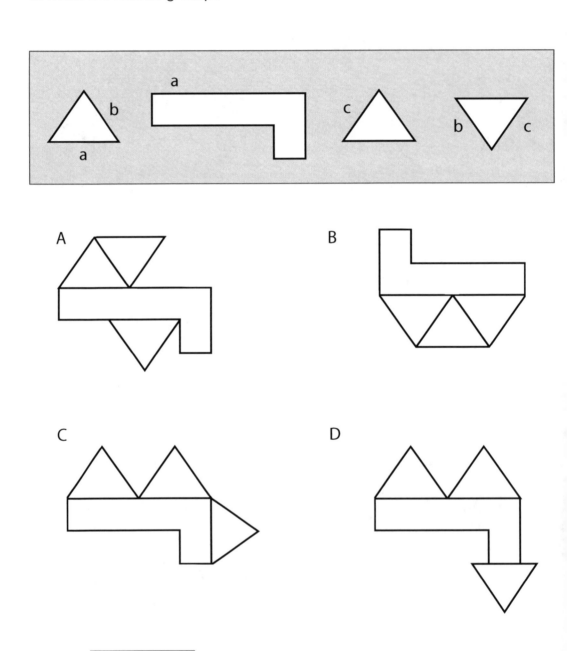

Answer ____

Question 20

Join all of the shapes together with the corresponding letters
to make the following shape.

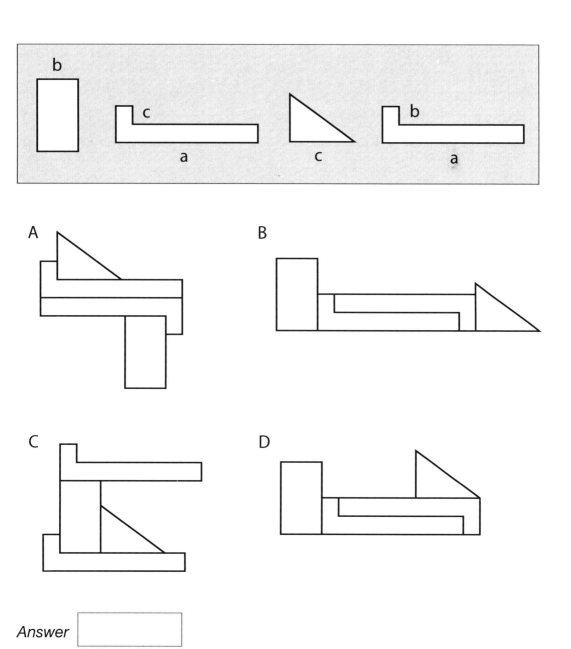

Answer

ANSWERS TO NON-VERBAL REASONING – SPATIAL REASONING

Q1. D

Q2. E

Q3. A

Q4. C

Q5. C

Q6. B

Q7. A

Q8. D

Q9. A

Q10. B

Q11. A

Q12. C

Q13. B

Q14. A

Q15. C

Q16. D

Q17. D

Q18. C

Q19. B

Q20. A

NON-VERBAL REASONING – ABSTRACT REASONING

Question 1

Work out which figure is a top-down 2D view of the 3D shape.

3D Question Figure

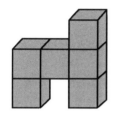

2D Views

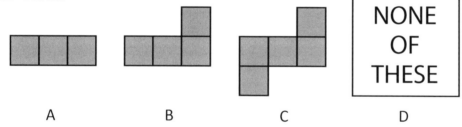

A   B   C   D

Answer

Question 2

Work out which option fits best in the missing square in order to complete the sequence.

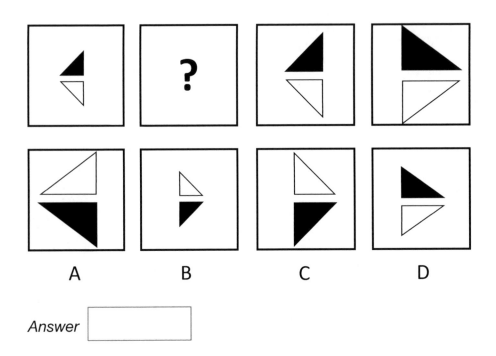

A   B   C   D

Answer

Question 3

Work out which 3D shapes from the answer figures are needed to create the Question Figure.

Question Figure

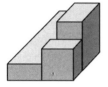

Answer Figures

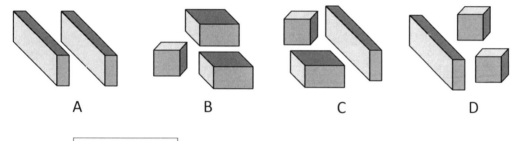

| A | B | C | D |

Answer

Question 4

Work out which 3D shapes from the answer figures are needed to create the Question Figure.

Question Figure

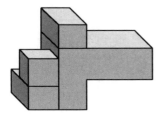

Answer Figures

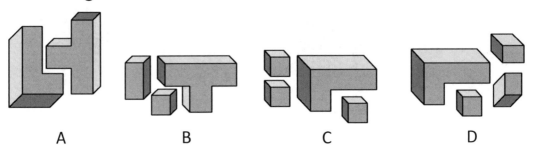

| A | B | C | D |

Answer

Question 5

Work out which option fits best in the missing square in order to complete the sequence.

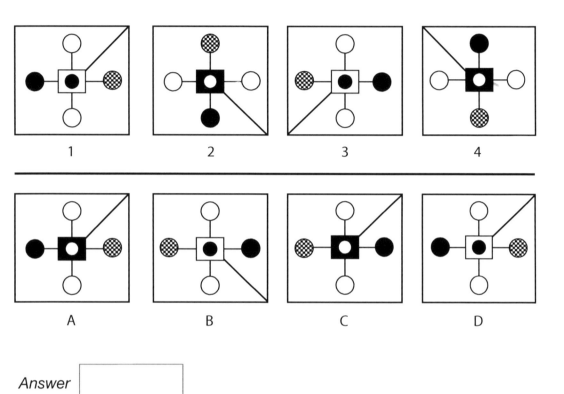

| 1 | 2 | 3 | 4 |

| A | B | C | D |

Answer _____

Question 6

Work out which of the cubes can be made from the net.

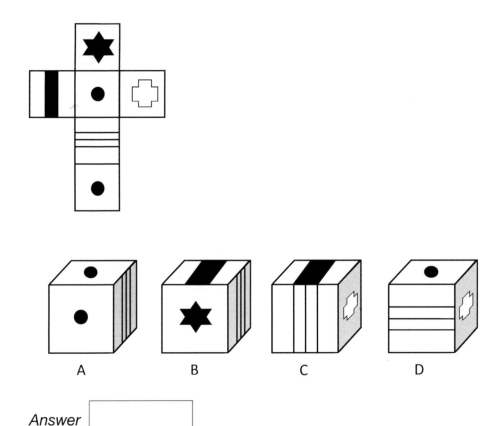

Answer [   ]

Question 7

Work out which two shapes are identical. (No rotation or reflection needed). TWO answers required.

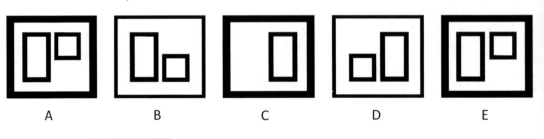

Answer [   ]

Question 8

Work out which option fits best in the missing square in order to complete the sequence.

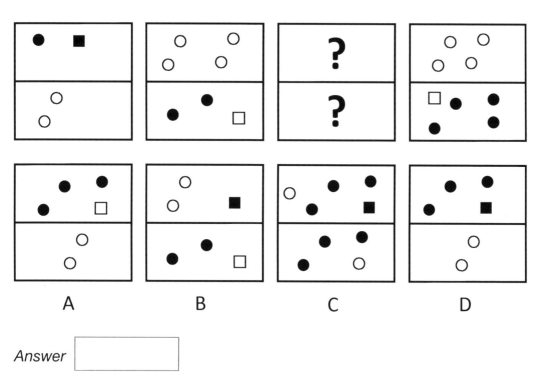

A   B   C   D

Answer [   ]

Question 9

Work out which two shapes are identical. (No rotation or reflection needed). TWO answers required.

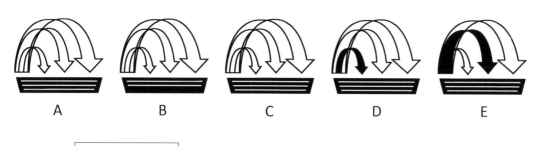

A   B   C   D   E

Answer [   ]

Question 10

Work out which two shapes are identical. (No rotation or reflection needed). TWO answers required.

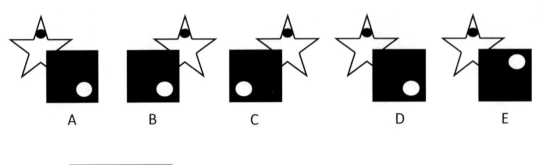

| A | B | C | D | E |

Answer

Question 11

Work out which two shapes are identical. (No rotation or reflection needed). TWO answers required.

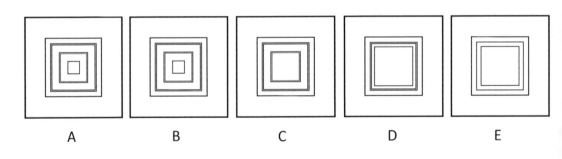

| A | B | C | D | E |

Answer

Question 12

Work out which option is a reflection of the Question Figure.

Question Figure

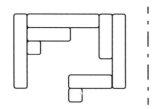

Answer Figures

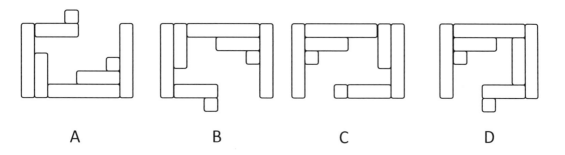

| A | B | C | D |

Answer [   ]

Question 13

Work out which option is a reflection of the Question Figure.

Question Figure

- - — - - - -

Answer Figures

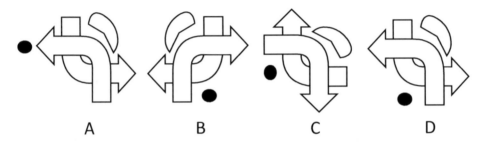

A	B	C	D

Answer

Question 14

Work out which option (A, B, C or D) would NOT look like the Question Figure if it was rotated.

Question Figure   Answer Figures

 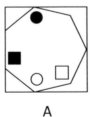 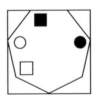 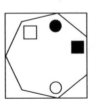 

A	B	C	D

Answer

Question 15

Work out which option (A, B, C or D) would NOT look like the Question Figure if it was rotated.

Question Figure   Answer Figures

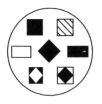

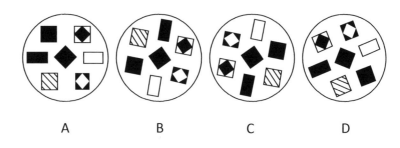

A   B   C   D

Answer

Question 16

Fill in the missing square in order to complete the grid.

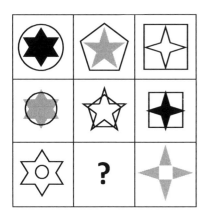

A   B   C   D

Answer

Question 17

Work out which figure is a top-down 2D view of the 3D Question Figure.

3D Question Figure

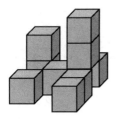

2D Views

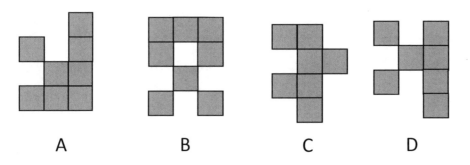

| A | B | C | D |

Answer [   ]

Question 18

Look at how the figure changes from box 1 to box 2. Apply the same changes in order to get the correct answer.

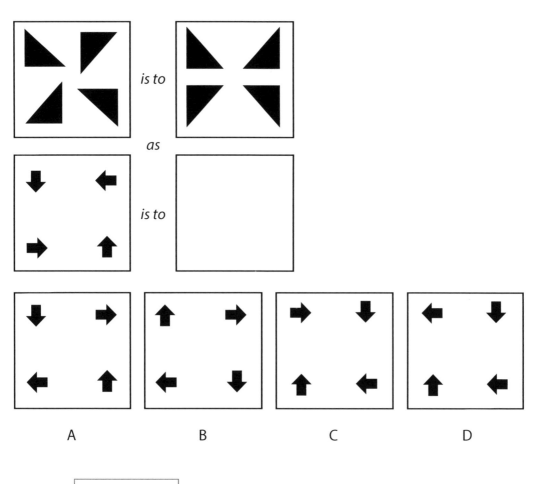

A   B   C   D

Answer

Question 19

Work out which option (A, B, C or D) would NOT look like the Question Figure if it was rotated.

Question Figure

Answer Figures

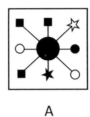 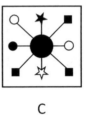 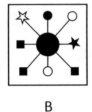 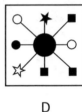

A   B   C   D

Answer

Question 20

Work out which option (A, B, C or D) would NOT look like the Question Figure if it was rotated.

Question Figure

Answer Figures

A   B   C   D

Answer

Question 21

Work out which option (A, B, C or D) would NOT look like the Question Figure if it was rotated.

Question Figure   Answer Figures

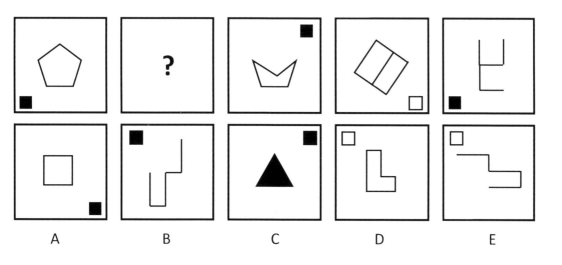

A   B   C   D

Answer

Question 22

What figure completes the sequence pattern?

A   B   C   D   E

Answer

Question 23

What figure completes the sequence pattern?

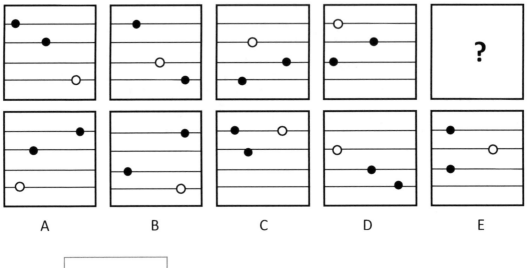

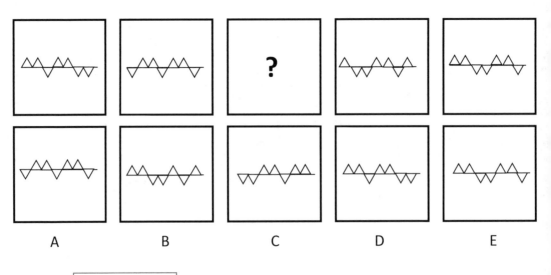

Answer

Question 24

What figure completes the sequence pattern?

Answer

Question 25

What figure completes the sequence pattern?

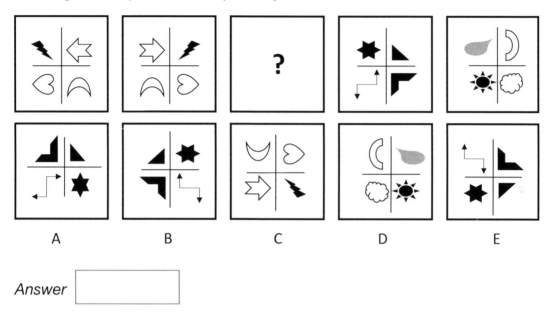

A   B   C   D   E

Answer

Question 26

What figure completes the sequence pattern?

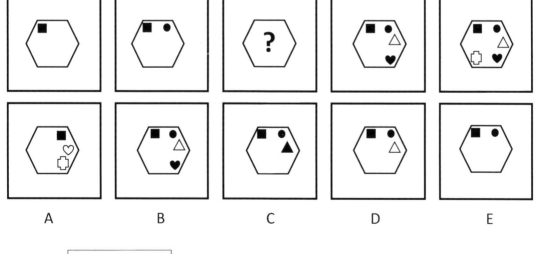

A   B   C   D   E

Answer

Question 27

What figure completes the sequence pattern?

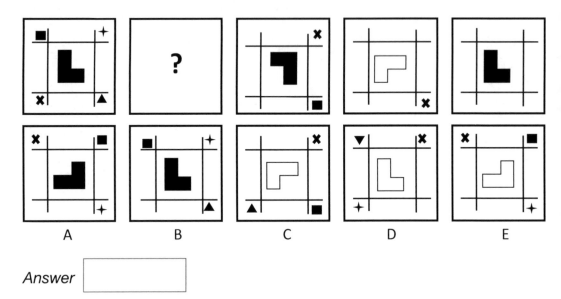

Answer

Question 28

What figure fits in with the sequence pattern?

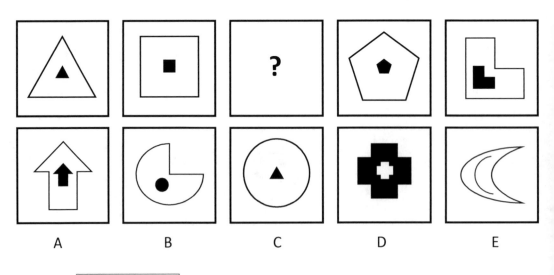

Answer

Question 29

What figure comes next in the series?

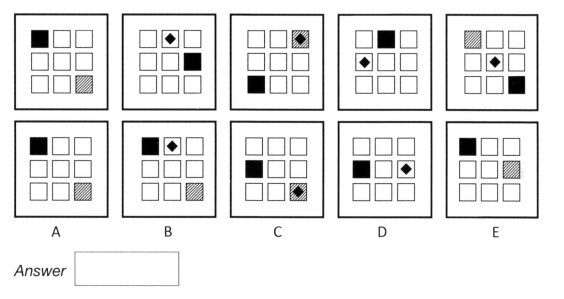

A   B   C   D   E

Answer

Question 30

What figure comes next in the series?

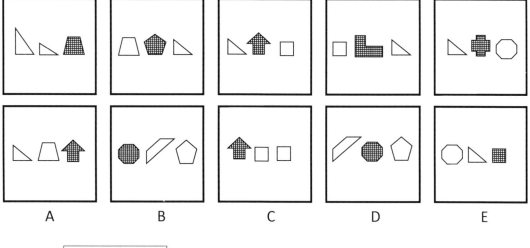

A   B   C   D   E

Answer

ANSWERS TO NON-VERBAL REASONING – ABSTRACT REASONING

Q1. A

EXPLANATION = a top-down 2D view of the 3D Question Figure would show three squares in a horizontal line.

Q2. D

EXPLANATION = the sequence follows: every even square contains triangles pointing in the right direction, every odd square has triangles pointing in the left direction. The triangles get bigger as the sequence progresses.

Q3.C

EXPLANATION = the Question Figure contains one cube, and two different sized cuboids.

Q4. D

EXPLANATION = the Question Figure contains an 'L' 3D shape, 2 cuboids of the same length, and a cube.

Q5. A

EXPLANATION = within each square the shapes are moving round 90 degrees anti-clockwise as the sequence progresses. You will also notice that the square and inner circle which forms the centre of each shape, are alternating between black and white as the sequence progresses. The diagonal line within each square is moving round clockwise as the sequence progresses.

Q6. D

EXPLANATION = Figure A can be ruled out because the two circles need to be on opposite sides. Figure B can be ruled out because the side with the three lines needs to be a circle instead. Figure C can be ruled out because the 'cross' sign would need to be a circle.

Q7. A and E

EXPLANATION = none of the other shapes are identical. Figures A and E are identical.

Q8. D

EXPLANATION = starting from the top left box in the first rectangle, the number of dots is one, and also includes a black square. The black square changes colour. One dot is added each time, as the sequence progresses. Starting from the bottom left box in the rectangle, it has two white dots, this follows a zig-zag pattern, of two dots then four dots, two dots then four dots and so forth.

Q9. A and C

EXPLANATION = Figures A and C are the only identical shapes.

Q10. A and D

EXPLANATION = Figures A and D are the only identical shapes.

Q11. A and B

EXPLANATION = Figures A and B are the only identical shapes.

Q12. B

EXPLANATION = Figure B is a reflection of the Question Figure. Figure A is a rotation not a reflection. Figures C and D have been manipulated but not rotated.

Q13. D

EXPLANATION = Figure D is a reflection of the Question Figure. Figure A has the black dot in the wrong position (even though the rest of the shape is a reflection). Figures B and C are rotations not reflections.

Q14. C

EXPLANATION = Figure C is the correct answer because it is not an exact rotation of the Question Figure. The black and white circles have swapped places, which means the shape has been manipulated.

Q15. A

EXPLANATION = in Figure A, the black square should be opposite to the black square with the white triangle. Also, the black square with the diamond should be side by side with the white square with the black diamond. Therefore Figure A is not identical.

Q16. B

EXPLANATION = the sequence follows: from box 1 to 3, a six sided star, a five sided star and a four sided star. These stars are placed inside a shape. The next row has the same star shapes, but is placed half in-half out of another shape. The colour sequence has moved along one space each time. So, the last row has the star shapes outside the other shape. The colour pattern has moved one space again. The missing box needs to contain a five sided black star with a white pentagon inside.

Q17. D

EXPLANATION = there are only seven blocks that you will see from above. This rules out Figures A and B. Four blocks in a vertical line forms the right hand side of the shape. Figure C has an extra block on the right side of the four blocks, therefore this can be ruled out.

Q18. A

EXPLANATION = within the top set of squares, the top left and bottom right shapes remain in the same position. The bottom left and top right shapes rotate 180 degrees.

Q19. C

EXPLANATION = Figure C is the correct answer because the black square and the white star have swapped places. Two of the black squares in the Question Figure should be next to each other. Whereas in Figure C, the black squares are all in the corners and therefore cannot be an exact rotation.

Q20. D

EXPLANATION = in Figure D, there is a black circle. The Question Figure does not contain a black circle and therefore cannot be an exact rotation.

Q21. C

EXPLANATION = Figure C is not a rotation of the Question Figure because the line through the middle of the diamond has been made longer (instead of remaining inside the diamond, it now touches the outside of the square).

Q22. E

Rule 1 = the small square moves around one place clockwise as the sequence progresses.

Rule 2 = the small square alternates from black to white as the sequence progresses.

Rule 3 = the shape in the centre must contain 5 sides.

Figure A can be ruled out because the shape in the centre has only 4 sides; also, the black square in the bottom right corner should be a white square in the top left corner. Figure B can be ruled out because the black square needs to be a white square. Figure C can be ruled out because the shape in the centre needs to have 5 sides; also the black square in the top right corner needs to be a white square, and in the top left corner. Figure D can be ruled out because the shape in the centre has 6 sides.

Q23. A

Rule 1 = the two black dots remain straight after one another (there is no line in between the two black dots).

Rule 2 = the white dot remains one line ahead of the last black dot.

Rule 3 = the dots move up one line each time.

Figure B can be ruled out because the black dots should not have a line in between them. Figure C can be ruled out because the black dot should not be on the same line as the white dot. Figure D can be ruled out because the white dot needs to be on the bottom line. Figure E can be ruled out because the two black dots have been separated by the white dot in the middle.

Q24. C

Rule 1 = the triangles move one place to the right as the sequence progresses.

Figure A can be ruled out because it is a replica of box 2. Figure B can be ruled out because the triangles at the end of the figure are incorrect. Figure D can be ruled out because it is a replica of box 1. Figure E can be ruled out because it is a replica of box 5.

Q25. B

Rule 1 = The sequence contains vertical reflections. Box 1 is reflected to box 2. Box 3 is reflected to box 4 and so on.

Figure A can be ruled out because this has been reflected and then rotated; it is not a mere reflection of the next box. Figure C can be ruled out because this is a horizontal reflection of box 2; we want a reflection of box 4. Figure D can be ruled out because this is a vertical reflection of box 5; we want a vertical reflection of box 4. Figure E can be ruled out because this is a horizontal reflection of box 4; we want a vertical reflection of box 4.

Q26. D

Rule 1 = a new shape is placed in each of the corners of the hexagon.

Rule 2 = these shapes start in the top left corner and are added in a clockwise manner.

Figure A can be ruled out because we are looking for a black square, a black circle and a white triangle. Figure B can be ruled out because we only need three shapes, not four. Figure C can be ruled out because the triangle needs to be white, not black. Figure E can be ruled out because we need three shapes, not two.

Q27. E

Rule 1 = the shape in the middle rotates 90° anti-clockwise as the sequence progresses.

Rule 2 = the shape in the middle alternates from black to white as the sequence progresses.

Rule 3 = the small shapes move one position to the next corner (in a clockwise manner).

Rule 4 = as the shapes rotate around, a shape is left off. You will notice, that the 'cross' shape appears the most, therefore this must be the beginning of this sequence, and so the last shape rotated (using the 'cross' to begin) will be left off.

Figure A can be ruled out because the shape in the middle needs to be white, not black. Figure B can be ruled out because the shape in the middle needs to be white and rotated 90° anti-clockwise. Also, the small shapes do not follow the correct pattern. Figure C can be ruled out because the shape in the middle needs to be rotated 180°. Also the small shapes do not follow the correct pattern. Figure D can be ruled out because the shape in the middle needs to be rotated 90° anti-clockwise. None of the small shapes are in the correct position.

Q28. A

Rule 1 = the large shape is white. The small shapes are black.

Rule 2 = the small shape inside the large shape is the same shape.

Figure B can be ruled out because the 'pac-man' shape does not contain the same shape in the centre of the shape, it contains a circle instead. Figure C can be ruled out because the large white circle should contain a small black circle, not a black triangle. Figure D can be ruled out because the large shape should be white, and the small shape should be black. Figure E can be ruled out because the moon shape only contains a curved line, not a small moon shape.

Q29. D

Rule 1 = the black square moves 3 spaces clockwise, around the outer edge of the squares.

Rule 2 = the shaded box moves 1 space anti-clockwise, around the outer edge of the squares. If this coincides with a black square, it turns into a black square.

Rule 3 = the black diamond moves along the sequence from left to right; and once it reaches the end, it begins on the next row.

Figure A can be ruled out because the black square needs to be the first square on the second row. The shaded square should have disappeared and the black diamond should be the third square on the second row. Figure B can be ruled out because none of shaded or black squares are in the correct place. The diamond shape is also in the incorrect position. Figure C can be ruled out because the diamond should be the third square on the second row. The shaded box should have disappeared. Figure E can be ruled out because the black square needs to be on the row underneath; the shaded box should have disappeared and instead, have a black diamond in it.

Q30. B

Rule 1 = the last shape in each figure begins the shape in the next box.

Rule 2 = the shape with the most sides is highlighted.

Figure A can be ruled out because the sequence must start with an octagon, not a triangle. Figure C can be ruled out because the first shape in the sequence needs to be an octagon as opposed to an arrow. Figure D can be ruled out because the sequence needs to start with an octagon. Figure E can be ruled out because the octagon needs to be shaded in (it has the most number of sides in that figure).

NON-VERBAL REASONING – INDUCTIVE REASONING

Question 1

Which figure is the odd one out?

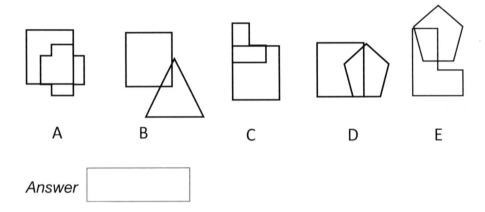

A   B   C   D   E

Answer

Question 2

Which figure fits in with the sequence?

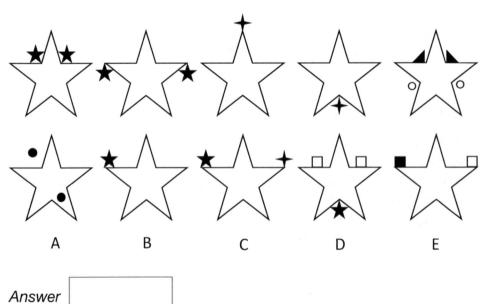

A   B   C   D   E

Answer

Question 3

Which answer fits in with the sequence?

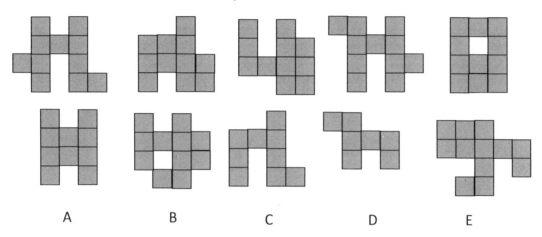

A   B   C   D   E

Answer

Question 4

Which figure fits in with the sequence?

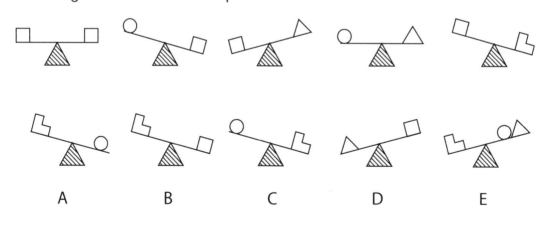

A   B   C   D   E

Answer

Question 5

What comes next in the sequence?

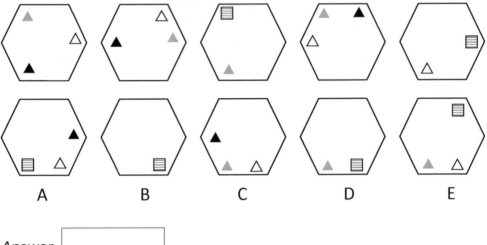

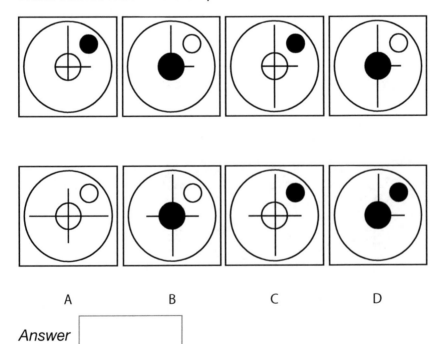

A   B   C   D   E

Answer

Question 6

What comes next in the sequence?

A   B   C   D

Answer

Question 7

What comes next in the sequence?

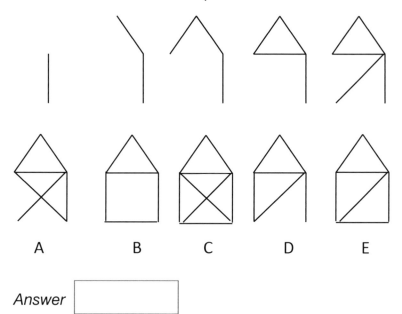

A   B   C   D   E

Answer

Question 8

What comes next in the sequence?

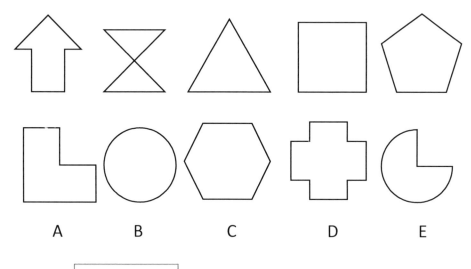

A   B   C   D   E

Answer

Question 9

What comes next in the sequence?

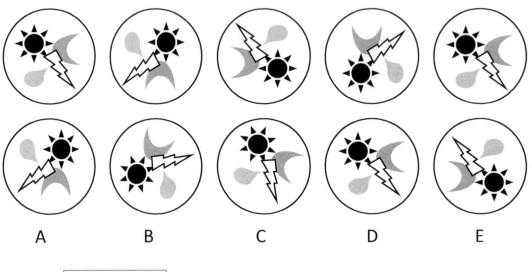

A   B   C   D   E

Answer

Question 10

What comes next in the sequence?

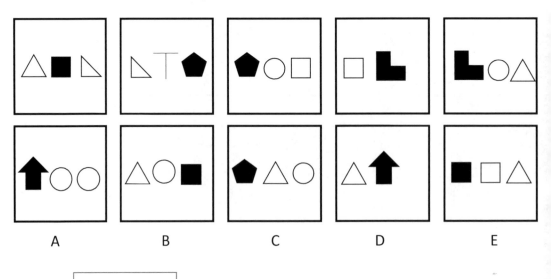

A   B   C   D   E

Answer

Question 11

What comes next in the sequence?

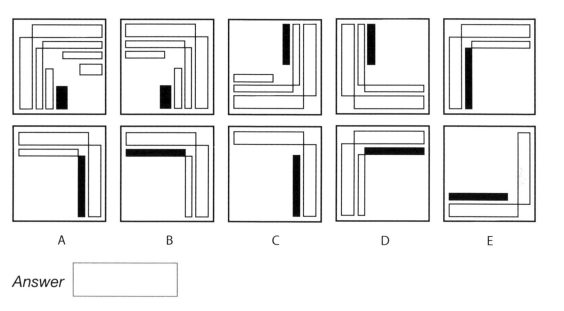

A	B	C	D	E

Answer

Question 12

Which answer fits in with the sequence?

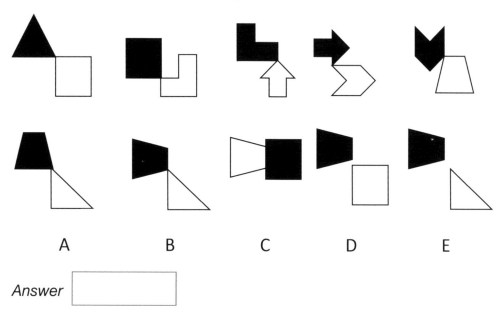

A	B	C	D	E

Answer

Question 13

Which answer fits in with the sequence?

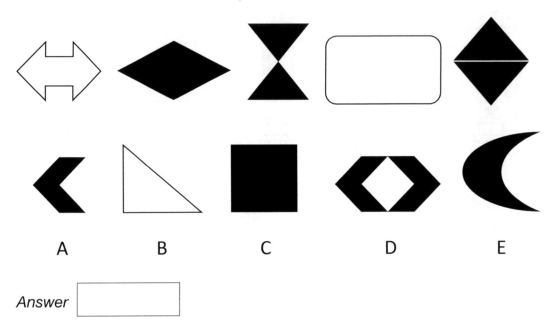

| A | B | C | D | E |

Answer [　　　　]

Question 14

What comes next in the sequence?

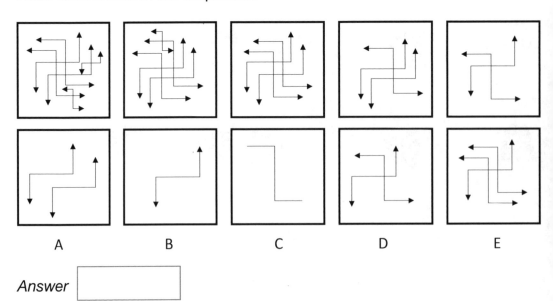

| A | B | C | D | E |

Answer [　　　　]

Question 15

What comes next in the sequence?

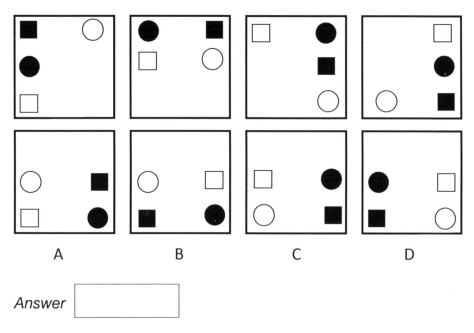

A   B   C   D

Answer

Question 16

What comes next in the sequence?

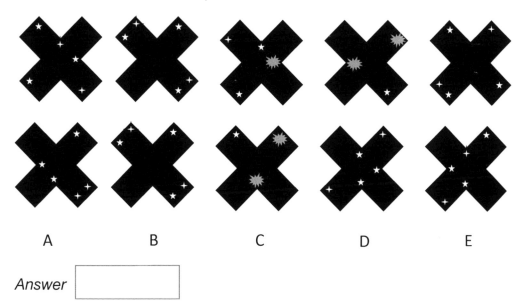

A   B   C   D   E

Answer

Question 17

What comes next in the sequence?

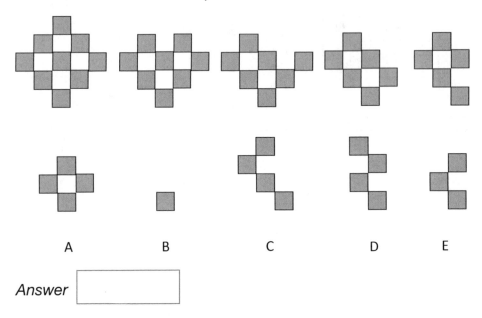

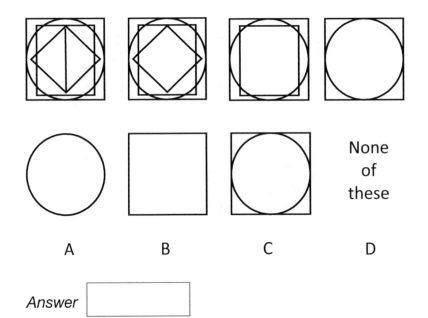

| A | B | C | D | E |

Answer [   ]

Question 18

What comes next in the sequence?

A   B   C   D

Answer [   ]

Question 19

What comes next in the sequence?

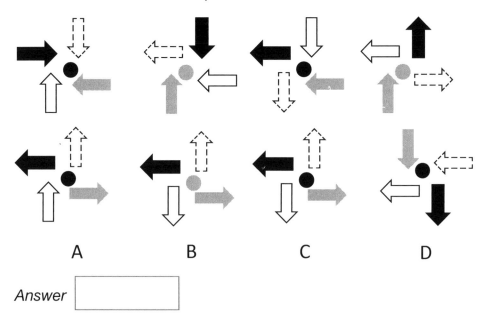

| A | B | C | D |

Answer

Question 20

What comes next in the sequence?

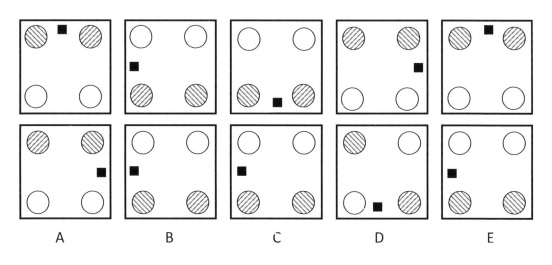

| A | B | C | D | E |

Answer

Question 21

Fill in the missing gap in order to complete the sequence.

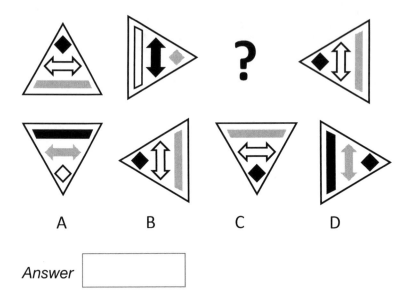

A   B   C   D

Answer [ ]

Question 22

Fill in the missing gap in order to complete the sequence.

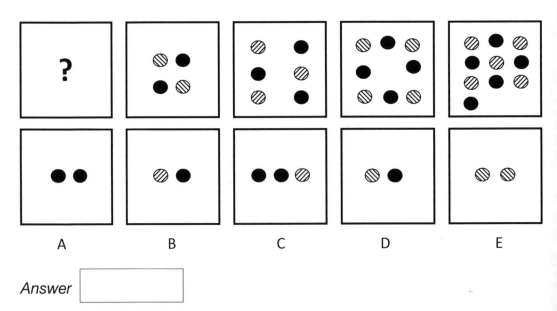

A   B   C   D   E

Answer [ ]

Question 23

What comes next in the sequence?

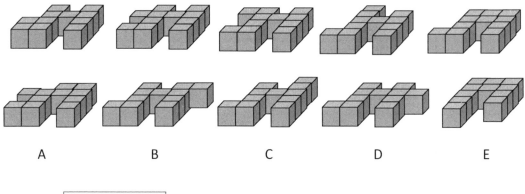

A   B   C   D   E

Answer

Question 24

What comes next in the sequence?

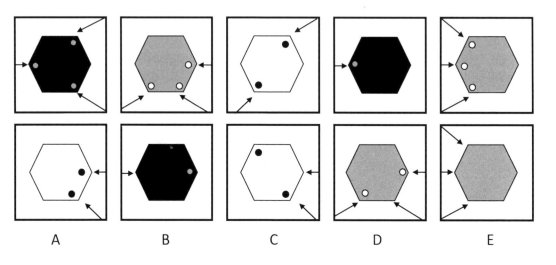

A   B   C   D   E

Answer

Question 25

Fill in the gap in order to complete the sequence.

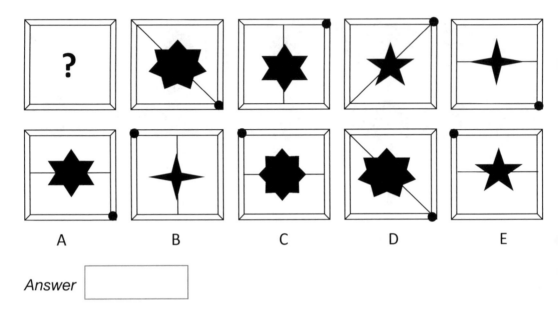

A   B   C   D   E

Answer

Question 26

Fill in the gap in order to complete the sequence.

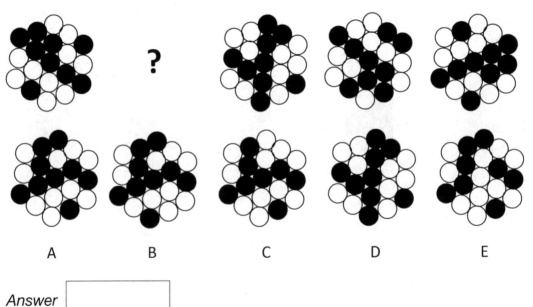

A   B   C   D   E

Answer

Question 27

Which figure is the odd one out?

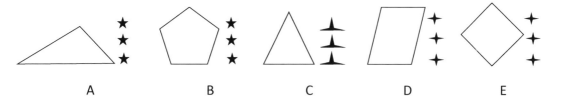

A B C D E

Answer

Question 28

Which figure is the odd one out?

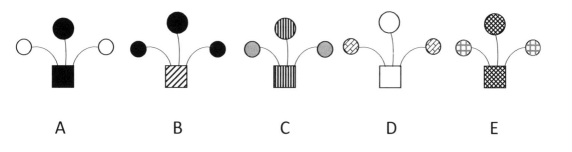

A B C D E

Answer

Question 29

Fill in the gap in order to complete the sequence.

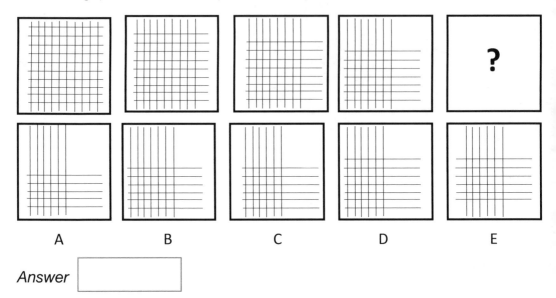

Answer

Question 30

Fill in the gap in order to complete the sequence.

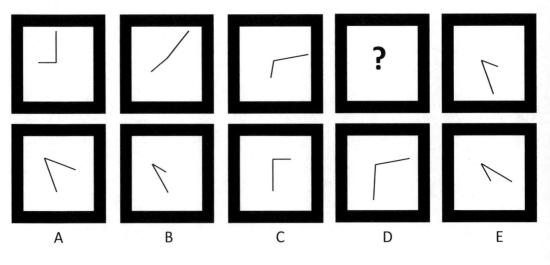

Answer

ANSWERS TO NON-VERBAL REASONING – INDUCTIVE REASONING

Q1. E

Rule 1 = each figure must contain a square.

Figure E is the odd one out because all of the other figures contain a square, whereas Figure E contains an 'L shape' and a pentagon.

Q2. D

Rule 1 = there must be at least one line of symmetry in the figure.

Figure A can be ruled out because it has no lines of symmetry. Figure B can be ruled out because it has no lines of symmetry. Figure C can be ruled out because the black star on the left would not reflect the black star on the right. Figure E can be ruled out because the black square on the left would not reflect the white square on the right.

Q3. B

Rule 1 = the pattern has to include 11 squares.

Figure A can be ruled out because it only contains 10 squares. Figure C can be ruled out because it only contains 9 squares. Figure D can be ruled out because it only contains 7 squares. Figure E can be ruled out because it contains 12 squares.

Q4. C

Rule 1 = squares weigh more than the circles.

Rule 2 = squares weigh more than the triangles.

Rule 3 = triangles and circles weigh the same.

Rule 4 = 'L' shapes weigh more than the squares.

Figure A can be ruled out because the 'L' shape weighs more than circles, therefore the scales are not correct. Figure B can be ruled out because the 'L' shape weighs more than squares; and therefore the scales are incorrect. Figure D can be ruled out because squares weigh more than triangles. Figure E can be ruled out because you are not given any indication as to whether the circle and the triangle together, would weigh less than the 'L' shape.

Q5. D

Rule 1 = the grey triangle moves around the points of the hexagon two places clockwise.

Rule 2 = the white triangle moves around the points of the hexagon one place anti-clockwise.

Rule 3 = the black triangle moves around the points of the hexagon one place clockwise.

Rule 4 = if any of the shapes coincide and end up at the same point, the shapes automatically become a patterned square.

Figure A can be ruled out because a grey triangle should be positioned in the bottom left corner, and a striped square should be positioned in the bottom right corner. Figure B can be ruled out because a grey triangle needs to be added to the bottom left corner. Figure C can be ruled out because the black triangle should not be there, and the white triangle should be a striped square instead. Figure E can be ruled out because the striped square should be in the position of the white triangle, and the white triangle should be removed.

Q6. C

Rule 1 = the centre circle alternates between white and black.

Rule 2 = the circle in the top right corner alternates between black and white.

Rule 3 = a line is added through the centre of the circle in a clockwise manner (forming a 'plus-like' shape).

Figure A can be ruled out because the white circle in the top right corner needs to be black. Also, the lines horizontally should be shorter than the lines vertically. Figure B can be ruled out because the black centred circle needs to be white. Figure D can be ruled out because the black centred circle needs to be white. Also, a vertical line and a horizontal line need to be added (to form a 'plus-like' shape).

Q7. D

Rule 1 = you need to draw the figure without the pen leaving the paper.

Rule 2 = you cannot go over any line more than once.

Figure A can be ruled out because the next line drawn will be a vertical line to form the left side of the house. Figure B can be ruled out because a diagonal line has disappeared and instead has drawn in the rest of the outer house. Figure C can be ruled out because your next figure will still have 2 lines missing. Figure E can be ruled out because you cannot draw both the bottom line of the house and the left horizontal line.

Q8. C

Rule 1 = an extra line of symmetry is added as the sequence progresses.

Figure A can be ruled out because this has no lines of symmetry. Figure B can be ruled out because a circle is symmetrical no matter what way you rotate it. Figure D can be ruled out because this shape has 4 lines of symmetry; we need a shape with 6 lines of symmetry. Figure E can be ruled out because this only has 1 line of symmetry.

Q9. A

Rule 1 = the figure is rotated 90° clockwise as the sequence progresses.

Figure B can be ruled out because it has been rotated approximateiy 90° anti-clockwise. Figure C can be ruled out because this has been rotated less than 90° clockwise. Figure D can be ruled out because this has been less than 90° rotated (anti-clockwise). Figure E can be ruled out because it has been rotated 180°.

Q10. D

Rule 1 = the first shape in each of the figures, must be the same as the last shape in the previous box.

Rule 2 = the shape with the most number of sides is black.

Rule 3 = all of the sides in each shape must add up to 10.

Figure A can be ruled out because the sides only add up to 9. Figure B can be ruled out because the sides only add up to 8. Figure C can be ruled out because the sides only add up to 9. Figure E can be ruled out because the sides add up to 11. Also, the shape with the most sides is a square; however there are two squares in this figure, so both squares should be black.

Q11. C

Rule 1 = the figure rotates 90° clockwise as the sequence progresses.

Rule 2 = as the sequence progresses, the black shape switches sides.

Rule 3 = the shaded shape disappears in the next box; and the shape closest to the middle becomes the next shaded shape.

Figure A can be ruled out because the small horizontal rectangle should have disappeared. Figure B can be ruled out because the shaded shape should be the small vertical rectangle, not the small horizontal rectangle. Figure D can be ruled out because the figure has been rotated the wrong way, and the black shape should be the vertical rectangle, not the horizontal rectangle. Figure E can be ruled out because the figure has been rotated the wrong way and the shaded rectangle, should be vertical not horizontal.

Q12. B

Rule 1 = the white shape at the end of the figure, becomes a black figure at the start of the next figure.

Rule 2 = the white shape is also rotated 90° clockwise to form the first shape of the next figure.

Rule 3 = both shapes need to be joined at the corner.

Figure A can be ruled out because the black shape has not been rotated 90° clockwise (from the previous figure). Figure C can be ruled out because the trapezoid should be black. Also, the shapes need to be joined at points from both shapes. Figure D can be ruled out because the shapes are not joining by the points of both shapes. Figure E can be ruled out because the shapes are not joining by the points of both shapes.

Q13. D

Rule 1 = each shape needs to contain two lines of symmetry.

Figure A can be ruled out because it only has 1 line of symmetry. Figure B can be ruled out because it has no lines of symmetry. Figure C can be ruled out because it has 4 lines of symmetry. Figure E can be ruled out because it has 1 line of symmetry.

Q14. B

Rule 1 = the figure is rotated 90° anti-clockwise, as the sequence progresses.

Rule 2 = one line is eliminated each time as the sequence progresses.

Figure A can be ruled out because one line should be left, not two. Figure C can be ruled out because the arrows on the end of the line would still remain. Figure D can be ruled out because there should only be one line left, not two. Figure E can be ruled out because only one line should remain, not three.

Q15. B

Rule 1 = the shapes move round one place clockwise.

Figure A can be ruled out because the two squares are in the wrong place; the black square should be where the white square is; and the white square should be where the black square is. Figure C can be ruled out because this is a horizontal reflection of answer option A. Figure D can be ruled out because this is a vertical reflection of answer option C.

Q16. E

Rule 1 = the five pointed stars move around all the points of the cross, two spaces clockwise.

Rule 2 = the four pointed stars move around all the points of the cross, one space anti-clockwise.

Rule 3 = if two or more stars interlink at the same point, the stars become a grey shape.

Figure A can be ruled out because the stars are in the incorrect position. Figure B can be ruled out because it is a replica of box 2. Figure C can be ruled out because none of the stars should overlap at the points. Figure D can be ruled out because the stars are in the incorrect position.

Q17. A

Rule 1 = starting from the top of the figure, and moving around the outer edge of the shape, in a clockwise motion, one square is removed each time.

Figure B can be ruled out because four squares would remain. Figure C can be ruled out because the four squares should form a cross-like shape. Figure D can be ruled out because the four squares should form a cross-like shape. Figure E can be ruled out because the shape should have four squares, not three.

Q18. B

Rule 1 = working from the inside of the shape, outwards, one shape disappears each time.

Figure A can be ruled out because the shape on the outside is a square; and therefore a square would remain. Figure C can be ruled out because this is a replica of box 4. Figure D can be ruled out because one of the answers is correct; so therefore it cannot be 'none'.

Q19. C

Rule 1 = the figure rotates 90° anti-clockwise as the sequence progresses.

Rule 2 = the dot in the centre alternates from black to grey, as the sequence progresses.

Rule 3 = the arrows begin all pointing inwards. As the sequence progresses, one arrow is turned outwards.

Figure A can be ruled out because the white arrow is pointing inwards; all the arrows should be pointing outwards. Figure B can be ruled out because the grey dot should be a black dot. Figure D can be ruled out because the dashed arrow should be pointing outwards as opposed to inwards.

Q20. C

Rule 1 = the black square rotates 90° anti-clockwise.

Rule 2 = the downward hatching circle follows the pattern of: top left, bottom right, bottom left, top right. The sequence then repeats.

Rule 3 = the upward hatching circle follows the pattern of: top right, bottom left, bottom right, top left. The sequence then repeats.

Q21. A

Rule 1 = the triangle is rotated 90° clockwise as the sequence progresses.

Rule 2 = the shapes inside the triangle remain in the same position; however the colour pattern changes. The colour pattern moves down one space each time, and once it reaches the bottom, it goes back to the top.

Q22. B

Rule 1 = the number of dots increase by 2 each time.

Rule 2 = the diagonal lines alternate from top left to bottom right; to top right to bottom left.

Rule 3 = the number of black dots increases by 1 each time.

Figure A can be ruled out because the first figure should contain one black dot and one striped dot. Figure C can be ruled out because the first figure should contain only two dots, not three. Figure D can be ruled out because the diagonal lines are going the wrong way; they should be top right to bottom left; not top left to bottom right. Figure E can be ruled out because there should be one black dot and one striped dot.

Q23. C

Rule 1 = the first square in the first column moves around the outer edge of the shape one space in a clockwise motion.

Figures A, B, D and E can all be ruled out because the square that is rotating around the outer edge is in the incorrect position for each figure, apart from Figure C.

Q24. A

Rule 1 = the hexagon alternates colour. It changes colour from black, to grey, to white.

Rule 2 = the black arrows must be touching the outer squared box.

Rule 3 = the black arrows are used to indicate where the circles should be inside the hexagon.

Rule 4 = the circles inside the shapes follow the colour pattern of: grey, white, black.

Figure B can be ruled out because the arrow on the left side of the square, in the middle, should have a circle directly next to it (inside the hexagon); instead the circle is in the middle right corner of the hexagon. Figure C can be ruled out because the circle in the top left corner of the hexagon should be positioned in the middle right corner of the hexagon. Figure D can be ruled out because the middle arrow is pointing to an empty space; either the arrow should be removed or a circle should be placed where the arrow is pointing. Figure E can be ruled out because there are three arrows, and no circles; the arrows are used to illustrate where the circles should be positioned.

Q25. C

Rule 1 = the black star-shape in the middle of the figure loses one point as the sequence progresses. For example, a six-sided star becomes a five-sided star and then a four-sided star and so on.

Rule 2 = the black dot on the corner of the square rotates clockwise one place, then two places, then three, then four. Once it reaches four it works backwards (anti-clockwise): three spaces, then two, then one and so forth.

Rule 3 = the line in the middle of the shape rotates 45° clockwise, as the sequence progresses.

Figure A can be ruled out because the black star needs to have eight points. Also, the black dot should be in the top left corner. Figure B can be ruled out because the black star needs to have eight points, not four. Also, the vertical line should be horizontal. Figure D can be ruled out because the black star needs to have eight points, not seven. Also, the diagonal line should be horizontal and the black dot should be in the top left corner. Figure E can be ruled out because the five-sided star should be an eight-sided star.

Q26. A

Rule 1 = the dot in the centre remains black throughout the sequence.

Rule 2 = the inner circle (minus the centre circle) moves one space anti-clockwise, as the sequence progresses.

Rule 3 = the outer circles move one space clockwise, as the sequence progresses.

Figure B can be ruled out because the black dot at the bottom centre, should be white, and the black circle should be one space anti-clockwise. Figure C can be ruled out because there should be a black circle at the top centre (outer edge). Figure D can be ruled out because this is an exact replica of figure 3. Figure E can be ruled out because the centred circle should be black, not white.

Q27. A

Rule 1 = the number of points on the large shape should match the number of points on the black star-shape.

Figure A is the odd one out because the large shape contains three points, whereas the number of points on the star is five.

Q28. B

Rule 1 = the shapes opposite each other should be of the same pattern.

Figure B is the odd one out because the pattern in the square (and opposite the black circle) are not of the same colour and pattern. Either the circle should be changed to the same diagonal black and white lines, or the square should be changed to black.

Q29. C

Rule 1 = one line from the top of the horizontal lines is removed as the sequence progresses.

Rule 2 = one line from the far right side of the vertical lines is removed as the sequence progresses.

Figure A can be ruled out because there should be six horizontal lines, not five. Figure B can be ruled out because there should be six vertical lines, not seven. Figure D can be ruled out because there should be six horizontal lines, not seven. Figure E can be ruled out because the lines have been removed from the wrong sides; the horizontal line should be removed from the top, not the bottom; and the vertical line should be removed from the far right side, not the left side.

Q30. E

Rule 1 = the big line moves 40° clockwise as the sequence progresses.

Rule 2 = the small line moves 40° anti-clockwise as the sequence progresses.

Figure A can be ruled out because only one line should be big, the other line should be shorter. Figure B can be ruled out because the short line should be a big line; and the big line should be the short line. Figure C can be ruled out because this is a rotation of the first figure in the sequence. Figure D can be ruled out because neither line is in the correct position.

CONCENTRATION
TESTS

WHAT ARE CONCENTRATION TESTS?

Concentration tests have become increasingly popular within job selection processes. Some recruiters want to see evidence of how effective you are at carrying out tasks that require high levels of concentration.

Concentration tests often require great attention to detail. You will usually be provided with a large set of information that you will need to take in quickly, and using that information, to work out the answer.

During this chapter, you will be provided with a variety of sample test questions that will go a long way to helping you improve your concentration skills.

WHO SITS A CONCENTRATION TEST?

Many technical posts require you to sit some form of Concentration test. Train drivers in particular, are certainly made to sit several concentration tests in order to show that they can focus for long periods of time. The Army, Royal Navy and Royal Air Force will also require candidates to take a Concentration test, as will any job that is highly technical and requires great concentration skills for an extended period of time.

As with any test, the more practice you undergo, the more likely you are to pass the assessment.

HOW WILL I BE TESTED?

The type of test that you will sit, will depend on the job for which you are applying. In order for you to gain a solid idea of what you can expect, and how to improve, we suggest that you work through all of the concentration questions in order to maximise your concentration ability.

Typical Concentration tests may include:

- Numerical Visual Comparison tests
- Work Rate tests
- Dots Concentration tests

NUMERICAL VISUAL COMPARISON TESTS

The Numerical Visual Comparison test is an online assessment whereby you will be given four pairs of combinations. This will include combinations of number digits, or a mixture of both letters and numbers. Your job is to find the pair that **does not match** in both columns.

An example below is illustrated so you can visualise the question:

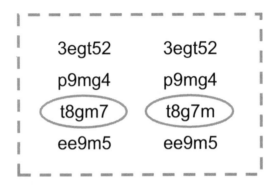

The test is relatively simple. All you have to do is spot which pair **does not match**. In the above example, the row that does not match is highlighted. You should be able to notice that the reason this combination does not match is because the 'm' and the '7' are in different places in each column.

However, what makes the test more challenging is the fact you will only be given 5 minutes in which to answer 150 questions. The key to the test is to work swiftly and accurately. The test is designed so that you are unable to finish it, so do not be put off by the thought of not being able to complete the assessment.

WORK RATE TESTS

This form of test assesses your ability to work quickly and accurately whilst carrying out simple routine tasks.

You will be given a code which consists of either numbers, letters or symbols.

Your task is to look at the provided alternative codes and decide which one has been taken from the SAME vertical columns as the original code.

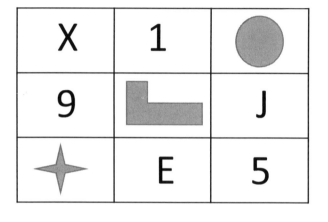

A. ● 9 1   **B.** 5EX   **C.** ●⌐ 1   **D.** 9 1●

Answer: if you had to find the code that corresponded with 915, you could use the **answer option D.** You would take the 9 from the first row, the 1 from the second row, and then take the circle. This uses the same columns as originally stated.

DOTS CONCENTRATION TESTS

The Dots Concentration tests are one of the hardest parts of the assessment process. It is the one test that most people fail and this is mainly due to a lack of preparation. Many candidates turn up to take the test without any prior knowledge of how the test works and what is expected of them.

- The test is designed to assess your ability to concentrate whilst performing tasks at high speed. The test will be carried out either with a pen and paper, or a computer and a computer screen.

- Whichever test you undertake, you will be presented with five pages or screens that each contains 25 columns.

- Each of the columns contains boxes with patterns of dots which are either in groups of 2, 3, 4, 5 or 6. Your task is to work quickly and accurately through each column, from left to right, identifying boxes of 4 dots only.

- You are allowed two minutes only per sheet and, once the two minutes are up, you are told to move onto the next page regardless of whether you have completed it or not.

Take a look at the following row of dots:

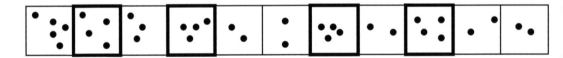

You will notice that the 2nd, 4th, 7th and 9th boxes each contain 4 dots. If you were taking the paper and pencil based version of the test, you would mark the boxes that contain 4 dots.

CONCENTRATION TESTS – NUMERICAL VISUAL COMPARISON

*Look at the four pairs of numerical digits. Circle or highlight the combination pair that **does not** match.*

QUESTION 1 - Sheet 1

9871	9871	7431	7431	4976	4676	7923	7293
1235	1235	1225	1255	4697	4697	3265	3265
7469	7496	3664	3664	6562	6562	2647	2647
6344	6344	3549	3549	3597	3597	4961	4961
7947	7947	4697	4697	5591	5591	5598	5598
4654	4564	7989	7989	6694	6694	6659	6659
4165	4165	6278	6278	1622	1662	4613	4613
1346	1346	4691	6691	4448	4448	3108	3018
7952	7952	8853	8853	7792	7792	4598	4598
0097	0097	8469	8669	7913	7931	6621	6621
0064	0664	1465	1465	7469	7469	5648	5648
1025	1025	4812	4812	7692	7692	8712	7812
4564	4564	5684	5684	6541	5641	3369	3369
0694	0694	5479	5479	2658	2658	3478	3478
1620	1620	2698	2698	7952	7952	3589	3859
4169	4196	1610	1601	2679	2679	1694	1694
4644	4444	6523	6523	7943	7943	9376	9376
6646	6646	0042	0042	3246	3246	9713	9713
1366	1366	0170	0070	0651	0551	0544	0544
3024	3024	0394	0394	3651	3651	4369	4339
5478	5478	7410	7410	5525	5525	7410	7401
9631	9631	4987	4987	5571	5571	6314	6314
3260	3260	7631	7613	5987	9587	9874	9874
0587	0857	6854	6854	5103	5103	1679	1679
4622	4622	4103	4103	4792	4792	4967	4667
2264	2624	3034	3034	5423	5423	4610	4610
1325	1325	0950	0590	6432	6432	6459	6459
4679	4679	1463	1463	0649	0469	6462	6462

Look at the four pairs of numerical digits. Circle or highlight the combination pair that **does not** match.

Sheet 2

49846 49846	97842 97842	44975 44975	79895 79995
46216 46216	64494 64494	69871 69871	97461 97461
87641 86741	65979 65979	36105 31605	46959 46959
47879 47879	14645 14465	49792 49792	46997 46997

49526 49526	79852 79852	79852 79852	84641 84641
25984 25948	59441 59414	25694 25694	00651 06051
16479 16479	19859 19859	41977 41977	03103 03103
49751 49751	49742 49742	10268 10286	13204 13204

98510 95810	95615 95615	79654 79654	46584 46584
97106 97106	49562 49562	97414 97414	69716 69716
65892 65892	16984 16894	47945 47945	62544 62554
15497 15497	49756 49756	65487 65478	69712 69712

96587 96587	47925 47925	47925 47925	79261 79261
95410 95410	96102 66102	79560 79650	41004 41004
01360 01360	23547 23547	06414 06414	47978 47778
46105 64105	46940 46940	49787 49787	98851 98851

98712 98712	98514 98514	89474 89447	96478 96478
36204 32604	54477 54477	49974 49974	46775 46775
79461 79461	61149 61149	49887 49887	16584 16584
13645 13645	49470 49770	46120 46120	23668 23688

98521 98521	96584 96584	74698 76498	62302 62302
56987 56987	46414 46414	58962 58962	56841 56841
14479 11479	02366 02666	13644 13644	36984 36984
36972 36972	56320 56320	47851 47851	27893 27895

86984 86984	74632 74632	63258 63258	48579 48579
36942 33942	03665 03655	85936 85996	69520 69520
47497 47497	46910 46910	97848 97848	26547 26547
46979 46979	03689 03689	96347 96347	79585 79558

*Look at the four pairs of numerical digits. Circle or highlight the combination pair that **does not** match.*

Sheet 3

494765	494765	498514	498514	796585	796558	798895	798895
498451	498451	497897	497897	874158	874158	498978	498978
469597	469597	798585	795885	895851	895851	479784	479784
798952	799852	568744	568744	498798	498798	154775	154575

745698	745698	798514	798514	467985	476985	498984	498984
798520	798220	498798	498798	598977	598977	465987	465987
795210	795210	798520	798520	789552	789552	495952	499552
462248	462248	795463	795436	469898	469898	798524	798524

798895	798995	794614	794414	978984	978984	978984	978984
798554	798554	498784	498784	494881	494481	465898	465598
498795	498795	978984	978984	497974	497974	741220	741220
495202	495202	798522	798522	499874	499874	023650	023650

798565	798565	498894	498894	794654	794654	795655	795655
565987	565987	794659	794659	469795	469795	746984	746984
477784	477784	895251	895551	465201	465210	468972	468972
465207	465270	465687	465687	469897	469897	136897	136879

741235	741235	968571	968571	698745	699745	741369	741369
869695	869695	146447	146447	596897	596897	699523	699523
579852	579552	797889	797899	798520	798520	232644	232644
265489	265489	568987	568987	236547	236547	465947	465974

794685	794885	465985	465985	794655	794655	798556	798556
856982	856982	598799	598799	565977	655977	565978	565978
003587	003587	798562	798662	798523	798523	798898	798998
594412	594412	265977	265977	265978	265978	895622	895622

895656	896556	562022	562022	699845	699845	798556	798556
569875	569875	226985	226985	565977	565977	565988	565988
331001	331001	450023	450023	788998	788998	787848	787848
012024	012024	232021	232010	595232	595532	487874	787848

*Look at the four pairs of numerical digits. Circle or highlight the combination pair that **does not** match.*

Sheet 4

8989	8989	9894	9894	7981	7981	79865	79865
9897	9897	4621	4221	1659	1569	49655	49655
7989	7989	0262	0262	5954	5954	41035	41035
5656	5556	4689	4689	4203	4203	56568	56668

79856	79865	46687	46887	79856	79856	95897	95897
56597	56597	79861	79861	26564	26664	46598	46598
46523	46523	46597	46597	49874	49874	79895	79985
26546	26546	79852	79852	10124	10124	59256	59256

7985	7885	7985	7985	79523	79523	59659	59659
5659	5659	1301	1301	25665	25565	49974	49974
8987	8987	3624	3664	59787	59787	49595	49995
7981	7981	4658	4658	25659	25659	26211	26211

59594	59549	62659	62569	62622	62622	46565	46565
46595	46595	49897	49897	62261	62261	56594	56594
98778	98778	79856	79856	12616	12616	46797	46797
46230	46230	62644	62644	64652	46652	13206	12306

46598	46589	56594	56594	49846	49846	5951	5915
89798	89798	42369	42639	56578	56578	2665	2665
89871	89871	66477	66477	78978	87978	5621	5621
13256	13256	56201	56201	95251	95251	1035	1035

2326	2326	2655	2655	7950	7950	7958	7958
5654	5654	5659	5559	1659	1659	2326	2362
4652	4652	7985	7985	8951	9851	2598	2598
2320	2302	4620	4620	4621	4621	7895	7895

23265	23665	46595	46595	56959	56959	59554	59554
56989	56989	78985	78985	65654	65654	46256	46256
89874	89874	56597	56597	13698	31698	98778	98778
43221	43221	74395	74359	78365	78365	95861	98561

*Look at the four pairs of numerical digits. Circle or highlight the combination pair that **does not** match.*

Sheet 5

79534	79334	75364	75346	56523	56523	79583	79583
62987	62987	56871	56871	35654	35654	26565	26565
45654	45654	25657	25657	49762	47962	59874	95874
46547	46547	47982	47982	23210	23210	46489	46489

79582	79582	46598	46958	59562	59562	46253	46253
26295	26295	89532	89532	26249	26249	23266	23266
98974	98974	23264	23264	98955	98855	59775	57975
36230	36330	46479	46479	56215	56215	45645	45645

46958	64958	46522	46522	56222	56222	25655	25655
89872	89872	23679	23679	26998	26988	59879	59879
32697	32697	98746	98476	89745	89745	79789	79889
46575	46575	56597	56597	16568	16568	59977	59977

79586	79586	2565	2565	4956	4956	4656	4656
56595	56595	5657	5667	2654	2654	5978	5978
97955	97955	7985	7985	4659	4659	0035	0035
56597	65597	2362	2362	7985	4659	0610	0601

65654	65654	4658	4658	49522	49552	84764	84764
20364	20364	8985	8895	26548	26548	46597	46597
03654	03654	2697	2697	89775	89775	98523	98523
13034	13304	7985	7985	26459	26459	23265	32265

46579	46579	45955	45955	59584	59584	79562	79562
89875	89855	56577	56577	59532	55532	26541	25541
26204	26204	98956	98966	23264	23264	49897	49897
89531	89531	26289	26289	46547	46547	79852	79852

79582	79582	97855	97855	79582	79582	79565	79565
26297	26297	56597	56597	26654	26654	56597	56597
79853	79853	79526	79562	49656	49656	74151	71451
26259	22659	26256	26256	26597	26579	26597	26597

*Look at the four pairs of numerical digits. Circle or highlight the combination pair that **does not** match.*

Sheet 6

957422	957422	798552	798552	795862	975862	46956	46956
262594	265294	268975	268975	262949	262949	52695	52695
479562	479562	565102	565102	498952	498952	59722	57922
262449	262449	236264	236246	236297	236297	26594	26594

49562	49562	995525	995525	79525	79525	79855	79855
26974	26974	565987	565978	26978	26978	89512	89512
16981	61981	798553	798553	79820	79820	45847	45847
16595	16595	236269	236269	16597	61597	78474	78874

79582	79582	79526	79256
26547	26457	56597	56597
12305	12305	79526	79526
54597	54597	56597	56597

ANSWERS TO **QUESTION 1**

Sheet 1

9871 9871	7431 7431	4976 4676	7923 7293
1235 1235	1225 1255	4697 4697	3265 3265
7469 7496	3664 3664	6562 6562	2647 2647
6344 6344	3549 3549	3597 3597	4961 4961
7947 7947	4697 4697	5591 5591	5598 5598
4654 4564	7989 7989	6694 6694	6659 6659
4165 4165	6278 6278	1622 1662	4613 4613
1346 1346	4691 6691	4448 4448	3108 3018
7952 7952	8853 8853	7792 7792	4598 4598
0097 0097	8469 8669	7913 7931	6621 6621
0064 0664	1465 1465	7469 7469	5648 5648
1025 1025	4812 4812	7692 7692	8712 7812
4564 4564	5684 5684	6541 5641	3369 3369
0694 0694	5479 5479	2658 2658	3478 3478
1620 1620	2698 2698	7952 7952	3589 3859
4169 4196	1610 1601	2679 2679	1694 1694
4644 4444	6523 6523	7943 7943	9376 9376
6646 6646	0042 0042	3246 3246	9713 9713
1366 1366	0170 0070	0651 0551	0544 0544
3024 3024	0394 0394	3651 3651	4369 4339
5478 5478	7410 7410	5525 5525	7410 7401
9631 9631	4987 4987	5571 5571	6314 6314
3260 3260	7631 7613	5987 9587	9874 9874
0587 0857	6854 6854	5103 5103	1679 1679
4622 4622	4103 4103	4792 4792	4967 4667
2264 2624	3034 3034	5423 5423	4610 4610
1325 1325	0950 0590	6432 6432	6459 6459
4679 4679	1463 1463	0649 0469	6462 6462

Sheet 2

49846	49846	97842	97842	44975	44975	79895	79995
46216	46216	64494	64494	69871	69871	97461	97461
87641	86741	65979	65979	36105	31605	46959	46959
47879	47879	14645	14465	49792	49792	46997	46997
49526	49526	79852	79852	79852	79852	84641	84641
25984	25948	59441	59414	25694	25694	00651	06051
16479	16479	19859	19859	41977	41977	03103	03103
49751	49751	49742	49742	10268	10286	13204	13204
98510	95810	95615	95615	79654	79654	46584	46584
97106	97106	49562	49562	97414	97414	69716	69716
65892	65892	16984	16894	47945	47945	62544	62554
15497	15497	49756	49756	65487	65478	69712	69712
96587	96587	47925	47925	47925	47925	79261	79261
95410	95410	96102	66102	79560	79650	41004	41004
01360	01360	23547	23547	06414	06414	47978	47778
46105	64105	46940	46940	49787	49787	98851	98851
98712	98712	98514	98514	89474	89447	96478	96478
36204	32604	54477	54477	49974	49974	46775	46775
79461	79461	61149	61149	49887	49887	16584	16584
13645	13645	49470	49770	46120	46120	23668	23688
98521	98521	96584	96584	74698	76498	62302	62302
56987	56987	46414	46414	58962	58962	56841	56841
14479	11479	02366	02666	13644	13644	36984	36984
36972	36972	56320	56320	47851	47851	27893	27895
86984	86984	74632	74632	63258	63258	48579	48579
36942	33942	03665	03655	85936	85996	69520	69520
47497	47497	46910	46910	97848	97848	26547	26547
46979	46979	03689	03689	96347	96347	79585	79558

Sheet 3

494765 494765	498514 498514	796585 796558	798895 798895
498451 498451	497897 497897	874158 874158	498978 498978
469597 469597	798585 795885	895851 895851	479784 479784
798952 799852	568744 568744	498798 498798	154775 154575

745698 745698	798514 798514	467985 476985	498984 498984
798520 798220	498798 498798	598977 598977	465987 465987
795210 795210	798520 798520	789552 789552	495952 499552
462248 462248	795463 795436	469898 469898	798524 798524

798895 798995	794614 794414	978984 978984	978984 978984
798554 798554	498784 498784	494881 494481	465898 465598
498795 498795	978984 978984	497974 497974	741220 741220
495202 495202	798522 798522	499874 499874	023650 023650

798565 798565	498894 498894	794654 794654	795655 795655
565987 565987	794659 794659	469795 469795	746984 746984
477784 477784	895251 895551	465201 465210	468972 468972
465207 465270	465687 465687	469897 469897	136897 136879

741235 741235	968571 968571	698745 699745	741369 741369
869695 869695	146447 146447	596897 596897	699523 699523
579852 579552	797889 797899	798520 798520	232644 232644
265489 265489	568987 568987	236547 236547	465947 465974

794685 794885	465985 465985	794655 794655	798556 798556
856982 856982	598799 598799	565977 655977	565978 565978
003587 003587	798562 798662	798523 798523	798898 798998
594412 594412	265977 265977	265978 265978	895622 895622

895656 896556	562022 562022	699845 699845	798556 798556
569875 569875	226985 226985	565977 565977	565988 565988
331001 331001	450023 450023	788998 788998	787848 787848
012024 012024	232021 232010	595232 595532	487874 787848

Sheet 4

8989 8989	9894 9894	7981 7981	79865 79865
9897 9897	4621 4221	1659 1569	49655 49655
7989 7989	0262 0262	5954 5954	41035 41035
5656 5556	4689 4689	4203 4203	56568 56668
79856 79865	46687 46887	79856 79856	95897 95897
56597 56597	79861 79861	26564 26664	46598 46598
46523 46523	46597 46597	49874 49874	79895 79985
26546 26546	79852 79852	10124 10124	59256 59256
7985 7885	7985 7985	79523 79523	59659 59659
5659 5659	1301 1301	25665 25565	49974 49974
8987 8987	3624 3664	59787 59787	49595 49995
7981 7981	4658 4658	25659 25659	26211 26211
59594 59549	62659 62569	62622 62622	46565 46565
46595 46595	49897 49897	62261 62261	56594 56594
98778 98778	79856 79856	12616 12616	46797 46797
46230 46230	62644 62644	64652 46652	13206 12306
46598 46589	56594 56594	49846 49846	5951 5915
89798 89798	42369 42639	56578 56578	2665 2665
89871 89871	66477 66477	78978 87978	5621 5621
13256 13256	56201 56201	95251 95251	1035 1035
2326 2326	2655 2655	7950 7950	7958 7958
5654 5654	5659 5559	1659 1659	2326 2362
4652 4652	7985 7985	8951 9851	2598 2598
2320 2302	4620 4620	4621 4621	7895 7895
23265 23665	46595 46595	56959 56959	59554 59554
56989 56989	78985 78985	65654 65654	46256 46256
89874 89874	56597 56597	13698 31698	98778 98778
43221 43221	74395 74359	78365 78365	95861 98561

Sheet 5

79534	79334	75364	75346	56523	56523	79583	79583
62987	62987	56871	56871	35654	35654	26565	26565
45654	45654	25657	25657	49762	47962	59874	95874
46547	46547	47982	47982	23210	23210	46489	46489
79582	79582	46598	46958	59562	59562	46253	46253
26295	26295	89532	89532	26249	26249	23266	23266
98974	98974	23264	23264	98955	98855	59775	57975
36230	36330	46479	46479	56215	56215	45645	45645
46958	64958	46522	46522	56222	56222	25655	25655
89872	89872	23679	23679	26998	26988	59879	59879
32697	32697	98746	98476	89745	89745	79789	79889
46575	46575	56597	56597	16568	16568	59977	59977
79586	79586	2565	2565	4956	4956	4656	4656
56595	56595	5657	5667	2654	2654	5978	5978
97955	97955	7985	7985	4659	4659	0035	0035
56597	65597	2362	2362	7985	4659	0610	0601
65654	65654	4658	4658	49522	49552	84764	84764
20364	20364	8985	8895	26548	26548	46597	46597
03654	03654	2697	2697	89775	89775	98523	98523
13034	13304	7985	7985	26459	26459	23265	32265
46579	46579	45955	45955	59584	59584	79562	79562
89875	89855	56577	56577	59532	55532	26541	25541
26204	26204	98956	98966	23264	23264	49897	49897
89531	89531	26289	26289	46547	46547	79852	79852
79582	79582	97855	97855	79582	79582	79565	79565
26297	26297	56597	56597	26654	26654	56597	56597
79853	79853	79526	79562	49656	49656	74151	71451
26259	22659	26256	26256	26597	26579	26597	26597

Sheet 6

957422	957422	798552	798552	795862	975862	46956	46956
262594	265294	268975	268975	262949	262949	52695	52695
479562	479562	565102	565102	498952	498952	59722	57922
262449	262449	236264	236246	236297	236297	26594	26594
49562	49562	995525	995525	79525	79525	79855	79855
26974	26974	565987	565978	26978	26978	89512	89512
16981	61981	798553	798553	79820	79820	45847	45847
16595	16595	236269	236269	16597	61597	78474	78874
79582	79582	79526	79256				
26547	26457	56597	56597				
12305	12305	79526	79526				
54597	54597	56597	56597				

*Look at the four pairs of alpha-numerical digits. Circle or highlight the combination pair that **does not** match.*

QUESTION 2 - Sheet 1

dl49f	dl49f	39dj5	39dj5	ep395	ep395	elp59	elp59
30f3r	30f3r	qp294	qp294	eptiy	petiy	jkow8	jkow8
lo3vr	lo3yr	doi39	doi39	39ri3	39ri3	do03r	do03r
or35k	or35k	d034i	d034l	k5o58	k5o58	mlg94	mlg49

move3	move3	39fjw	39fjw	35957	35957	wp20e	wp20e
yijn5	yijn5	pyk5k	ypk5k	vmpw3	vmpw3	fmog4	fmog4
fkp30	fk3p0	fmv93	fmv93	deok5	deok5	vmpeg	mvpeg
deklp	deklp	dmp24	dmp24	rpk60	rpk06	204dk	204dk

ri40e	ri40e	fjo39	fjo93	wpa10	wpa01	fejmo	fejmo
or30r	or30r	powe2	powe2	dld93	dld93	308jo	308jo
fk04j	fk04j	dk035	dk035	dkv92	dkv92	r30ie	r30ie
t40gj	t04gj	358fj	358fj	s024k	s024k	20oew	20eow

395kr	395kr	fem34	fem34	09668	09668	trjo3	trjo3
mcl39	mci39	dkp30	dkp30	jig7t	jij7t	lpeea	lpeaa
jlgt0	jlgt0	20dmv	2odmv	o9ubj	o9ubj	f3k63	f3k63
r04ir	r04ir	dkf30	dkf30	k0i76	k0i76	fpk46	fpk46

tk303	tk303	gfo3k5	gfo3k5	35fe3	35fe3	lr39fp	lr39fp
rlpf2	rlfp2	59eu3	59ue3	350dk	350kd	flp30	flp03
flp3d	flp3d	34oiro	34oiro	q130e	q130e	fro46	fro46
dkp20	dkp20	3058d	3058d	vmlt3	vmlt3	t4240	t4240

gml45	gml45	dwo14	dwo14	35erp	53erp	3fjo3p	3fjo3p
340rk	340rk	304or	304ro	wp24r	wp24r	eoo42	eoo42
e2l04	e2i04	092lp	092lp	fm40e	fm40e	mv3o4	mv34o
r3k05	r3k05	2dwp2	2dwp2	emp53	emp53	kop94	kop94

f46ju	f46ju	roi3q	roi3p	aklq9u1	aklq9u1	35fap1	35fpa1
ssu9s	ssu9s	249dj	249dj	dkpc96	dkpc96	dl304r	dl304r
skp97	skp97	djo07	djo07	bkpw08	bkpw08	cmp29	cmp29
mo906	mo960	hoit7	hoit7	n08dpp	no8dpp	rkp30	rkp30

*Look at the four pairs of alpha-numerical digits. Circle or highlight the combination pair that **does not** match.*

Sheet 2

fdsp2	fdsp2	eok35	eko35	adp53	adp53	aoj53	aoj53
sa245	sa245	dkwp3	dkwp3	sdlp4	sdlp4	vmpt4	vmpt4
dfvm4	dfvm4	wek46	wek46	fnk3k	fnk3k	repk3	repk3
w563g	w536g	kp57d	kp57d	aslk5	asl5k	dwl53	dwi53
5r9t4	5r9t4	359fj	359fj	qk4kg	gk4kg	grkl3	grkl3
grkp4	grkp4	aru95	aru95	fmlfe4	fmlfe4	frk3r	frkr3
gfm35	gfn35	ryy85	ryy85	tkp40	tkp40	vmlf9	vmlf9
dl35jt	dl35jt	a9u47	a9u74	40irjw	40irjw	dpl69	dpl69
fek42	fek42	gh39a	gh39a	the93	the93	g349fn	g349fn
wij3n	wij3n	amm6f	amm6f	tpe38r	tpe38r	fel48r	fel48r
tmp46	tmp46	flk64	fik64	mfep4	mfep4	twnl3	townl3
m35ja	m35ga	polk5	polk5	r39fe	r93fe	rjow3	rjow3
grtlm4	grtlm4	g9345	g9345	euiorw	eiuorw	35992	35992
bvm3r	bvm3r	38702	38702	wero35	wero35	fnsk3	fns23
5jre30	5lre30	etnkd	entkd	gf35ir	gf35ir	39nr3	39nr3
35793	35793	34098	34098	nro3nr	nro3nr	em6l7	em6l7
gfn4nt	gfn4nt	68753	68753	xdkl4	xdkj4	kjhfy	kjhfy
rm3l2	rm321	freojr	freoir	zprli	zprli	hui96	hui96
yml34	yml34	vcmne	vcmne	itu38	itu38	oj97g	0j97g
plghi3	plghi3	35089	35089	nml30	nml30	nlk9t	nlk9t
kgy7f	kgy7f	gdkn4	gdkn4	campt3	campt3	fajioj	fajioj
987jl	987jli	fejio5	fejio5	dfsfm6	dfsfm6	wplai	wplai
mb905	mb905	plhih8	plhih8	gjasp5	gjsap5	caaop	caaop
cyt86r	cyt86r	nkr39	nrk39	hsk64	hsk64	oarji	oarjil
35983	35983	yaok5	yaok5	29082	29028	fla35a	fla35a
20957	60957	iimpy7	iimpy7	qpalfm	qpalfm	al38gh	al38gh
247d9	247d9	gkdpm	gkdmp	mcao4	mcao4	daml46	dami46
ae3k4	ae3k4	3598j	3598j	nb39f	nb39f	faml57	faml57

Look at the four pairs of alpha-numerical digits. Circle or highlight the combination pair that does not match.

Sheet 3

03ke3	03ke3	d63ju	d63ju	sal35k	sal53k	30irwk	30irwk
xmcl9	xmci9	qpel29	qpel29	oiu48a	oiu48a	ewpe2	wepe2
e3lmr	e3lmr	drlp35	drlp35	m38ak	m38ak	wwekp	wwekp
46lgm	46lgm	nfl3pq	nfl3qp	as29sk	as29sk	2394e	2394e

3580ak	358oak	salp3	salp3	salpt	salpt	cxa4l3	cxa4l3
dasl53	dasl53	rel86	rel86	gdko4	gdko4	l23lr5	l32lr5
adkl34	adkl34	ro35j	ro35g	39dj3	39dj3	tlep4k	tlep4k
gdlok5	gdlok5	lpsa2	lpsa2	vek2k	vekk2	rk4kar	rk4kar

3lp5g	3lp5g	w29di	w29dd	sal238	sal238	etplgf	etpglf
ktgr4	ktgr4	dsko3	dsko3	249716	294716	grmo4	grmo4
5l3j2	5l3i2	hspl2	hspl2	aso2kr	aso2kr	trmeo	trmeo
a90fg	a90fg	k120d	k120d	rek3ko	rek3ko	3048d	3048d

uialpa	uialpa	cemuv	cemuv	yafm4l	yafm4l	49738	94738
apslfm	paslfm	eokwa	eokwa	49frj3	49frj3	42980	42980
dskape	dskape	s2le0e	s2leeo	0ds2j	ods2j	asjoe	asjoe
oial30	oial30	lp30a	lp30a	198dw	198dw	dsok2	dsok2

bnr3if	bnr3if	rei301	rei031	a9dt4	a9dt4	93jd1	93jd1
x20ala	x20ala	aspl11	aspl11	4m6l7	4m6i7	10sk2	10ks2
z19al6	z19al6	pyt94a	pyt94a	ly4pd	ly4pd	ek20p	ek20p
q204ld	g204ld	idsjwa	idsjwa	d3u9r	d3u9r	y02jr	y02jr

s92md	s92md	694fk	694fk	ou92m	ou92m	29ap2k	29ap2k
d19am	d19am	e2i01	e2i01	mc92a	mc92a	dsk2a9	ds2ka9
wpqa0	wpqao	cm30a	mc30a	nap29	nap92	ma02la	ma02la
prm28	prm28	kao2a	kao2a	ka17s	ka17s	a9dk39	a9dk39

k29ak	k29ak	45da7	45da7	op08a	op08a	28ak9	28ak9
7al20	7ai20	92mf2	92mf2	a7rn5	a7rn5	19sk1	19ks1
20lda	20lda	al8f9j	la8f9j	vm48a	vm48a	a8sh7	a8sh7
97dj2	97dj2	m7foa	m7foa	ama39	ama93	29a26	29a26

*Look at the four pairs of alpha-numerical digits. Circle or highlight the combination pair that **does not** match.*

Sheet 4

w038f	w038f	e03ld4	e03ld4	lam48	lma48	a0lsn	a0lsn
28fj53	28fj53	0ld73h	0ld73h	amb58	amb58	rj39d	rg39d
38rsiw	38rsiw	d7i3bd	d73ibd	27dh3	27dh3	2e20d	2e20d
q2oe0	q20e0	k926ai	k926ai	n9j23	n9j23	fe0k2	fe0k2
dalpfn	dalpfn	ask348	ask348	qwplam	qwplam	29alpa	29alpa
fdmla	fdmla	347ash	347ahs	amw28	amw28	se19d	es19d
3f9am	3f9am	da37fh	da37fh	29dj20	29dj20	v9s6w	v9s6w
mda20	mad20	hs8j02	hs8j02	lp18jd	lpi8jd	l29aq	l29aq
249ame	249mae	rel29a	rel29a	498fao	498fao	ja93h3	ja93h3
ppo8ye	ppo8ye	al20r8	al20r8	23amrt	23mart	28snma	28snma
9euige	9euige	vbgu4	vbgu4	tra92m	tra92m	sm28ag	sm2a8g
cdn385	cdn385	49gjra	49gira	am20d	am20d	fdmla2	fdmla2
gh47sl	gh47sl	348gfj	348gfj	39fja0	39fja0	1e27rt	1e27rt
sk38rp	sk83rp	29en2	29en2	1047f	1047f	0gle79	ogle79
d83hfe	d83hfe	208fm	208fm	37659	37569	tr8fl3e	tr8fl3e
39lp82	39lp82	opww7	opwu7	m8c62	m8c62	c93ma	c93ma
l2a74	i2a74	38fk19	38fk19	wp39sl	wp39sl	34927	34927
itu38d	itu38d	193753	193573	lsmc37	lscm37	lpqun	lpqun
bmdk2	bmdk2	e9r8t6	e9r8t6	dh37ql	dh37ql	frn37	frn37
am38d	am38d	l9689w	l9689w	io16ah	io16ah	29do3	29d03
398daj	398daj	w93mc	w93mc	cm39al	cm39al	h92jd6	h92jd6
10ripa	10rlpa	ep28a	ep82a	al28rua	al28ura	29s1la	29s1la
amd21	amd21	0ql173	0ql173	e382f0	e382f0	a81l03	8a1l03
p08j7a	p08j7a	2479a	2479a	fek381	fek381	936el2	936el2
gh38sk	gh38sk	x3d6g8	x3d6g8	xmsl37	xsml37	bb37dka	bb37kda
29sl28	29sl28	0nmf6s	0nmf6s	2846fw	2846fw	vm389fe	vm389fe
s6g9j0	s9g6j0	6bf93m	6fb93m	m97gd6	m97gd6	lfdh38g	lfdh38g
v745n2	v745n2	dk291n	dk291n	dh28q8	dh28q8	dsj3476	dsj3476

Look at the four pairs of alpha-numerical digits. Circle or highlight the combination pair that **does not** match.

Sheet 5

389am2	389am2	jfjs238	jfjs238	3895fj	3895fj	a5h8f5	a5h8f5
20d86g	208d6g	39475	39475	ek28a	ek28a	me17eb	me17eb
cmd76	cmd76	397da	397da	pef28l	pel28f	me18eo	me18eo
r9846d	r9846d	24dj98	24jd98	fcn38	fcn38	st176a	st167a

van8s7	van8s7	vma7f9	vma7f9	348f37	348f37	mv83ah	mv38ah
xbos7z	xbox7z	fj37ara	fj37ara	29dm2	22dm9	dka18a	dka18a
qpal7fe	qpal7fe	0mv7fh	0mv7bh	18sn26	18sn26	pl8mfra	pl8mfra
e8mwa	e8mwa	hsd38a	hsd38a	2348hl	2348hl	aor237	aor237

na84	na84	awu38	awu38	8976f	8966f	y5f8h	y5f8h
ld72	ld72	bc894	bc894	768kl	768kl	0nh8f	0nh8f
29fg	29fg	387fh	387hf	58d3t	58d3t	d8gs2	dogs2
mcw6	mc26	29752	29752	t7ki0	t7ki0	58dv8	58dv8

vnd7l	vnd7l	nc7ek4	nc7ek4	nc63	nc63	2579	2579
0k76s	0k76s	gh30al	hg30al	2378	2378	dajp	dajp
me28a	me28e	cm20gf	cm20gf	piwr	piwr	394h	349h
ple8ah	ple8ah	s8pm2a	s8pm2a	fa8g	fag8	rqo2	rqo2

h83dk0	h38dk0	mc30g	mc30g	n7924	n7924	7420f	7420f
289hfa	289hfa	g4bh8	g4bh8	7420a	7402a	fsjfr3	fsjrf3
294875	294875	ry93t	ry93t	fjal3o	fjal3o	3573g	3573g
5389fs	5389fs	7539h	75e9h	r239a	r239a	c3b8g	c3b8g

chg84j	cha84j	kl926s	kl962s	qpri58	qpri58	cm349f	cm349f
dj38sg	dj38sg	djk27h	djk27h	39fpl3	39flp3	295fh7	259fh7
fkc823	fkc823	2749d0	2749d0	3k6bn	3k6bn	537dn3	537dn3
2846dh	2846dh	xdj278	xdj278	s9wn7	s9wn7	385792	385792

lsk389	lsk389	eilw18a	eilw18a	q8fm4n	q8fm4n	ldj72h	idj72h
38eb35	38be35	al4rnm	al4rnm	sm28da	sm82da	afkr3k	afkr3k
63ma98	63ma98	zcwr39	zcwr39	0kc3h8	0kc3h8	td9nm	td9nm
mcd3l0	mcd3l0	dal53nj	dai53nj	fh38ka	fh38ka	ud308t	ud308t

Look at the four pairs of alpha-numerical digits. Circle or highlight the combination pair that **does not** match.

Sheet 6

387aj3	387ja3	a5f8hk	a5f8hk	tuwopa	tuwopa	e82kfr	e82kfr
l037dg	l037dg	m56n3	m56n3	2084al	2484al	gvvn5	gavn5
kla73n	kla73n	lfm4ea	lm4ea	skfhj47	skfhj47	308fka	308fka
dm38a	dm38a	mrk48e	mrk48e	vkfh7c	vkfh7c	pal7fm	pal7fm

49an56	94an56	nv0f78	nv0f78	boot8a	boat8a	xmcl38	xmcl38
239pl3	239pl3	sl54j9	sl5499	rmnn5l	rmnn5l	qwok5o	qwko5o
3457r8	3457r8	mi5a82	mi5a82	alprmy	alprmy	m5nhjc	m5nhjc
2cm79r	2cm79r	akr308	akr308	30586	30586	h5820a	h5820a

938728	938278	emc84h	emc84h
953jf05	953jf05	03ldj63	03ldj63
po398a	po398a	qlpe28	qlpe28
vb39ala	vb39ala	xcpoi24	xcpol24

ANSWERS TO *QUESTION 2*

Sheet 1

dl49f dl49f	39dj5 39dj5	ep395 ep395	elp59 elp59
30f3r 30f3r	qp294 qp294	eptiy petiy	jkow8 jkow8
lo3vr lo3yr	doi39 doi39	39ri3 39ri3	do03r do03r
or35k or35k	d034i d034l	k5o58 k5o58	mlg94 mlg49
move3 move3	39fjw 39fjw	35957 35957	wp20e wp20e
yijn5 yijn5	pyk5k ypk5k	vmpw3 vmpw3	fmog4 fmog4
fkp30 fk3p0	fmv93 fmv93	deok5 deok5	vmpeg mvpeg
deklp deklp	dmp24 dmp24	rpk60 rpk06	204dk 204dk
ri40e ri40e	fjo39 fjo93	wpa10 wpa01	fejmo fejmo
or30r or30r	powe2 powe2	dld93 dld93	308jo 308jo
fk04j fk04j	dk035 dk035	dkv92 dkv92	r30ie r30ie
t40gj t04gj	358fj 358fj	s024k s024k	20oew 20eow
395kr 395kr	fem34 fem34	09668 09668	trjo3 trjo3
mcl39 mci39	dkp30 dkp30	jig7t jij7t	lpeea lpeaa
jlgt0 jlgt0	20dmv 2odmv	o9ubj o9ubj	f3k63 f3k63
r04ir r04ir	dkf30 dkf30	k0i76 k0i76	fpk46 fpk46
tk303 tk303	gfo3k5 gfo3k5	35fe3 35fe3	lr39fp lr39fp
rlpf2 rlfp2	59eu3 59ue3	350dk 350kd	flp30 flp03
flp3d flp3d	34oiro 34oiro	q130e q130e	fro46 fro46
dkp20 dkp20	3058d 3058d	vmlt3 vmlt3	t4240 t4240
gml45 gml45	dwo14 dwo14	35erp 53erp	3fjo3p 3fjo3p
340rk 340rk	304or 304ro	wp24r wp24r	eoo42 eoo42
e2l04 e2i04	092lp 092lp	fm40e fm40e	mv3o4 mv34o
r3k05 r3k05	2dwp2 2dwp2	emp53 emp53	kop94 kop94
f46ju f46ju	roi3q roi3p	aklq9u1 aklq9u1	35fap1 35fpa1
ssu9s ssu9s	249dj 249dj	dkpc96 dkpc96	dl304r dl304r
skp97 skp97	djo07 djo07	bkpw08 bkpw08	cmp29 cmp29
mo906 mo960	hoit7 hoit7	n08dpp no8dpp	rkp30 rkp30

Sheet 2

fdsp2 fdsp2	eok35 eko35	adp53 adp53	aoj53 aoj53
sa245 sa245	dkwp3 dkwp3	sdlp4 sdlp4	vmpt4 vmpt4
dfvm4 dfvm4	wek46 wek46	fnk3k fnk3k	repk3 repk3
w563g w536g	kp57d kp57d	aslk5 asl5k	dwl53 dwi53
5r9t4 5r9t4	359fj 359fj	qk4kg gk4kg	grkl3 grkl3
grkp4 grkp4	aru95 aru95	fmlfe4 fmlfe4	frk3r frkr3
gfm35 gfn35	ryy85 ryy85	tkp40 tkp40	vmlf9 vmlf9
dl35jt dl35jt	a9u47 a9u74	40irjw 40irjw	dpl69 dpl69
fek42 fek42	gh39a gh39a	the93 the93	g349fn g349fn
wij3n wij3n	amm6f amm6f	tpe38r tpe38r	fel48r fel48r
tmp46 tmp46	flk64 fik64	mfep4 mfep4	twnl3 townl3
m35ja m35ga	polk5 polk5	r39fe r93fe	rjow3 rjow3
grtlm4 grtlm4	g9345 g9345	euiorw eiuorw	35992 35992
bvm3r bvm3r	38702 38702	wero35 wero35	fnsk3 fns23
5jre30 5lre30	etnkd entkd	gf35ir gf35ir	39nr3 39nr3
35793 35793	34098 34098	nro3nr nro3nr	em6l7 em6l7
gfn4nt gfn4nt	68753 68753	xdkl4 xdkj4	kjhfy kjhfy
rm3l2 rm321	freojr freoir	zprli zprli	hui96 hui96
yml34 yml34	vcmne vcmne	itu38 itu38	oj97g 0j97g
plghi3 plghi3	35089 35089	nml30 nml30	nlk9t nlk9t
kgy7f kgy7f	gdkn4 gdkn4	campt3 campt3	fajioj fajioj
987jl 987jli	fejio5 fejio5	dfsfm6 dfsfm6	wplai wplai
mb905 mb905	plhih8 plhih8	gjasp5 gjsap5	caaop caaop
cyt86r cyt86r	nkr39 nrk39	hsk64 hsk64	oarji oarjil
35983 35983	yaok5 yaok5	29082 29028	fla35a fla35a
20957 60957	iimpy7 iimpy7	qpalfm qpalfm	al38gh al38gh
247d9 247d9	gkdpm gkdmp	mcao4 mcao4	daml46 dami46
ae3k4 ae3k4	3598j 3598j	nb39f nb39f	faml57 faml57

Sheet 3

03ke3	03ke3	d63ju	d63ju	sal35k	sal53k	30irwk	30irwk
xmcl9	xmci9	qpel29	qpel29	oiu48a	oiu48a	ewpe2	wepe2
e3lmr	e3lmr	drlp35	drlp35	m38ak	m38ak	wwekp	wwekp
46lgm	46lgm	nfl3pq	nfl3qp	as29sk	as29sk	2394e	2394e

3580ak	358oak	salp3	salp3	salpt	salpt	cxa4l3	cxa4l3
dasl53	dasl53	rel86	rel86	gdko4	gdko4	l23lr5	l32lr5
adkl34	adkl34	ro35j	ro35g	39dj3	39dj3	tlep4k	tlep4k
gdlok5	gdlok5	lpsa2	lpsa2	vek2k	vekk2	rk4kar	rk4kar

3lp5g	3lp5g	w29di	w29dd	sal238	sal238	etplgf	etpglf
ktgr4	ktgr4	dsko3	dsko3	249716	294716	grmo4	grmo4
5l3j2	5l3i2	hspl2	hspl2	aso2kr	aso2kr	trmeo	trmeo
a90fg	a90fg	k120d	k120d	rek3ko	rek3ko	3048d	3048d

uialpa	uialpa	cemuv	cemuv	yafm4l	yafm4l	49738	94738
apslfm	paslfm	eokwa	eokwa	49frj3	49frj3	42980	42980
dskape	dskape	s2le0e	s2leeo	0ds2j	ods2j	asjoe	asjoe
oial30	oial30	lp30a	lp30a	198dw	198dw	dsok2	dsok2

bnr3if	bnr3if	rei301	rei031	a9dt4	a9dt4	93jd1	93jd1
x20ala	x20ala	aspl11	aspl11	4m6l7	4m6i7	10sk2	10ks2
z19al6	z19al6	pyt94a	pyt94a	ly4pd	ly4pd	ek20p	ek20p
q204ld	g204ld	idsjwa	idsjwa	d3u9r	d3u9r	y02jr	y02jr

s92md	s92md	694fk	694fk	ou92m	ou92m	29ap2k	29ap2k
d19am	d19am	e2i01	e2i01	mc92a	mc92a	dsk2a9	ds2ka9
wpqa0	wpqao	cm30a	mc30a	nap29	nap92	ma02la	ma02la
prm28	prm28	kao2a	kao2a	ka17s	ka17s	a9dk39	a9dk39

k29ak	k29ak	45da7	45da7	op08a	op08a	28ak9	28ak9
7al20	7ai20	92mf2	92mf2	a7rn5	a7rn5	19sk1	19ks1
20lda	20lda	al8f9j	la8f9j	vm48a	vm48a	a8sh7	a8sh7
97dj2	97dj2	m7foa	m7foa	ama39	ama93	29a26	29a26

Sheet 4

w038f w038f	e03ld4 e03ld4	lam48 lma48	a0lsn a0lsn
28fj53 28fj53	0ld73h 0ld73h	amb58 amb58	rj39d rg39d
38rsiw 38rsiw	d7i3bd d73ibd	27dh3 27dh3	2e20d 2e20d
q2oe0 q20e0	k926ai k926ai	n9j23 n9j23	fe0k2 fe0k2
dalpfn dalpfn	ask348 ask348	qwplam qwplam	29alpa 29alpa
fdmla fdmla	347ash 347ahs	amw28 amw28	se19d es19d
3f9am 3f9am	da37fh da37fh	29dj20 29dj20	v9s6w v9s6w
mda20 mad20	hs8j02 hs8j02	lp18jd lpi8jd	l29aq l29aq
249ame 249mae	rel29a rel29a	498fao 498fao	ja93h3 ja93h3
ppo8ye ppo8ye	al20r8 al20r8	23amrt 23mart	28snma 28snma
9euige 9euige	vbgu4 vbgu4	tra92m tra92m	sm28ag sm2a8g
cdn385 cdn385	49gjra 49gira	am20d am20d	fdmla2 fdmla2
gh47sl gh47sl	348gfj 348gfj	39fja0 39fja0	1e27rt 1e27rt
sk38rp sk83rp	29en2 29en2	1047f 1047f	0gle79 ogle79
d83hfe d83hfe	208fm 208fm	37659 37569	tr8fl3e tr8fl3e
39lp82 39lp82	opww7 opwu7	m8c62 m8c62	c93ma c93ma
l2a74 i2a74	38fk19 38fk19	wp39sl wp39sl	34927 34927
itu38d itu38d	193753 193573	lsmc37 lscm37	lpqun lpqun
bmdk2 bmdk2	e9r8t6 e9r8t6	dh37ql dh37ql	frn37 frn37
am38d am38d	l9689w l9689w	io16ah io16ah	29do3 29d03
398daj 398daj	w93mc w93mc	cm39al cm39al	h92jd6 h92jd6
10ripa 10rlpa	ep28a ep82a	al28rua al28ura	29s1la 29s1la
amd21 amd21	0ql173 0ql173	e382f0 e382f0	a81l03 8a1l03
p08j7a p08j7a	2479a 2479a	fek381 fek381	936el2 936el2
gh38sk gh38sk	x3d6g8 x3d6g8	xmsl37 xsml37	bb37dka bb37kda
29sl28 29sl28	0nmf6s 0nmf6s	2846fw 2846fw	vm389fe vm389fe
s6g9j0 s9g6j0	6bf93m 6fb93m	m97gd6 m97gd6	lfdh38g lfdh38g
v745n2 v745n2	dk291n dk291n	dh28q8 dh28q8	dsj3476 dsj3476

Sheet 5

389am2	389am2	jfjs238	jfjs238	3895fj	3895fj	a5h8f5	a5h8f5
20d86g	208d6g	39475	39475	ek28a	ek28a	me17eb	me17eb
cmd76	cmd76	397da	397da	pef28l	pel28f	me18eo	me18eo
r9846d	r9846d	24dj98	24jd98	fcn38	fcn38	st176a	st167a

van8s7	van8s7	vma7f9	vma7f9	348f37	348f37	mv83ah	mv38ah
xbos7z	xbox7z	fj37ara	fj37ara	29dm2	22dm9	dka18a	dka18a
qpal7fe	qpal7fe	0mv7fh	0mv7bh	18sn26	18sn26	pl8mfra	pl8mfra
e8mwa	e8mwa	hsd38a	hsd38a	2348hl	2348hl	aor237	aor237

na84	na84	awu38	awu38	8976f	8966f	y5f8h	y5f8h
ld72	ld72	bc894	bc894	768kl	768kl	0nh8f	0nh8f
29fg	29fg	387fh	387hf	58d3t	58d3t	d8gs2	dogs2
mcw6	mc26	29752	29752	t7ki0	t7ki0	58dv8	58dv8

vnd7l	vnd7l	nc7ek4	nc7ek4	nc63	nc63	2579	2579
0k76s	0k76s	gh30al	hg30al	2378	2378	dajp	dajp
me28a	me28e	cm20gf	cm20gf	piwr	piwr	394h	349h
ple8ah	ple8ah	s8pm2a	s8pm2a	fa8g	fag8	rqo2	rqo2

h83dk0	h38dk0	mc30g	mc30g	n7924	n7924	7420f	7420f
289hfa	289hfa	g4bh8	g4bh8	7420a	7402a	fsjfr3	fsjrf3
294875	294875	ry93t	ry93t	fjal3o	fjal3o	3573g	3573g
5389fs	5389fs	7539h	75e9h	r239a	r239a	c3b8g	c3b8g

chg84j	cha84j	kl926s	kl962s	qpri58	qpri58	cm349f	cm349f
dj38sg	dj38sg	djk27h	djk27h	39fpl3	39flp3	295fh7	259fh7
fkc823	fkc823	2749d0	2749d0	3k6bn	3k6bn	537dn3	537dn3
2846dh	2846dh	xdj278	xdj278	s9wn7	s9wn7	385792	385792

lsk389	lsk389	eilw18a	eilw18a	q8fm4n	q8fm4n	ldj72h	idj72h
38eb35	38be35	al4rnm	al4rnm	sm28da	sm82da	afkr3k	afkr3k
63ma98	63ma98	zcwr39	zcwr39	0kc3h8	0kc3h8	td9nm	td9nm
mcd3l0	mcd3l0	dal53nj	dai53nj	fh38ka	fh38ka	ud308t	ud308t

Sheet 6

387aj3	387ja3	a5f8hk	a5f8hk	tuwopa	tuwopa	e82kfr	e82kfr
l037dg	l037dg	m56n3	m56n3	2084al	2484al	gvvn5	gavn5
kla73n	kla73n	lfm4ea	lm4ea	skfhj47	skfhj47	308fka	308fka
dm38a	dm38a	mrk48e	mrk48e	vkfh7c	vkfh7c	pal7fm	pal7fm
49an56	94an56	nv0f78	nv0f78	boot8a	boat8a	xmcl38	xmcl38
239pl3	239pl3	sl54j9	sl5499	rmnn5l	rmnn5l	qwok5o	qwko5o
3457r8	3457r8	mi5a82	mi5a82	alprmy	alprmy	m5nhjc	m5nhjc
2cm79r	2cm79r	akr308	akr308	30586	30586	h5820a	h5820a
938728	938278	emc84h	emc84h				
953jf05	953jf05	03ldj63	03ldj63				
po398a	po398a	qlpe28	qlpe28				
vb39ala	vb39ala	xcpoi24	xcpol24				

*Look at the four pairs of alpha-numerical digits. Circle or highlight the combination pair that **does not** match.*

QUESTION 3 - Sheet 1

la0s	la0s	w5f8	w5f8	e6t9	e6t9	a8fm	8afm
a0d8	aod8	7mw2	7mw2	74b2	742b	47rb	47rb
48fm	48fm	das3	das3	046f	046f	v7sa	v7sa
s7f5	s7f5	935f	953f	0od8	0od8	9gdm	9gdm
d5h8	d5h8	r6i0	r6l0	gh78	gh78	ed58	ed58
m9b7	m9b7	0md3	0md3	hj9f	hj9f	9ki6	9kl6
git7	git7	35f7	35f7	6897	6987	76hi	76hi
79g7	76g7	y4ma	y4ma	gu72	gu72	458y	458y
d76h	d76h	df7h	df7h	w2r5	w2r5	t8y3	toy3
g8i9	g8i9	8yhg	8yhg	o0u7	o0u7	mc32	mc32
78yt	78yt	7t03	7to3	y5y7	y57y	5378	5378
87yj	87yg	nc4f	nc4f	ty38	ty38	ru93	ru93
dajk	dajk	de0k	de0k	q34i	q34i	67dk	67dk
353a	353a	87yu	87uy	m8d4	m8d4	k907	k907
su89	su89	9uit	9uit	f87o	f870	7689	7869
35jf	35if	6r98	6r98	ghi6	ghi6	v68j	v68j
ryi9	ryi9	3e46	3a46	m9g6	m9j6	mce8	mce8
wert	wetr	f8hk	f8hk	wfr8	wfr8	g4j9	g4l9
mnbv	mnbv	bn8f	bn8f	i764	i764	248f	248f
c678	c678	df94	df94	oiu7	oiu7	539a	539a
5rg8	5rg8	t7i9	t7i9	z69m	z69m	e5i9	e5i9
tj85	tj85	r6gh	r6gh	z6ag	z6ag	lo90	io90
hdd2	hdd2	kju6	kuj6	an8o	an8o	r7yu	r7yu
sam2	san2	g7hf	g7hf	m964	m694	n8y5	n8y5
e5u8	e5u8	rt8y	rt8j	fj49	fi49	ul19	ul91
l0j7	l0j7	hhfd	hhfd	cm39	cm39	o486	o486
g7k0	g7k0	asdn	asdn	th92	th92	dm37	dm37
mv7u	mu7u	rj38	rj38	akld	akld	vmd7	vmd7

*Look at the four pairs of alpha-numerical digits. Circle or highlight the combination pair that **does not** match.*

Sheet 2

mv83	mv83	f3h8	f3h8	qopl	qopl	la9r	la9r
gj3j	gj3j	c3m9	cm39	w348	w348	39ey	39ye
so28	s028	2508	2508	vma2	vma2	w925	w925
ajk3	ajk3	8yud	8yud	397f	937f	vnb3	vnb3

2745	2745	5237	5327	ka85	ka85	e2o0	e2o0
apru	apru	daj9	daj9	j85a	g85a	i9e7	i97e
gvm7	gum7	r3u9	r3u9	fa56	fa56	yt47	yt47
eh37	eh37	iuy7	iuy7	zb75	zb75	t472	t472

nfr7	nfr7	t4u8	t4v8	eo28	eo28	ooeu	ooeu
r382	r482	f3j9	f3j9	298e	298e	3857	3587
q947	q947	2395	2395	cma6	cma6	fdk9	fdk9
mfdh	mfdh	v9vm	v9vm	m705	n705	4358	4358

m86f	m86f	kjs8	kis8	lap8	lap8	p9l7	p9l7
578j	578i	sjf7	sjf7	r38a	r38a	i8yu	i8uy
5e8h	5e8h	3rn6	3rn6	2349	2349	t5e3	t5e3
g853	g853	63n3	63n3	v39a	v93a	na6a	na6a

th38	th38	q760	q760	r6i9	r6i9	cb37	cb37
dfjk	dfik	l975	l975	m8f5	m8f5	e38f	e38f
32e2	32e2	ej3n	ej3m	sd56	sd65	t3m6	t3m6
q3w0	q3w0	4m37	4m37	i974	i974	69g6	69g9

qp29	qp29	e29c	e29c	a6d9	a6d9	qt70	qt70
gm5b	gmb5	38f7	38f7	04m6	04n6	m389	m389
s7ch	s7ch	4m67	4n67	5n59	5n59	38yf	38yf
5mg7	5mg7	2b5m	2b5m	5n38	5n38	398j	389j

r4t7	r4t7	u8t6	u8t6	s4y8	s4y8	pl8a	pl8a
lu9t	lu9t	u895	u895	8hjl	8hjl	aj85	ay85
y487	x487	678u	678v	f6ih	f6ih	a576	a576
488t	488t	iuy6	iuy6	r68g	r68j	g789	g789

*Look at the four pairs of alpha-numerical digits. Circle or highlight the combination pair that **does not** match.*

Sheet 3

f6yu8	f6yu8	ar69k	ar69k	lo87t	lo87t	ft5ei	ft5ei
h875r	h875r	mia7s	mia7s	dj8d6	dj8d6	tro54	tro54
j9m76	jm976	su89d	su89d	cmcr3	cmcr3	bv8sd	bvosd
d5tr8	d5tr8	cu86s	cu68s	ru38a	ru83a	sr8g5	sr8g5

t39tj	t93tj	d6h9b	d6h9b	78yut	78yut	um7b6	um7b6
4j47f	4j47f	28sju	28sju	4r7y4	4r7u4	6n5v4	6n5v4
r47f9	r47f9	2n46k	2n46k	9hj4b	9hj4b	5g8je	5g8ej
h8f5a	h8f5a	7nm53	7mn53	4mg8a	4mg8a	y834d	y834d

8m76h	8m76h	y47fj	y47fj	fdi39	fdl39	asm36	ams36
45f79	45f79	4d76h	4a76h	34ryt	34ryt	48ty4	48ty4
juu89	juu89	pal78	pal78	459ir	459ir	t483g	t483g
a58ha	a5h8a	vm57f	vm57f	456ua	456ua	hu459	hu459

jfi47	jfi47	3478r	3478r	bb7e4	bb7e4	85mf7	85mf7
g48v7	g48v7	39ik0	39ik0	nj3b8	nj3b8	4jkf7	4jkf7
y40kh	y40hk	y58h8	y85h8	48gm4	48mg4	d04mf	d04mf
389m3	389m3	hg4o0	hg4o0	27d0t	27d0t	sl48k	si48k

4jfs0	4fjs0	e6th9	e6th9	gl59m	gl95m	a2f5h	a2f5h
m6s74	m6s74	383m7	388m7	t89s6	t89s6	m56f4	n56f4
fkt84	fkt84	m3x85	m3x85	fm40f	fm40f	lf39g	lf39g
gtk38	gtk38	s6ns7	s6ns7	49r3y	49r3y	t4i0t	t4i0t

56gf3	56gf3	ry4n8	ry4n8	n8d64	n8d64	48t07	48t07
78jg4	78j4g	g94hf	g94hf	d6g9h	d6g9h	334m9	334n9
67htg	67htg	fdm8g	fmd8g	5mf73	5mf37	64n36	64n36
mju5s	mju5s	g93jf	g93jf	b85oh	b85oh	348a7	348a7

7vd5m	7vd5m	6g9j3	6g9j3	vm49f	vm49f	3578p	3578p
y8s54	y8s54	3edy4	3edu4	fu93k	fu93k	49it4	49it4
h9r7s	h9r7s	48tj0	48tj0	af378	af738	64u88	49ti4
g7as5	glas5	426f6	426f6	cu9r3	cu9r3	r4y73	r4y73

Look at the four pairs of alpha-numerical digits. Circle or highlight the combination pair that **does not** match.

Sheet 4

37r3y	37r3y	t49fn	t49fn	6d03m	6d03m	us9gf	us9gf
3c957	3d957	3bvj6	3bvj6	38cve	38cve	gkg83	gkg83
loda7	loda7	gn7s6	gn76s	e93jr	e93jr	39f8k	39f8k
va84g	va84g	6na68	6na68	yi5j2	yl5j2	648dg	648gd
21674	21674	e69jl	e69jl	53g05	53g05	a5f8h	a5f8h
truip	truip	d845b	d845b	496s4	469s4	7m5b3	7m5b3
gfhjk	gjhjk	h836a	h386a	50hk7	50hk7	g84d5	g48d5
vcmbn	vcmbn	am3n5	am3n5	7j5g6	7j5g6	7nt4r	7nt4r
e2u9f	e2v9f	mbn48	mbn48	k7b5x	k7b5x	g7hj0	g7hjo
0hm6b	0hm6b	t49rv	t49rv	zv4b5	zv4b5	n5b27	n5b27
4b8f4	4b8f4	rhf97	rhf97	q6g8h	q9g8h	fgh83	fgh83
79hk5	79hk5	fj9b5	fy9b5	dk9g6	dk9g6	v0p3l	v0p3l
k7h56	k7h56	t7kim	t7kim	26db0	26db0	7n9tf	7n9tf
g6df8	g6fd8	96g90	96g90	034nf	o34nf	97nkd	97nkd
k96bs	k96bs	mk9de	m9kde	93ms5	93ms5	8ch3k	8ch3k
j97tv	j97tv	2f6j9	2f6j9	92m3c	92m3c	3nm53	3mn53
s37g9	s37g9	v8m78	v8m78	64b0l	64bol	24748	24748
9uj64	9uj64	6g3a7	6g3a7	6tjgf	6tjgf	8753f	8753f
7gjn3	7gyn3	987k8	978k8	954df	954df	086g3	086g3
9mxr6	9mxr6	742u0	742u0	f456k	f456k	53ky5	53yk5
7m5v3	7m5v3	589j5	589j5	86h94	86h94	g8k96	g89k6
9nm4s	9nm4s	ekn74	ekn74	866d4	866d4	86hj9	86hj9
9y3df	9u3df	hmj95	hmy95	i9g64	i9g46	d6bj6	d6bj6
64h6n	64h6n	nkl76	nkl76	8j5d5	8j5d5	9jne4	9jne4
87g5d	87g5d	08m5s	08m5s	0kl7h	0kl7h	a5d8h	a5d8h
9j7d3	9j7d3	85b84	8b584	6b4s3	6b43s	n9f75	n97f5
e5bg8	eb5g8	mvc8j	mvc8j	86hi8	86hi8	s7fg4	s7fg4
j9y5e	j9y5e	m974d	m974d	095f8	095f8	49gw4	49gw4

Look at the four pairs of alpha-numerical digits. Circle or highlight the combination pair that **does not** match.

Sheet 5

d8gn27	d8gn27	fy378m	fy378m	a8dm58	a8dm58	d73kf9	d73kf9
plday3	plday3	397d4a	397d4a	dlr75c	dlr75c	0l3f6h	0l3f6h
4g8j6g	4g8j6g	0m7g54	om7g54	97548c	97548c	6dg8dj	6gd8dj
3d760j	3e760j	8dkb7a	8dkb7a	cm38bs	mc38bs	s5f8hm	s5f8hm
a4d7c9	a4d7c9	q6r8m5	q6r8m5	h75f7k	h75f7k	s539gm	s539gm
ldjk73	ldjk73	gm94nb	gm94nb	k96bhd	k69bhd	03r8g4	03r8g4
395gj5	395gi5	v894ml	v894ml	5d9ghr	5d9ghr	r37h8t	r37h8t
e945kr	e945кr	hk04ny	hk04yn	mv84nf	mv84nf	4nmvg3	4mnvg3
vgf740	vgf740	q478tk	q478tk	74mc8j	74mc8j	q438k6	q438k6
39it3y	39it3y	034m5n	033m5n	fdj4nfd	fdj4nfd	pl58gn	pi58gn
r380i4	r380j4	64n49t	64n49t	83h8d2	83hd82	uin85n	uin85n
ad9j3f	ad9j3f	36f9m8	36f9m8	03lu4a	03lu4a	yun68f	yun68f
9k7h6d	9k76hd	e3j6mt	e3j6mt	f6j9k7	f6j9k7	q6u80o	q6u80o
378f94	378f94	94mpg7	94mgp7	mn79kl	mn79kl	m76h5d	m76h5d
48hjg4	48hjg4	g94bgu	g94bgu	eh97k0	eh97k0	39gdj8	39adj8
akamto	akamto	g9gouy	g9gouy	l074gh	l704gh	97hkid	97hkid
l98hf6	l98hf6	56jkn7	56jkn7	w4u9km	w4uk9m	i86t8o	i86t8o
ung74f	ung74f	974df7	974df7	kh78ok	kh78ok	oi6fh8	o6ifh8
0m7n5d	0n7n5d	9kyer6	9kjer6	m64257	m64257	mk75gf	mk75gf
97f48j	97f48j	9634md	9634md	864h90	864h90	jkuu36	jkuu36
ty84gh	ty84gh	m85t79i	m85t79i	r68kna	r68kna	965yu9	965yu9
o986nk	o986nk	kg34gh	kg34gh	ld7cn6	ld7cn6	ui85e4	ui85e4
k976fj	k976fj	uy6rfv	uy6rfv	9e6sn2	96esn2	49ug47	49gu47
876rhn	876hrn	qpla8f	pqla8f	679ed8	679ed8	97nu64	97nu64
08u75g	08u75g	t669j6	t669j6	468hf5	468hf5	124q79	214q79
86h5f7	86h5f7	j865g6	j865g6	8uin64	8uin64	875h85	875h85
98mf57	98m5f7	l905f6	l905f6	23jd78	23dj78	7u5d8o	7u5d8o
i975gj	i975gj	854f7h	845f7h	69jka4	69jka4	8654de	8654de

*Look at the four pairs of alpha-numerical digits. Circle or highlight the combination pair that **does not** match.*

Sheet 6

348g4	348g4	4eds8	4eds8	285fh	285fh	357hf8	357hf8
t348a	t438a	9jh46	9jh46	34jf3	34jf3	83f3g7	83t3g7
84k5f	84k5f	3738f	7338f	9jfa6	9jfa6	jg8497	jg8497
93ja5	93ja5	3bm6f	3bm6f	mc367	mc637	3hf6k3	3hf6k3

qy79jf	qy79jf	83mf9p	83mf9p	t4da	t4da	328a7	328a7
dd7aya	dd7aya	348tu7	348tu7	faj7	faj7	ut4o5	ut405
04mv74	04mv74	3y7t39	3u7t39	64g7	64g7	du84m	du84m
r84jf9	r84fj9	93may7	93may7	46a3	64a3	4g7m8	4g7m8

3mc7h	3mc7h	q6g9m	q6g9m
48g0k	48g0k	f7d6g	f7dog
5g9a6	5g9a6	39g53	39g53
n79v7	n97v7	vm96h	vm96h

ANSWERS TO *QUESTION 3*

Sheet 1

la0s	la0s	w5f8	w5f8	e6t9	e6t9	a8fm	8afm
a0d8	aod8	7mw2	7mw2	74b2	742b	47rb	47rb
48fm	48fm	das3	das3	046f	046f	v7sa	v7sa
s7f5	s7f5	935f	953f	0od8	0od8	9gdm	9gdm

d5h8	d5h8	r6i0	r6l0	gh78	gh78	ed58	ed58
m9b7	m9b7	0md3	0md3	hj9f	hj9f	9ki6	9kl6
git7	git7	35f7	35f7	6897	6987	76hi	76hi
79g7	76g7	y4ma	y4ma	gu72	gu72	458y	458y

d76h	d76h	df7h	df7h	w2r5	w2r5	t8y3	toy3
g8i9	g8i9	8yhg	8yhg	o0u7	o0u7	mc32	mc32
78yt	78yt	7t03	7to3	y5y7	y57y	5378	5378
87yj	87yg	nc4f	nc4f	ty38	ty38	ru93	ru93

dajk	dajk	de0k	de0k	q34i	q34i	67dk	67dk
353a	353a	87yu	87uy	m8d4	m8d4	k907	k907
su89	su89	9uit	9uit	f87o	f870	7689	7869
35jf	35if	6r98	6r98	ghi6	ghi6	v68j	v68j

ryi9	ryi9	3e46	3a46	m9g6	m9j6	mce8	mce8
wert	wetr	f8hk	f8hk	wfr8	wfr8	g4j9	g4l9
mnbv	mnbv	bn8f	bn8f	i764	i764	248f	248f
c678	c678	df94	df94	oiu7	oiu7	539a	539a

5rg8	5rg8	t7i9	t7i9	z69m	z69m	e5i9	e5i9
tj85	tj85	r6gh	r6gh	z6ag	z6ag	lo90	io90
hdd2	hdd2	kju6	kuj6	an8o	an8o	r7yu	r7yu
sam2	san2	g7hf	g7hf	m964	m694	n8y5	n8y5

e5u8	e5u8	rt8y	rt8j	fj49	fi49	ul19	ul91
l0j7	l0j7	hhfd	hhfd	cm39	cm39	o486	o486
g7k0	g7k0	asdn	asdn	th92	th92	dm37	dm37
mv7u	mu7u	rj38	rj38	akld	akld	vmd7	vmd7

Sheet 2

mv83	mv83	f3h8	f3h8	qopl	qopl	la9r	la9r
gj3j	gj3j	c3m9	cm39	w348	w348	39ey	39ye
so28	s028	2508	2508	vma2	vma2	w925	w925
ajk3	ajk3	8yud	8yud	397f	937f	vnb3	vnb3

2745	2745	5237	5327	ka85	ka85	e2o0	e2o0
apru	apru	daj9	daj9	j85a	g85a	i9e7	i97e
gvm7	gum7	r3u9	r3u9	fa56	fa56	yt47	yt47
eh37	eh37	iuy7	iuy7	zb75	zb75	t472	t472

nfr7	nfr7	t4u8	t4v8	eo28	eo28	ooeu	ooeu
r382	r482	f3j9	f3j9	298e	298e	3857	3587
q947	q947	2395	2395	cma6	cma6	fdk9	fdk9
mfdh	mfdh	v9vm	v9vm	m705	n705	4358	4358

m86f	m86f	kjs8	kis8	lap8	lap8	p9l7	p9l7
578j	578i	sjf7	sjf7	r38a	r38a	i8yu	i8uy
5e8h	5e8h	3rn6	3rn6	2349	2349	t5e3	t5e3
g853	g853	63n3	63n3	v39a	v93a	na6a	na6a

th38	th38	q760	q760	r6i9	r6i9	cb37	cb37
dfjk	dfik	l975	l975	m8f5	m8f5	e38f	e38f
32e2	32e2	ej3n	ej3m	sd56	sd65	t3m6	t3m6
q3w0	q3w0	4m37	4m37	i974	i974	69g6	69g9

qp29	qp29	e29c	e29c	a6d9	a6d9	qt70	qt70
gm5b	gmb5	38f7	38f7	04m6	04n6	m389	m389
s7ch	s7ch	4m67	4n67	5n59	5n59	38yf	38yf
5mg7	5mg7	2b5m	2b5m	5n38	5n38	398j	389j

r4t7	r4t7	u8t6	u8t6	s4y8	s4y8	pl8a	pl8a
lu9t	lu9t	u895	u895	8hjl	8hjl	aj85	ay85
y487	x487	678u	678v	f6ih	f6ih	a576	a576
488t	488t	iuy6	iuy6	r68g	r68j	g789	g789

Sheet 3

f6yu8	f6yu8	ar69k	ar69k	lo87t	lo87t	ft5ei	ft5ei
h875r	h875r	mia7s	mia7s	dj8d6	dj8d6	tro54	tro54
j9m76	jm976	su89d	su89d	cmcr3	cmcr3	bv8sd	bvosd
d5tr8	d5tr8	cu86s	cu68s	ru38a	ru83a	sr8g5	sr8g5

t39tj	t93tj	d6h9b	d6h9b	78yut	78yut	um7b6	um7b6
4j47f	4j47f	28sju	28sju	4r7y4	4r7u4	6n5v4	6n5v4
r47f9	r47f9	2n46k	2n46k	9hj4b	9hj4b	5g8je	5g8ej
h8f5a	h8f5a	7nm53	7mn53	4mg8a	4mg8a	y834d	y834d

8m76h	8m76h	y47fj	y47fj	fdi39	fdl39	asm36	ams36
45f79	45f79	4d76h	4a76h	34ryt	34ryt	48ty4	48ty4
juu89	juu89	pal78	pal78	459ir	459ir	t483g	t483g
a58ha	a5h8a	vm57f	vm57f	456ua	456ua	hu459	hu459

jfi47	jfi47	3478r	3478r	bb7e4	bb7e4	85mf7	85mf7
g48v7	g48v7	39ik0	39ik0	nj3b8	nj3b8	4jkf7	4jkf7
y40kh	y40hk	y58h8	y85h8	48gm4	48mg4	d04mf	d04mf
389m3	389m3	hg4o0	hg4o0	27d0t	27d0t	sl48k	si48k

4jfs0	4fjs0	e6th9	e6th9	gl59m	gl95m	a2f5h	a2f5h
m6s74	m6s74	383m7	388m7	t89s6	t89s6	m56f4	n56f4
fkt84	fkt84	m3x85	m3x85	fm40f	fm40f	lf39g	lf39g
gtk38	gtk38	s6ns7	s6ns7	49r3y	49r3y	t4i0t	t4i0t

56gf3	56gf3	ry4n8	ry4n8	n8d64	n8d64	48t07	48t07
78jg4	78j4g	g94hf	g94hf	d6g9h	d6g9h	334m9	334n9
67htg	67htg	fdm8g	fmd8g	5mf73	5mf37	64n36	64n36
mju5s	mju5s	g93jf	g93jf	b85oh	b85oh	348a7	348a7

7vd5m	7vd5m	6g9j3	6g9j3	vm49f	vm49f	3578p	3578p
y8s54	y8s54	3edy4	3edu4	fu93k	fu93k	49it4	49it4
h9r7s	h9r7s	48tj0	48tj0	af378	af738	64u88	49ti4
g7as5	glas5	426f6	426f6	cu9r3	cu9r3	r4y73	r4y73

Sheet 4

37r3y	37r3y	t49fn	t49fn	6d03m	6d03m	us9gf	us9gf
3c957	3d957	3bvj6	3bvj6	38cve	38cve	gkg83	gkg83
loda7	loda7	gn7s6	gn76s	e93jr	e93jr	39f8k	39f8k
va84g	va84g	6na68	6na68	yi5j2	yl5j2	648dg	648gd
21674	21674	e69jl	e69jl	53g05	53g05	a5f8h	a5f8h
truip	truip	d845b	d845b	496s4	469s4	7m5b3	7m5b3
gfhjk	gjhjk	h836a	h386a	50hk7	50hk7	g84d5	g48d5
vcmbn	vcmbn	am3n5	am3n5	7j5g6	7j5g6	7nt4r	7nt4r
e2u9f	e2v9f	mbn48	mbn48	k7b5x	k7b5x	g7hj0	g7hjo
0hm6b	0hm6b	t49rv	t49rv	zv4b5	zv4b5	n5b27	n5b27
4b8f4	4b8f4	rhf97	rhf97	q6g8h	q9g8h	fgh83	fgh83
79hk5	79hk5	fj9b5	fy9b5	dk9g6	dk9g6	v0p3l	v0p3l
k7h56	k7h56	t7kim	t7kim	26db0	26db0	7n9tf	7n9tf
g6df8	g6fd8	96g90	96g90	034nf	o34nf	97nkd	97nkd
k96bs	k96bs	mk9de	m9kde	93ms5	93ms5	8ch3k	8ch3k
j97tv	j97tv	2f6j9	2f6j9	92m3c	92m3c	3nm53	3mn53
s37g9	s37g9	v8m78	v8m78	64b0l	64bol	24748	24748
9uj64	9uj64	6g3a7	6g3a7	6tjgf	6tjgf	8753f	8753f
7gjn3	7gyn3	987k8	978k8	954df	954df	086g3	086g3
9mxr6	9mxr6	742u0	742u0	f456k	f456k	53ky5	53yk5
7m5v3	7m5v3	589j5	589j5	86h94	86h94	g8k96	g89k6
9nm4s	9nm4s	ekn74	ekn74	866d4	866d4	86hj9	86hj9
9y3df	9u3df	hmj95	hmy95	i9g64	i9g46	d6bj6	d6bj6
64h6n	64h6n	nkl76	nkl76	8j5d5	8j5d5	9jne4	9jne4
87g5d	87g5d	08m5s	08m5s	0kl7h	0kl7h	a5d8h	a5d8h
9j7d3	9j7d3	85b84	8b584	6b4s3	6b43s	n9f75	n97f5
e5bg8	eb5g8	mvc8j	mvc8j	86hi8	86hi8	s7fg4	s7fg4
j9y5e	j9y5e	m974d	m974d	095f8	095f8	49gw4	49gw4

Sheet 5

d8gn27	d8gn27	fy378m	fy378m	a8dm58	a8dm58	d73kf9	d73kf9
plday3	plday3	397d4a	397d4a	dlr75c	dlr75c	0l3f6h	0l3f6h
4g8j6g	4g8j6g	0m7g54	om7g54	97548c	97548c	6dg8dj	6gd8dj
3d760j	3e760j	8dkb7a	8dkb7a	cm38bs	mc38bs	s5f8hm	s5f8hm

a4d7c9	a4d7c9	q6r8m5	q6r8m5	h75f7k	h75f7k	s539gm	s539gm
ldjk73	ldjk73	gm94nb	gm94nb	k96bhd	k69bhd	03r8g4	03r8g4
395gj5	395gi5	v894ml	v894ml	5d9ghr	5d9ghr	r37h8t	r37h8t
e945kr	e945kr	hk04ny	hk04yn	mv84nf	mv84nf	4nmvg3	4mnvg3

vgf740	vgf740	q478tk	q478tk	74mc8j	74mc8j	q438k6	q438k6
39it3y	39it3y	034m5n	033m5n	fdj4nfd	fdj4nfd	pl58gn	pi58gn
r380i4	r380j4	64n49t	64n49t	83h8d2	83hd82	uin85n	uin85n
ad9j3f	ad9j3f	36f9m8	36f9m8	03lu4a	03lu4a	yun68f	yun68f

9k7h6d	9k76hd	e3j6mt	e3j6mt	f6j9k7	f6j9k7	q6u80o	q6u80o
378f94	378f94	94mpg7	94mgp7	mn79kl	mn79kl	m76h5d	m76h5d
48hjg4	48hjg4	g94bgu	g94bgu	eh97k0	eh97k0	39gdj8	39adj8
akamto	akamto	g9gouy	g9gouy	l074gh	l704gh	97hkid	97hkid

l98hf6	l98hf6	56jkn7	56jkn7	w4u9km	w4uk9m	i86t8o	i86t8o
ung74f	ung74f	974df7	974df7	kh78ok	kh78ok	oi6fh8	o6ifh8
0m7n5d	0n7n5d	9kyer6	9kjer6	m64257	m64257	mk75gf	mk75gf
97f48j	97f48j	9634md	9634md	864h90	864h90	jkuu36	jkuu36

ty84gh	ty84gh	m85t79i	m85t79i	r68kna	r68kna	965yu9	965yu9
o986nk	o986nk	kg34gh	kg34gh	ld7cn6	ld7cn6	ui85e4	ui85e4
k976fj	k976fj	uy6rfv	uy6rfv	9e6sn2	96esn2	49ug47	49gu47
876rhn	876hrn	qpla8f	pqla8f	679ed8	679ed8	97nu64	97nu64

08u75g	08u75g	t669j6	t669j6	468hf5	468hf5	124q79	214q79
86h5f7	86h5f7	j865g6	j865g6	8uin64	8uin64	875h85	875h85
98mf57	98m5f7	l905f6	l905f6	23jd78	23dj78	7u5d8o	7u5d8o
i975gj	i975gj	854f7h	845f7h	69jka4	69jka4	8654de	8654de

Sheet 6

348g4	348g4	4eds8	4eds8	285fh	285fh	357hf8	357hf8
t348a	t438a	9jh46	9jh46	34jf3	34jf3	83f3g7	83t3g7
84k5f	84k5f	3738f	7338f	9jfa6	9jfa6	jg8497	jg8497
93ja5	93ja5	3bm6f	3bm6f	mc367	mc637	3hf6k3	3hf6k3
qy79jf	qy79jf	83mf9p	83mf9p	t4da	t4da	328a7	328a7
dd7aya	dd7aya	348tu7	348tu7	faj7	faj7	ut4o5	ut405
04mv74	04mv74	3y7t39	3u7t39	64g7	64g7	du84m	du84m
r84jf9	r84fj9	93may7	93may7	46a3	64a3	4g7m8	4g7m8
3mc7h	3mc7h	q6g9m	q6g9m				
48g0k	48g0k	f7d6g	f7dog				
5g9a6	5g9a6	39g53	39g53				
n79v7	n97v7	vm96h	vm96h				

*Look at the four pairs of numerical digits. Circle or highlight the combination pair that **does not** match.*

QUESTION 4 - Sheet 1

938-917 938-917	452-417 452-417	058-174 058-174	497-961 497-961
178-815 178-815	148-163 148-163	287-427 287-247	104-952 140-952
193-131 193-113	964-642 964-642	248-186 248-186	745-438 745-438
410-137 410-137	427-246 472-246	193-164 193-164	258-735 258-735

749-556 749-556	160-035 160-035	794-795 974-795	416-494 416-494
336-464 336-464	064-635 064-635	135-579 135-579	795-920 795-920
564-759 546-759	790-164 790-164	146-905 146-905	113-792 113-792
795-295 795-295	136-498 136-489	354-561 354-561	194-795 149-795

497-795 497-795	264-561 264-561	716-405 716-405	794-792 794-792
792-715 729-715	176-792 176-792	298-594 298-594	678-792 678-792
120-097 120-097	126-045 126-045	146-460 146-460	284-684 234-684
791-496 791-496	015-461 051-461	166-790 166-970	283-278 283-278

791-425 791-425	578-364 578-364	756-479 756-279	465-796 465-796
284-462 284-462	963-416 963-416	963-741 963-741	548-514 548-154
689-861 689-861	324-464 324-446	201-064 201-064	636-464 636-464
167-462 167-642	269-561 269-561	097-971 097-971	438-462 438-462

497-456 497-456	547-962 574-962	369-461 369-461	764-462 746-462
369-410 369-410	632-102 632-102	316-421 316-421	269-798 269-798
468-790 486-790	367-461 367-461	048-751 048-751	467-461 467-461
308-710 308-710	795-405 795-405	187-461 187-641	168-840 168-840

795-450 795-450	465-795 465-795	019-735 109-735	069-479 069-479
369-796 369-796	397-725 397-725	369-705 369-705	479-791 479-971
167-461 167-461	497-796 947-796	068-462 068-462	567-795 567-795
169-789 169-987	398-894 398-894	568-784 568-784	029-741 029-741

029-791 029-791	458-769 458-769	460-462 406-462	634-497 634-497
497-952 497-952	899-675 899-657	569-894 569-894	894-795 894-795
367-861 367-891	597-746 597-746	794-562 794-562	569-713 569-731
456-795 456-795	369-795 369-795	297-541 297-541	638-745 638-745

Look at the four pairs of numerical digits. Circle or highlight the combination pair that **does not** match.

Sheet 2

79-8645 79-8645	69-7895 69-7895	47-8945 47-8945	97-9856 97-9856
63-7459 63-7459	21-4587 21-4578	72-4259 72-4529	48-7958 48-7958
15-8652 15-8562	63-8956 63-8956	36-7198 36-7198	39-7849 93-7849
21-4510 21-4510	58-7963 58-7963	91-7932 91-7932	92-2648 92-2648

47-8564 47-8564	78-7926 78-7962	49-7621 49-7621	78-8954 87-8954
36-7155 36-7155	36-8541 36-8541	96-7951 96-7951	96-9715 96-9715
59-7951 59-7915	15-9578 15-9578	16-4692 19-4692	23-5647 23-5647
02-5631 02-5631	10-2057 10-2057	25-4761 25-4761	10-2504 10-2504

78-8953 78-8953	45-8965 54-8965	15-9657 15-9657	35-9874 35-9874
23-6478 23-6478	57-4561 57-4561	96-9745 99-9745	36-4761 36-4716
02-3620 02-6320	36-5475 36-5475	28-7894 28-7894	18-6946 18-6946
04-9018 04-9018	15-7951 15-7951	25-8974 25-8974	27-5861 27-5861

58-7769 58-7769	79-7952 79-7952	96-8423 96-8423	48-8654 84-8654
36-7615 36-7615	02-8944 20-8944	42-7615 42-7615	25-9645 25-9645
26-7651 26-7650	10-7106 10-7106	05-9846 05-9846	27-1456 27-1456
56-7954 56-7954	07-5610 07-5610	93-8442 93-8842	12-6479 12-6479

74-8964 74-8964	78-8545 88-8545	74-5245 74-5245	47-9954 47-9954
25-9648 25-9648	36-6104 36-6104	69-4610 69-4601	68-4105 68-4105
10-7145 10-7415	36-7105 36-7105	35-8941 35-8941	46-4617 46-4617
03-8964 03-8964	39-8412 39-8412	25-6514 25-6514	57-9451 75-9451

97-7944 97-7944	49-7921 49-7921	79-6465 79-6465	02-4754 02-4754
26-4764 62-4764	15-7469 15-7469	15-6954 15-6594	36-7914 36-7914
12-4560 12-4560	09-7761 90-7761	23-3654 23-3654	42-7924 42-7924
08-4604 08-4604	45-9654 45-9654	26-4561 26-4561	97-4612 79-4612

75-8696 75-8696	74-9624 74-9624	09-7446 90-7446	40-9642 04-9642
36-4614 36-4614	36-8642 36-8642	71-4604 71-4604	48-7620 48-7620
97-6447 97-6647	15-7614 51-7614	25-5954 25-5954	46-9781 46-9781
92-0579 92-0579	09-4761 09-4761	52-8942 52-8942	09-8645 09-8645

Look at the four pairs of numerical digits. Circle or highlight the combination pair that **does not** match.

Sheet 3

79-746 79-746	19-762 19-762	79-761 79-761	79-936 79-936
16-795 16-795	79-864 79-846	29-476 29-476	36-460 36-460
39-746 93-746	44-564 44-564	16-441 16-411	08-719 08-719
24-461 24-461	26-764 26-764	15-704 15-704	09-764 09-746

08-923 80-923	19-078 19-087	09-746 07-746	15-984 15-984
05-464 05-464	13-085 13-085	04-975 04-975	25-674 25-674
85-510 85-510	63-941 63-941	64-547 64-547	96-971 96-970
96-714 96-714	10-164 10-164	95-841 95-841	25-546 25-546

98-725 98-725	75-936 75-936	09-761 09-661	96-745 96-745
69-059 69-059	36-154 36-154	75-915 75-915	15-964 15-964
23-647 23-647	36-542 36-544	39-954 39-954	25-875 25-875
09-446 90-446	74-951 74-951	05-361 05-361	95-190 95-109

48-965 48-965	08-974 08-974	09-735 90-735	74-952 74-952
68-951 68-915	96-872 96-872	62-715 62-715	70-308 70-308
14-766 14-766	36-056 36-506	60-100 60-100	79-059 79-059
04-936 04-936	04-647 04-647	06-691 06-691	76-535 67-535

74-561 74-561	09-791 09-791	47-947 47-947	79-485 76-485
69-789 69-789	96-495 96-495	54-421 54-421	29-864 29-864
02-918 02-918	56-795 56-795	05-647 05-647	59-764 59-764
57-460 57-640	24-971 24-917	63-058 63-958	15-465 15-465

47-465 47-456	58-746 58-746	47-564 47-564	74-856 74-856
09-765 09-765	69-851 69-851	69-846 69-846	96-423 66-423
08-345 08-345	05-945 05-945	39-764 93-764	09-974 09-974
94-761 94-761	45-746 55-746	06-647 06-647	49-764 49-764

78-864 78-864	48-964 48-964	49-764 49-764	47-964 41-964
86-641 86-641	69-761 69-761	69-886 69-886	69-864 69-864
59-461 59-461	26-456 26-456	69-696 69-669	05-476 05-476
37-649 73-649	58-942 85-942	96-745 96-745	59-994 59-994

Look at the four pairs of numerical digits. Circle or highlight the combination pair that **does not** match.

Sheet 4

36-476 36-476	45-791 45-791	49-765 49-765	96-461 96-461
26-464 26-464	36-642 36-642	02-765 02-765	09-674 09-674
14-791 14-791	50-761 50-761	29-567 92-567	09-641 06-641
36-464 63-464	68-897 88-897	08-756 08-756	58-641 58-641

79-644 79-644	95-791 95-791	58-964 58-964	97-876 97-876
69-764 96-764	29-764 29-764	75-643 75-643	75-621 57-621
09-476 09-476	15-894 15-894	29-735 29-735	36-458 36-458
48-674 48-674	29-764 29-746	39-671 39-677	12-457 12-457

25-369 25-369	85-746 85-746	47-856 47-856	75-965 57-965
59-754 59-754	69-854 69-854	98-745 89-745	15-467 15-467
20-954 20-954	25-645 25-645	25-157 25-157	69-410 69-410
23-974 32-974	67-108 67-180	06-910 06-910	05-756 05-756

96-751 96-751	96-741 96-741	96-745 69-745	58-658 56-658
25-964 25-964	25-357 25-357	25-965 25-965	74-635 74-635
36-542 63-542	12-362 12-362	42-354 42-354	25-671 25-671
12-015 12-015	05-753 50-753	23-410 23-410	05-843 05-843

85-742 85-724	65-428 65-428	58-558 58-558	15-360 15-360
06-581 06-581	36-985 63-985	66-616 66-661	12-745 12-745
03-050 03-050	25-194 25-194	96-689 96-689	63-452 63-852
04-587 04-587	48-508 48-508	69-668 69-668	74-064 74-064

69-854 69-854	59-684 59-684	48-692 48-692	78-100 78-100
36-452 36-542	26-405 26-405	36-521 36-521	02-254 02-254
10-936 10-936	63-804 36-804	05-486 05-846	36-460 36-460
09-753 09-753	75-904 75-904	06-752 06-752	89-461 98-461

85-965 85-965	78-645 78-465	75-995 57-995	58-964 58-964
39-461 39-461	09-754 09-754	98-845 98-845	48-571 48-571
06-461 09-461	69-751 69-751	26-475 26-475	36-520 36-520
79-478 79-478	25-706 25-706	36-257 36-257	24-227 24-272

Look at the four pairs of numerical digits. Circle or highlight the combination pair that **does not** match.

Sheet 5

1-7954 1-7954	7-8974 7-8974	4-7923 4-7923	5-7986 5-7989
5-7984 5-7984	3-6442 3-6444	0-4647 0-4647	3-5647 3-5647
6-7897 6-7987	5-5476 5-5476	0-9665 0-9695	2-9796 2-9796
6-7641 6-7641	3-4561 3-4561	6-4567 6-4567	2-9861 2-9861
4-7956 4-7956	0-8976 0-8967	5-6345 5-6345	9-7941 9-7941
3-6797 3-7697	6-9759 6-9759	3-5647 3-5647	8-7972 8-7973
3-6741 3-6741	7-6494 7-6494	9-9971 9-9671	2-5647 2-5647
0-8944 0-8944	5-9796 5-9796	2-6919 2-6919	2-6972 2-6972
5-9479 5-9479	7-9792 7-9792	4-7953 4-7953	4-9479 4-9479
6-7972 6-7972	3-9472 3-9472	3-4978 1-4978	3-5697 3-5697
5-9785 6-9785	6-7941 6-7941	6-9721 6-9721	2-9448 2-9948
8-9715 8-9715	2-5647 2-6547	0-8947 0-8947	6-5642 6-5642
7-4576 7-4576	8-7946 9-7946	4-9476 4-9276	5-5647 5-5647
5-9725 5-9725	3-4567 3-4567	3-9417 3-9417	2-9497 2-9497
2-6472 2-6742	5-6941 5-6941	2-9647 2-9647	2-4672 2-4972
1-9715 1-9715	2-9657 2-9657	0-5694 0-5694	0-5678 0-5678
7-5694 7-5694	7-4794 7-4794	4-7945 4-7945	9-6647 9-6647
5-5972 5-5972	2-7943 2-7493	2-4678 2-4678	7-7915 7-7951
3-6471 3-6471	3-4647 3-4647	0-2698 0-2698	6-9752 6-9752
0-2647 0-2947	6-5892 6-5892	6-4972 9-4972	5-6512 5-6512
8-8947 8-8947	0-5976 0-5976	9-7895 9-7895	9-7953 9-7953
3-4564 3-4564	3-4975 3-4975	3-6497 3-6497	3-6497 3-4697
2-5647 2-5467	2-8775 2-8715	3-1028 3-0128	6-7915 6-7915
6-6791 6-6791	3-6549 3-6549	4-0974 4-0974	2-5894 2-5894
7-4792 7-4792	4-1264 4-1264	7-7946 7-7946	7-7715 7-7175
6-7895 6-7895	6-5497 6-5497	9-5974 9-5974	6-6448 6-6448
2-8954 2-8954	3-6914 3-6941	5-5597 5-5597	6-9641 6-9641
6-5614 6-6514	0-5947 0-5947	6-6698 6-6968	2-6971 2-6971

Look at the four pairs of numerical digits. Circle or highlight the combination pair that **does not** match.

Sheet 6

594-564 594-564	587-652 587-652	758-674 758-674	759-697 579-697
798-461 798-461	369-415 369-415	364-715 364-715	126-064 126-064
134-764 134-674	254-731 254-731	675-642 755-642	047-560 047-560
369-741 369-741	059-350 509-350	375-651 375-651	370-460 370-460

589-751 589-751	859-854 859-584	475-698 475-698	065-149 065-149
239-764 239-746	698-654 698-654	365-541 635-541	302-087 302-087
298-543 298-543	268-354 268-354	297-354 297-354	350-597 350-597
279-764 279-764	368-379 368-379	297-461 297-461	389-587 839-587

796-358 799-358	497-765 497-765
369-475 369-475	394-764 934-764
348-189 348-189	597-761 597-761
167-098 167-098	375-154 375-154

ANSWERS TO **QUESTION 4**

Sheet 1

938-917 938-917	452-417 452-417	058-174 058-174	497-961 497-961
178-815 178-815	148-163 148-163	287-427 287-247	104-952 140-952
193-131 193-113	964-642 964-642	248-186 248-186	745-438 745-438
410-137 410-137	427-246 472-246	193-164 193-164	258-735 258-735
749-556 749-556	160-035 160-035	794-795 974-795	416-494 416-494
336-464 336-464	064-635 064-635	135-579 135-579	795-920 795-920
564-759 546-759	790-164 790-164	146-905 146-905	113-792 113-792
795-295 795-295	136-498 136-489	354-561 354-561	194-795 149-795
497-795 497-795	264-561 264-561	716-405 716-405	794-792 794-792
792-715 729-715	176-792 176-792	298-594 298-594	678-792 678-792
120-097 120-097	126-045 126-045	146-460 146-460	284-684 234-684
791-496 791-496	015-461 051-461	166-790 166-970	283-278 283-278
791-425 791-425	578-364 578-364	756-479 756-279	465-796 465-796
284-462 284-462	963-416 963-416	963-741 963-741	548-514 548-154
689-861 689-861	324-464 324-446	201-064 201-064	636-464 636-464
167-462 167-642	269-561 269-561	097-971 097-971	438-462 438-462
497-456 497-456	547-962 574-962	369-461 369-461	764-462 746-462
369-410 369-410	632-102 632-102	316-421 316-421	269-798 269-798
468-790 486-790	367-461 367-461	048-751 048-751	467-461 467-461
308-710 308-710	795-405 795-405	187-461 187-641	168-840 168-840
795-450 795-450	465-795 465-795	019-735 109-735	069-479 069-479
369-796 369-796	397-725 397-725	369-705 369-705	479-791 479-971
167-461 167-461	497-796 947-796	068-462 068-462	567-795 567-795
169-789 169-987	398-894 398-894	568-784 568-784	029-741 029-741
029-791 029-791	458-769 458-769	460-462 406-462	634-497 634-497
497-952 497-952	899-675 899-657	569-894 569-894	894-795 894-795
367-861 367-891	597-746 597-746	794-562 794-562	569-713 569-731
456-795 456-795	369-795 369-795	297-541 297-541	638-745 638-745

Sheet 2

79-8645 79-8645	69-7895 69-7895	47-8945 47-8945	97-9856 97-9856
63-7459 63-7459	21-4587 21-4578	72-4259 72-4529	48-7958 48-7958
15-8652 15-8562	63-8956 63-8956	36-7198 36-7198	39-7849 93-7849
21-4510 21-4510	58-7963 58-7963	91-7932 91-7932	92-2648 92-2648

47-8564 47-8564	78-7926 78-7962	49-7621 49-7621	78-8954 87-8954
36-7155 36-7155	36-8541 36-8541	96-7951 96-7951	96-9715 96-9715
59-7951 59-7915	15-9578 15-9578	16-4692 19-4692	23-5647 23-5647
02-5631 02-5631	10-2057 10-2057	25-4761 25-4761	10-2504 10-2504

78-8953 78-8953	45-8965 54-8965	15-9657 15-9657	35-9874 35-9874
23-6478 23-6478	57-4561 57-4561	96-9745 99-9745	36-4761 36-4716
02-3620 02-6320	36-5475 36-5475	28-7894 28-7894	18-6946 18-6946
04-9018 04-9018	15-7951 15-7951	25-8974 25-8974	27-5861 27-5861

58-7769 58-7769	79-7952 79-7952	96-8423 96-8423	48-8654 84-8654
36-7615 36-7615	02-8944 20-8944	42-7615 42-7615	25-9645 25-9645
26-7651 26-7650	10-7106 10-7106	05-9846 05-9846	27-1456 27-1456
56-7954 56-7954	07-5610 07-5610	93-8442 93-8842	12-6479 12-6479

74-8964 74-8964	78-8545 88-8545	74-5245 74-5245	47-9954 47-9954
25-9648 25-9648	36-6104 36-6104	69-4610 69-4601	68-4105 68-4105
10-7145 10-7415	36-7105 36-7105	35-8941 35-8941	46-4617 46-4617
03-8964 03-8964	39-8412 39-8412	25-6514 25-6514	57-9451 75-9451

97-7944 97-7944	49-7921 49-7921	79-6465 79-6465	02-4754 02-4754
26-4764 62-4764	15-7469 15-7469	15-6954 15-6594	36-7914 36-7914
12-4560 12-4560	09-7761 90-7761	23-3654 23-3654	42-7924 42-7924
08-4604 08-4604	45-9654 45-9654	26-4561 26-4561	97-4612 79-4612

75-8696 75-8696	74-9624 74-9624	09-7446 90-7446	40-9642 04-9642
36-4614 36-4614	36-8642 36-8642	71-4604 71-4604	48-7620 48-7620
97-6447 97-6647	15-7614 51-7614	25-5954 25-5954	46-9781 46-9781
92-0579 92-0579	09-4761 09-4761	52-8942 52-8942	09-8645 09-8645

Sheet 3

79-746 79-746	19-762 19-762	79-761 79-761	79-936 79-936
16-795 16-795	79-864 79-846	29-476 29-476	36-460 36-460
39-746 93-746	44-564 44-564	16-441 16-411	08-719 08-719
24-461 24-461	26-764 26-764	15-704 15-704	09-764 09-746
08-923 80-923	19-078 19-087	09-746 07-746	15-984 15-984
05-464 05-464	13-085 13-085	04-975 04-975	25-674 25-674
85-510 85-510	63-941 63-941	64-547 64-547	96-971 96-970
96-714 96-714	10-164 10-164	95-841 95-841	25-546 25-546
98-725 98-725	75-936 75-936	09-761 09-661	96-745 96-745
69-059 69-059	36-154 36-154	75-915 75-915	15-964 15-964
23-647 23-647	36-542 36-544	39-954 39-954	25-875 25-875
09-446 90-446	74-951 74-951	05-361 05-361	95-190 95-109
48-965 48-965	08-974 08-974	09-735 90-735	74-952 74-952
68-951 68-915	96-872 96-872	62-715 62-715	70-308 70-308
14-766 14-766	36-056 36-506	60-100 60-100	79-059 79-059
04-936 04-936	04-647 04-647	06-691 06-691	76-535 67-535
74-561 74-561	09-791 09-791	47-947 47-947	79-485 76-485
69-789 69-789	96-495 96-495	54-421 54-421	29-864 29-864
02-918 02-918	56-795 56-795	05-647 05-647	59-764 59-764
57-460 57-640	24-971 24-917	63-058 63-958	15-465 15-465
47-465 47-456	58-746 58-746	47-564 47-564	74-856 74-856
09-765 09-765	69-851 69-851	69-846 69-846	96-423 66-423
08-345 08-345	05-945 05-945	39-764 93-764	09-974 09-974
94-761 94-761	45-746 55-746	06-647 06-647	49-764 49-764
78-864 78-864	48-964 48-964	49-764 49-764	47-964 41-964
86-641 86-641	69-761 69-761	69-886 69-886	69-864 69-864
59-461 59-461	26-456 26-456	69-696 69-669	05-476 05-476
37-649 73-649	58-942 85-942	96-745 96-745	59-994 59-994

Sheet 4

36-476 36-476	45-791 45-791	49-765 49-765	96-461 96-461
26-464 26-464	36-642 36-642	02-765 02-765	09-674 09-674
14-791 14-791	50-761 50-761	29-567 92-567	09-641 06-641
36-464 63-464	68-897 88-897	08-756 08-756	58-641 58-641
79-644 79-644	95-791 95-791	58-964 58-964	97-876 97-876
69-764 96-764	29-764 29-764	75-643 75-643	75-621 57-621
09-476 09-476	15-894 15-894	29-735 29-735	36-458 36-458
48-674 48-674	29-764 29-746	39-671 39-677	12-457 12-457
25-369 25-369	85-746 85-746	47-856 47-856	75-965 57-965
59-754 59-754	69-854 69-854	98-745 89-745	15-467 15-467
20-954 20-954	25-645 25-645	25-157 25-157	69-410 69-410
23-974 32-974	67-108 67-180	06-910 06-910	05-756 05-756
96-751 96-751	96-741 96-741	96-745 69-745	58-658 56-658
25-964 25-964	25-357 25-357	25-965 25-965	74-635 74-635
36-542 63-542	12-362 12-362	42-354 42-354	25-671 25-671
12-015 12-015	05-753 50-753	23-410 23-410	05-843 05-843
85-742 85-724	65-428 65-428	58-558 58-558	15-360 15-360
06-581 06-581	36-985 63-985	66-616 66-661	12-745 12-745
03-050 03-050	25-194 25-194	96-689 96-689	63-452 63-852
04-587 04-587	48-508 48-508	69-668 69-668	74-064 74-064
69-854 69-854	59-684 59-684	48-692 48-692	78-100 78-100
36-452 36-542	26-405 26-405	36-521 36-521	02-254 02-254
10-936 10-936	63-804 36-804	05-486 05-846	36-460 36-460
09-753 09-753	75-904 75-904	06-752 06-752	89-461 98-461
85-965 85-965	78-645 78-465	75-995 57-995	58-964 58-964
39-461 39-461	09-754 09-754	98-845 98-845	48-571 48-571
06-461 09-461	69-751 69-751	26-475 26-475	36-520 36-520
79-478 79-478	25-706 25-706	36-257 36-257	24-227 24-272

Sheet 5

1-7954 1-7954	7-8974 7-8974	4-7923 4-7923	5-7986 5-7989
5-7984 5-7984	3-6442 3-6444	0-4647 0-4647	3-5647 3-5647
6-7897 6-7987	5-5476 5-5476	0-9665 0-9695	2-9796 2-9796
6-7641 6-7641	3-4561 3-4561	6-4567 6-4567	2-9861 2-9861
4-7956 4-7956	0-8976 0-8967	5-6345 5-6345	9-7941 9-7941
3-6797 3-7697	6-9759 6-9759	3-5647 3-5647	8-7972 8-7973
3-6741 3-6741	7-6494 7-6494	9-9971 9-9671	2-5647 2-5647
0-8944 0-8944	5-9796 5-9796	2-6919 2-6919	2-6972 2-6972
5-9479 5-9479	7-9792 7-9792	4-7953 4-7953	4-9479 4-9479
6-7972 6-7972	3-9472 3-9472	3-4978 1-4978	3-5697 3-5697
5-9785 6-9785	6-7941 6-7941	6-9721 6-9721	2-9448 2-9948
8-9715 8-9715	2-5647 2-6547	0-8947 0-8947	6-5642 6-5642
7-4576 7-4576	8-7946 9-7946	4-9476 4-9276	5-5647 5-5647
5-9725 5-9725	3-4567 3-4567	3-9417 3-9417	2-9497 2-9497
2-6472 2-6742	5-6941 5-6941	2-9647 2-9647	2-4672 2-4972
1-9715 1-9715	2-9657 2-9657	0-5694 0-5694	0-5678 0-5678
7-5694 7-5694	7-4794 7-4794	4-7945 4-7945	9-6647 9-6647
5-5972 5-5972	2-7943 2-7493	2-4678 2-4678	7-7915 7-7951
3-6471 3-6471	3-4647 3-4647	0-2698 0-2698	6-9752 6-9752
0-2647 0-2947	6-5892 6-5892	6-4972 9-4972	5-6512 5-6512
8-8947 8-8947	0-5976 0-5976	9-7895 9-7895	9-7953 9-7953
3-4564 3-4564	3-4975 3-4975	3-6497 3-6497	3-6497 3-4697
2-5647 2-5467	2-8775 2-8715	3-1028 3-0128	6-7915 6-7915
6-6791 6-6791	3-6549 3-6549	4-0974 4-0974	2-5894 2-5894
7-4792 7-4792	4-1264 4-1264	7-7946 7-7946	7-7715 7-7175
6-7895 6-7895	6-5497 6-5497	9-5974 9-5974	6-6448 6-6448
2-8954 2-8954	3-6914 3-6941	5-5597 5-5597	6-9641 6-9641
6-5614 6-6514	0-5947 0-5947	6-6698 6-6968	2-6971 2-6971

Sheet 6

594-564	594-564	587-652	587-652	758-674	758-674	759-697	579-697
798-461	798-461	369-415	369-415	364-715	364-715	126-064	126-064
134-764	134-674	254-731	254-731	675-642	755-642	047-560	047-560
369-741	369-741	059-350	509-350	375-651	375-651	370-460	370-460
589-751	589-751	859-854	859-584	475-698	475-698	065-149	065-149
239-764	239-746	698-654	698-654	365-541	635-541	302-087	302-087
298-543	298-543	268-354	268-354	297-354	297-354	350-597	350-597
279-764	279-764	368-379	368-379	297-461	297-461	389-587	839-587
796-358	799-358	497-765	497-765				
369-475	369-475	394-764	934-764				
348-189	348-189	597-761	597-761				
167-098	167-098	375-154	375-154				

CONCENTRATION TESTS – WORK RATE TESTS

Question 1

Which of the answers below, is an alternative to the code **459**?

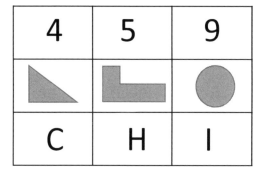

4	5	9
◤	⌐	●
C	H	I

A. C 5 ⌐   **B.** 4 5 H   **C.** ●C I   **D.** C 5 ●

Answer

Question 2

Which of the answers below, is an alternative to the code **3B7**?

A	B	C
3	9	✦
▬	▢	7

A. A 7 9   **B.** ▬ B ✦   **C.** 3 B ▢   **D.** ✦ 9 A

Answer

Question 3

Which of the answers below, is an alternative to the code **JXE**?

X	1	⬤
9	⌐	J
✦	E	5

A. ⬤ 9 1   **B.** 5EX   **C.** ⬤⌐1   **D.** 9 1⬤

Answer [   ]

Question 4

Which of the answers below, is an alternative to the code **56B**?

U	5	✚
✖	⬤	B
6	7	V

A. 7 U V   **B.** U 7 B   **C.** ⬤V✖   **D.** ✖⬤✚

Answer [   ]

Question 5

Which of the answers below, is an alternative to the code **E** 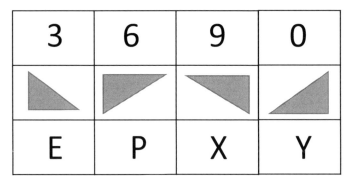 **X 0?**

3	6	9	0
E	P	X	Y

A. 9 0 P ◣   **B.** ◢ 3 Y 9   **C.** ◣ 6 9 ◢   **D.** ◣ 6 X ◣

Answer

Question 6

Which of the answers below, is an alternative to the code **F7W** ⬅ ?

8	T	F	➡
K	⬇	5	⬆
⬅	7	9	W

A. 9 ⬇ WK   **B.** T5KW   **C.** 57 ⬅ W   **D.** 9587

Answer

Question 7

Which of the answers below, is an alternative to the code **R04** 🖤 ?

F	Y	I	🖤
R	⭕	0	9
1	4	◖	6

A. 4691   **B.** 1◖⭕9 **C.** I🖤◖ 9   **D.** F⭕ I🖤

Answer

Question 8

Which of the answers below, is an alternative to the code **O219**?

8	1	5	6
R	N	M	O
2	4	9	7

A. 86NM   **B.** R7NM   **C.** 7RNM   **D.** 7RMN

Answer

Question 9

Which of the answers below, is an alternative to the code **BR7**?

R	A	F	S
1	3	5	7
D	◀	B	➡

A. DF3   **B.** 5S1   **C.** F1◀   **D.** 5D➡

Answer

Question 10

Which of the answers below, is an alternative to the code ☀ **Q2**?

◆	◖	☀	★
Y	5	C	2
Q	M	W	K

A. ◆MK   **B.** CMQ   **C.** W◆K   **D.** Y5★

Answer

Question 11

Which of the answers below, is an alternative to the code **800**?

S	3	8	
0		5	7
D	O	B	1

A. 15B   **B.** BD3   **C.** D81   **D.** OB

Answer [　　　　　]

Question 12

Which of the answers below, is an alternative to the code **QZ9**?

■	➡	♥	☀
◀	★	◖	⬌
2	Z	Q	9

A. ◖➡⬌   **B.** ♥★■   **C.** ■◖★   **D.** ◖☀➡

Answer [　　　　　]

Question 13

Which of the answers below, is an alternative to the code **8MT**?

T	G		5
2		N	M
	9	0	F
7	8	X	

A. 9N2   **B.** F2   **C.** 9X   **D.** M9N

Answer

Question 14

Which of the answers below, is an alternative to the code **7AP**?

I	L		P
	7	1	6
A		G	

A. 16P   **B.** 7I1   **C.** LI6   **D.** GLA

Answer

Question 15

Which of the answers below, is an alternative to the code **3X5OL**?

Y	S	H	O	A	L
1	2	3	4	5	6
X	Q	B	N	K	J

A. JA4S1   **B.** BYA4J   **C.** H1Q4B   **D.** Q5O4S

Answer [   ]

Question 16

Which of the answers below, is an alternative to the code **3 ◖ Q ● ?**

N	S	◖	1	X	L
A	▤	◈	4	●	Q
3	▲	▰	⤴	K	B

A. N◢XL   **B.** AS4X   **C.** A▤ LB   **D.** N◈BK

Answer [   ]

Question 17

Which of the answers below, is an alternative to the code **A96**?

E	M	5	Q
A			6
	9	C	

A. EMQ   **B.** EMC   **C.** C95   **D.** 95C

Answer

Question 18

Which of the answers below, is an alternative to the code **B5E**?

E	◖		B
	9	5	
⬥		●	4

A. 4 ⬥ ●   **B.** 4 ● ⬥   **C.** ● ⬥ 4   **D.** ⬥ 4 ●

Answer

Question 19

Which of the answers below, is an alternative to the code **F2IR**?

R	A	G	1	2	3
B	✚	6	↕	U	ᐸ
⚡	F	◗	L	≠	I

A. A ≠ ᐸ   **B.** ✚ 3BU   **C.** AU2R   **D.** A ≠ ᐸ B

Answer [   ]

Question 20

Which of the answers below, is an alternative to the code **P04**?

⟩	H	O	5
F	⬆	T	N
8	P	0	✖
4	★	X	1

A. HX1   **B.** ⬆ O ⟩   **C.** ⟩ ⬆ O   **D.** 1 ⟩ O

Answer [   ]

ANSWERS TO CONCENTRATION TEST – WORK RATE TEST

Q1. D

Q2. B

Q3. A

Q4. A

Q5. C

Q6. A

Q7. B

Q8. C

Q9. D

Q10. C

Q11. B

Q12. A

Q13. B

Q14. C

Q15. B

Q16. D

Q17. A

Q18. B

Q19. D

Q20. B

CONCENTRATION TESTS – GENERAL CONCENTRATION TESTS

Question 1

Cross out the letter 'n' (lower case) in each row. Write down the total number that you cross out in each row, in the box provided at the end of the row. You have 60 seconds to complete the test.

1.	Q	r	B	g	y	U	h	J	B	j	B	k	L	B	n	
2.	B	B	B	v	B	n	B	U	B	d	f	O	p	T	R	
3.	C	x	X	F	B	G	B	p	A	R	f	V	B	y	U	
4.	B	R	R	t	G	N	H	B	r	r	F	P	B	R	r	
5.	Q	a	Z	x	R	t	I	o	M	B	B	D	x	A	S	
6.	B	s	a	A	e	E	R	C	Y	U	B	j	P	o	R	
7.	T	R	r	B	F	r	S	N	b	B	c	F	F	R	R	
8.	B	v	R	r	R	y	R	B	R	r	D	e	B	R	F	
9.	T	R	K	B	o	u	b	g	t	m	R	r	X	r	R	
10.	C	B	n	h	j	Y	I	p	R	R	R	r	R	C	d	
11.	R	R	r	Y	B	B	v	M	n	h	K	j	R	E	R	
12.	B	W	r	E	R	f	p	U	I	H	B	y	U	B	R	
13.	R	r	Q	q	B	G	R	t	Q	B	E	F	T	y	R	
14.	T	B	A	I	N	D	P	I	V	E	R	B	T	y	S	
15.	d	x	z	Z	R	n	K	i	i	R	r	R	O	p	o	
16.	Q	R	r	E	D	D	e	w	K	B	I	O	P	R	R	
17.	H	O	B	B	e	E	R	r	R	R	V	B	H	j	R	
18.	K	B	u	U	Y	B	Y	r	R	R	D	B	z	q	B	
19.	P	y	g	h	B	I	r	t	r	e	B	e	R	q	B	
20.	B	h	B	h	B	r	R	r	N	B	B	y	Y	B	B	

Question 2

Cross out the letter 'a' (lower case). Write down the total number that you cross out in each row, in the box provided at the end of the row. You have 60 seconds to complete the test.

1.	a	O	t	Q	a	q	O	o	a	A	a	U	o	o	O	
2.	O	a	g	Y	t	a	c	C	c	O	a	o	a	D	w	
3.	B	a	O	g	a	a	S	q	Q	a	Q	q	O	o	a	
4.	a	L	N	h	U	u	a	o	H	y	t	R	a	O	o	
5.	G	V	a	R	t	Y	o	o	P	i	O	O	o	O	R	
6.	G	t	y	a	J	P	p	O	o	D	d	O	a	S	Q	
7.	O	o	O	a	o	o	Y	a	Y	q	Q	q	a	c	c	
8.	I	u	V	c	c	F	r	d	w	H	y	h	u	o	o	
9.	a	o	o	U	o	O	a	y	D	e	q	A	a	O	o	
10.	R	r	a	o	u	y	G	b	t	r	a	o	o	o	P	
11.	O	a	c	o	d	a	D	O	c	a	O	o	o	a	R	
12.	B	v	c	f	R	a	y	f	D	r	d	r	a	A	a	
13.	F	t	t	a	d	r	e	o	o	p	u	o	Q	t	r	
14.	F	g	r	t	y	N	H	N	a	o	p	O	o	I	y	
15.	T	r	e	d	w	a	u	i	y	F	c	r	D	e	W	
16.	a	a	O	a	p	O	u	i	S	t	d	r	a	S	O	
17.	I	a	O	A	a	a	c	C	c	g	o	a	o	R	t	
18.	G	g	a	g	o	t	f	d	r	t	a	u	o	o	j	
19.	Q	c	v	a	g	t	y	u	O	o	O	o	G	y	c	
20.	K	I	a	i	u	a	t	r	e	o	a	y	o	j	h	

Question 3

Cross out the letters 'v' (lower case) and 'W' (upper case). Search for both of these letters at the same time. Write down the total combined number that you cross out in each row, in the box provided at the end of the row. You have 60 seconds to complete the test.

1.	v	W	w	V	e	w	h	j	U	i	X	x	W	w	v	
2.	V	u	U	w	G	t	y	u	W	w	V	v	W	o	o	
3.	W	W	V	V	v	v	w	w	y	u	i	p	v	W	W	
4.	V	g	h	j	K	O	p	t	Y	V	v	W	W	w	V	
5.	Y	U	u	u	v	v	W	M	m	w	e	V	v	N	n	
6.	q	q	Q	G	g	H	Y	u	i	R	T	y	V	w	v	
7.	V	y	u	Y	u	o	p	N	h	j	W	w	V	V	v	
8.	t	y	m	k	m	N	b	C	x	W	w	V	v	b	v	
9.	O	o	V	v	f	g	h	j	k	n	h	N	h	V	X	
10.	T	V	v	X	c	d	W	w	W	v	V	v	f	r	p	
11.	V	V	v	w	W	w	v	V	v	W	w	g	y	Y	v	
12.	R	t	y	u	i	B	g	v	f	r	D	r	Q	w	W	
13.	R	t	y	V	c	V	c	v	f	r	W	w	W	w	V	
14.	G	y	u	i	O	p	R	t	y	E	w	V	V	v	W	
15.	Y	Y	y	Y	X	v	W	W	w	w	r	t	y	u	v	
16.	W	w	w	v	t	u	i	n	h	v	V	w	W	w	f	
17.	r	t	y	y	u	i	V	b	n	h	g	w	w	W	w	
18.	i	o	q	w	S	S	X	W	V	Z	z	V	v	W	y	
19.	P	o	Y	u	i	V	v	X	w	W	w	R	t	R	y	
20.	y	u	V	x	s	t	Y	u	y	W	w	C	d	V	w	

Question 4

Cross out the number 3 and the letter 'g' (lower case). Search for both letter and number at the same time. Write down the total combined number that you cross out in each row, in the box provided at the end of the row. You have 60 seconds to complete the test.

1.	8	B	8	V	v	W	q	P	p	r	g	B	b	8	u	
2.	B	b	R	r	r	y	U	i	8	8	B	B	b	g	G	
3.	j	u	p	P	b	v	f	r	B	b	w	3	6	7	R	
4.	8	3	2	h	y	U	x	W	w	v	X	v	b	B	8	
5.	f	G	g	B	p	h	b	b	b	B	B	8	8	5	3	
6.	y	u	U	7	6	5	8	e	r	d	r	w	8	B	b	
7.	o	O	o	P	7	8	5	b	3	8	3	R	r	S	I	
8.	B	b	3	8	B	B	b	h	h	V	c	b	B	7	1	
9.	1	3	c	V	f	I	u	y	t	r	B	b	8	8	8	
10.	y	B	b	8	4	3	3	3	X	x	x	f	F	r	t	
11.	Q	q	H	b	B	b	8	B	6	3	3	2	u	B	b	
12.	G	G	g	B	b	8	3	8	3	D	d	D	I	P	p	
13.	G	b	b	8	8	6	5	4	0	L	o	P	p	P	B	
14.	3	B	b	8	3	B	B	b	3	E	e	3	8	4	P	
15.	t	Y	y	D	e	e	D	f	g	W	8	8	P	P	B	
16.	C	C	b	n	B	8	B	8	B	b	8	3	9	3	9	
17.	6	6	b	B	8	8	d	k	I	p	o	U	S	y	Y	
18.	P	p	8	F	d	D	c	C	8	B	b	8	f	F	f	
19.	8	8	C	f	z	s	W	w	R	r	T	8	3	B	b	
20.	H	y	y	b	B	8	8	8	H	H	h	D	r	e	W	

Question 5

Cross out the letter 'E' (upper case) and the number '8'. Search for both letter and number at the same time. Write down the total combined number that you cross out in each row, in the box provided at the end of the row. You have 60 seconds to complete the test.

1.	E	6	e	8	8	e	3	p	b	d	e	E	3	8	T	
2.	e	8	3	6	7	y	u	I	V	f	E	e	b	B	E	
3.	W	w	q	D	d	c	x	z	O	p	e	R	6	8	3	
4.	y	u	I	o	p	P	t	T	Y	e	E	3	8	6	F	
5.	g	B	4	3	2	7	8	3	e	E	3	4	E	e	3	
6.	e	3	3	e	E	d	W	q	h	j	K	8	7	N	9	
7.	3	e	E	8	B	8	3	e	E	k	K	3	e	8	7	
8.	f	C	x	b	g	t	T	r	6	8	3	4	X	d	e	
9.	3	3	3	b	8	b	e	3	E	3	8	3	4	0	1	
10.	e	E	j	H	g	b	3	E	e	3	w	b	V	v	E	
11.	8	3	B	v	C	f	v	e	8	4	3	3	3	e	v	
12.	6	7	8	v	c	D	f	3	7	8	6	E	e	e	V	
13.	e	3	e	3	E	8	E	3	e	E	3	2	8	G	g	
14.	7	y	h	n	g	f	d	e	E	4	E	e	3	D	d	
15.	k	I	L	j	h	y	V	v	8	4	2	b	V	v	E	
16.	g	Y	y	i	9	8	7	0	3	O	o	v	V	v	e	
17.	8	2	B	b	v	e	W	e	r	5	5	R	r	e	V	
18.	3	e	E	e	3	4	b	V	v	e	W	w	q	A	a	
19.	5	e	3	V	f	r	6	5	4	e	e	E	e	3	E	
20.	e	E	e	R	3	4	2	1	3	E	e	h	G	f	d	

Question 6

Place a diagonal line across each box that contains 4 dots only. You have 30 seconds to complete the test.

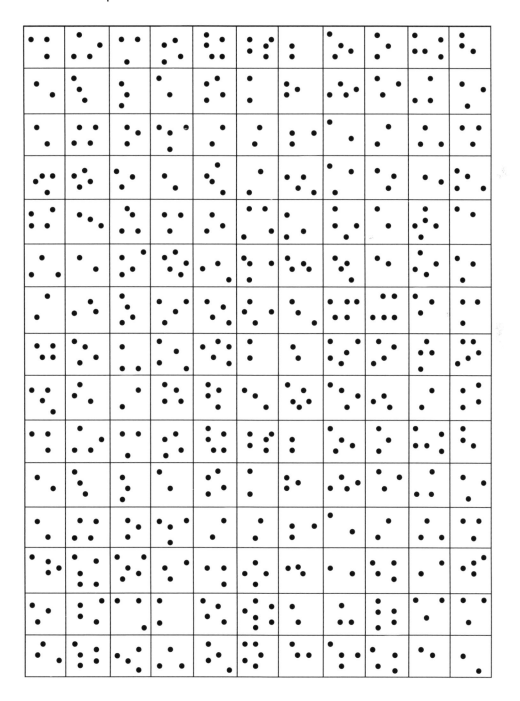

Question 7

Place a diagonal line across each box that contains 4 dots only. You have 30 seconds to complete the test.

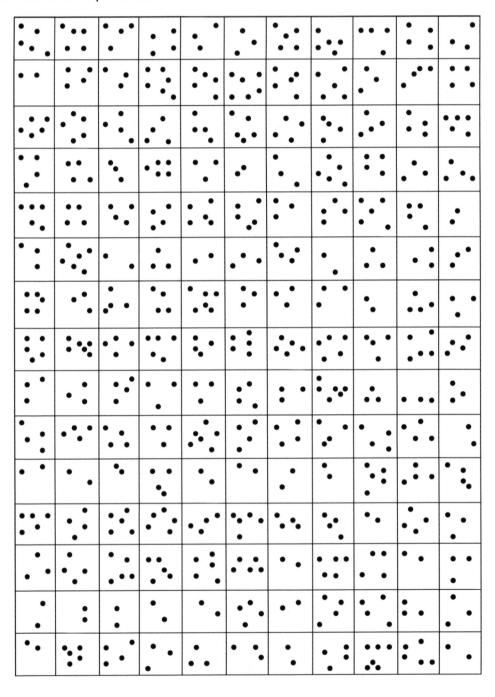

Question 8

Place a diagonal line across each box that contains 4 dots only. You have 30 seconds to complete the test.

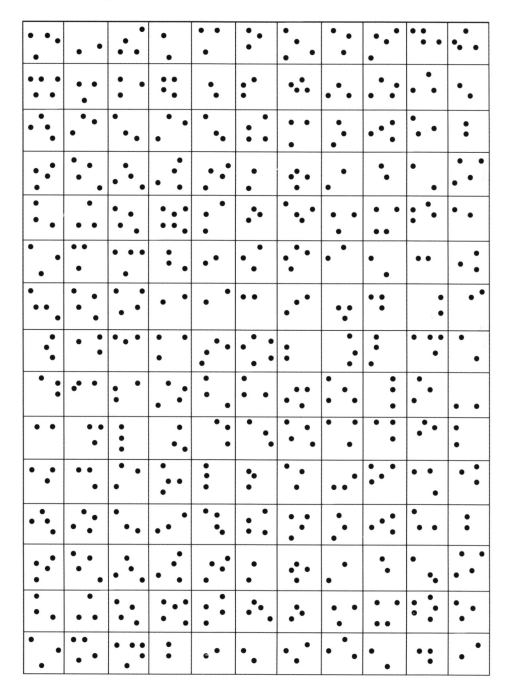

Question 9

Place a diagonal line across each box that contains 4 dots only. You have 30 seconds to complete the test.

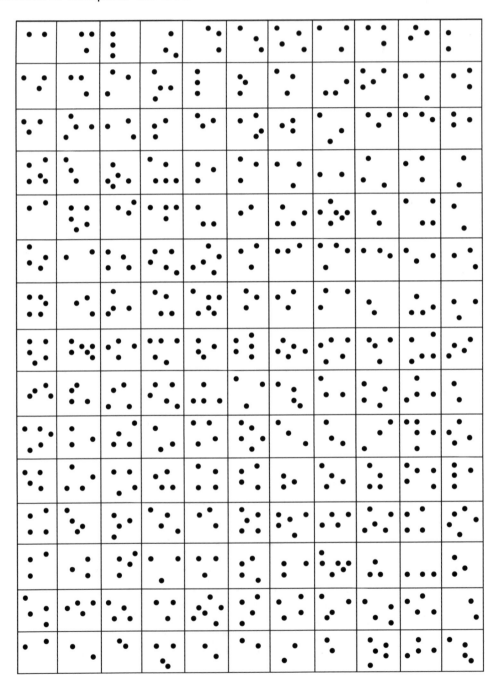

Question 10

Place a diagonal line across each box that contains 4 dots only. You have 30 seconds to complete the test.

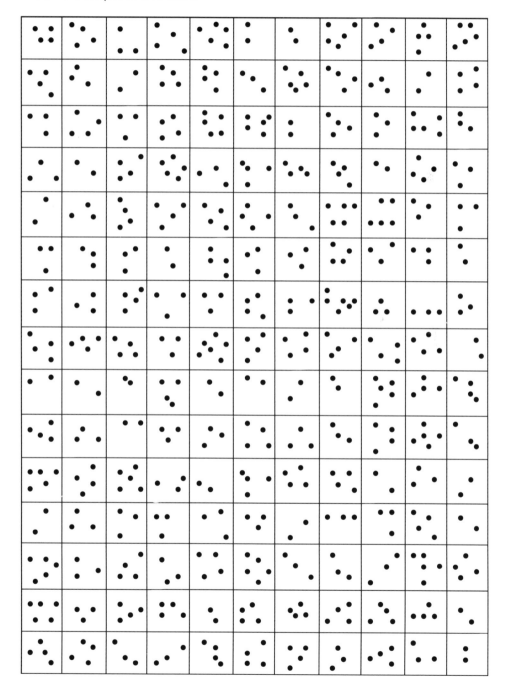

Study the below sequence for one minute. Once the minute is up, cover the sequence and answer the following questions.

G	I	P	B	M	E

Question 11

How many letters are in between the letter G and the letter E?

Answer [   ]

Question 12

How many letters were there in the sequence?

Answer [   ]

Question 13

What letter was between the letter I and the letter B?

Answer [   ]

Study the below sequence for one minute. Once the minute is up, cover the sequence and answer the following questions.

| S | L | S | A | E | S |

Question 14

How many letter S's were in the sequence?

Answer

Question 15

What was the third letter in the sequence?

Answer

Question 16

How many letters were there in between the letter L and the letter A?

Answer

Study the below sequence for one minute. Once the minute is up, cover the sequence and answer the following questions.

E	X	P	E	W	E	Z

Question 17

What was the first letter in the sequence?

Answer [   ]

Question 18

What was the fifth letter in the sequence?

Answer [   ]

Question 19

How many letters were there in the whole sequence?

Answer [   ]

Study the following grids for 5 seconds. Then turn the page and decide from the four options available which grid contains the collective group of coloured squares from the grids.

Question 20

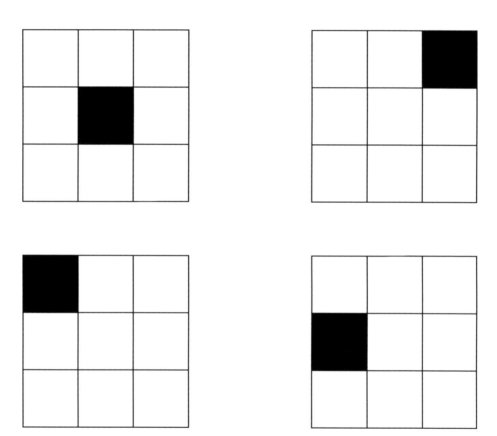

Question 20 Answer Options

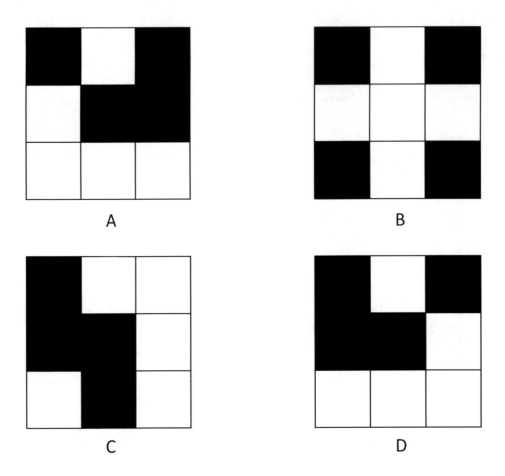

A

B

C

D

Answer

Study the following grids for 5 seconds. Then turn the page and decide from the four options available which grid contains the collective group of coloured squares from the grids.

Question 21

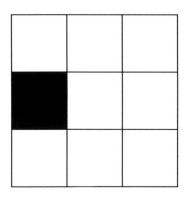

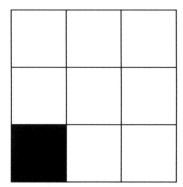

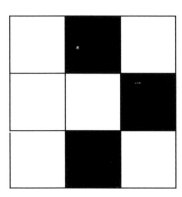

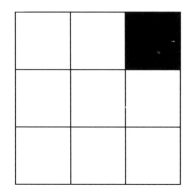

Question 21 Answer Options

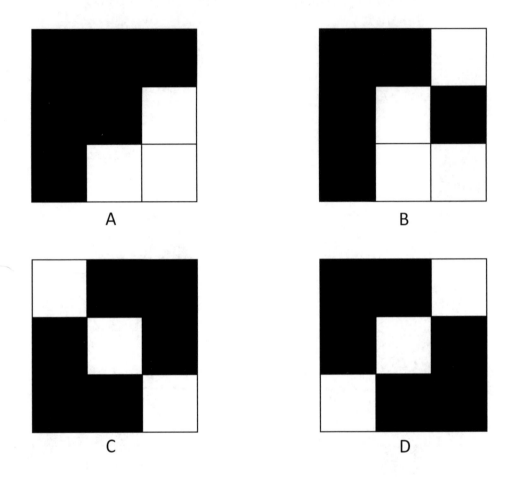

A

B

C

D

Answer

Study the following grids for 5 seconds. Then turn the page and decide from the four options available which grid contains the collective group of coloured squares from the grids.

Question 22

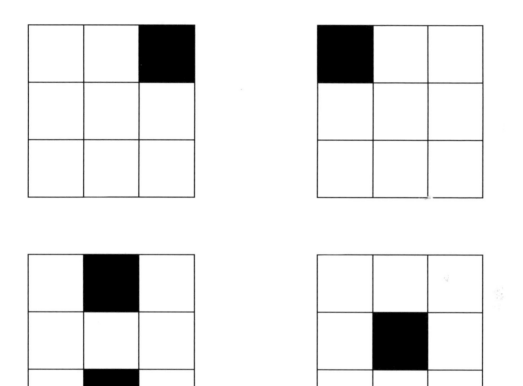

Question 22 Answer Options

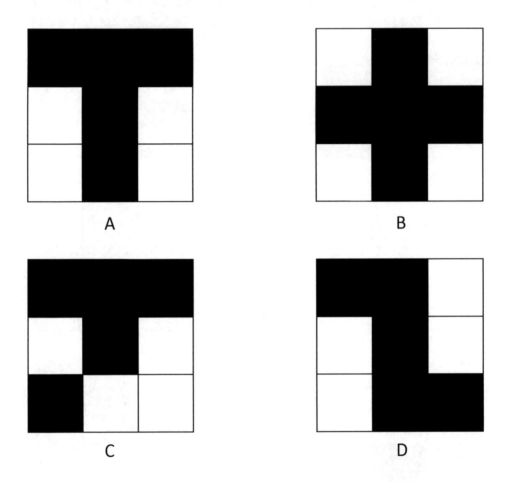

A

B

C

D

Answer

Study the following grids for 5 seconds. Then turn the page and decide from the four options available which grid contains the collective group of coloured squares from the grids.

Question 23

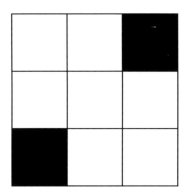

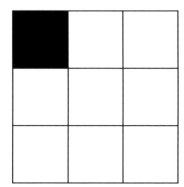

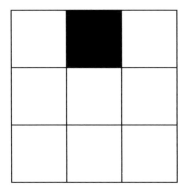

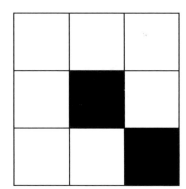

Question 23 Answer Options

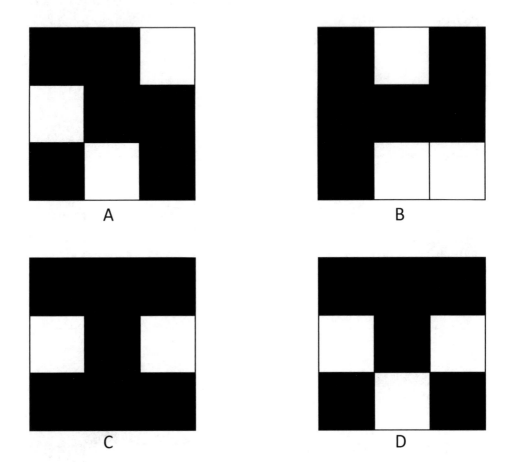

A

B

C

D

Answer

Study the following grids for 5 seconds. Then turn the page and decide from the four options available which grid contains the collective group of coloured squares from the grids.

Question 24

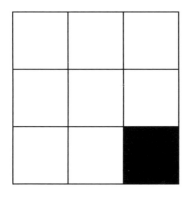

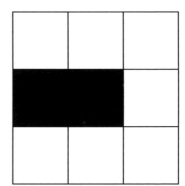

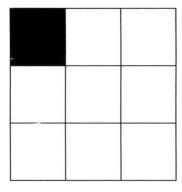

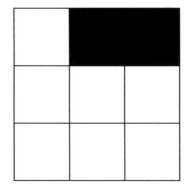

Question 24 Answer Options

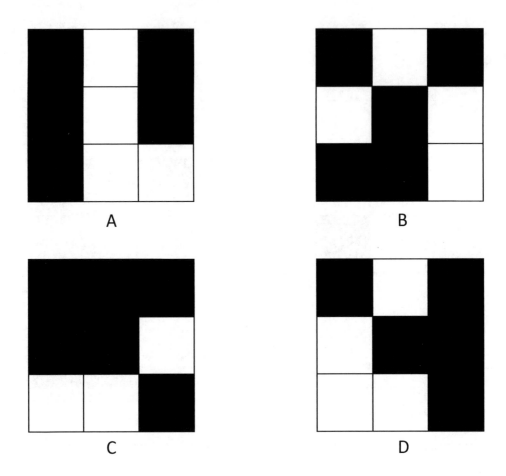

A

B

C

D

Answer

Study the following grids for 5 seconds. Then turn the page and decide from the four options available which grid contains the collective group of coloured squares from the grids.

Question 25

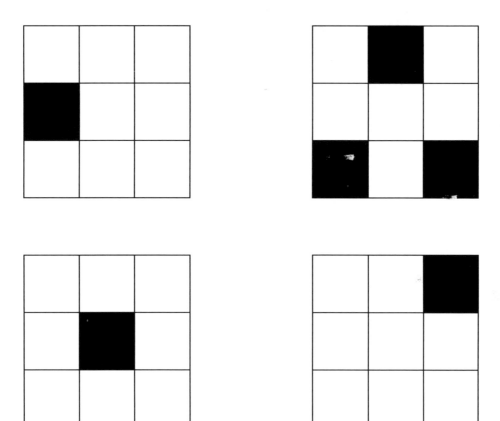

Question 25 Answer Options

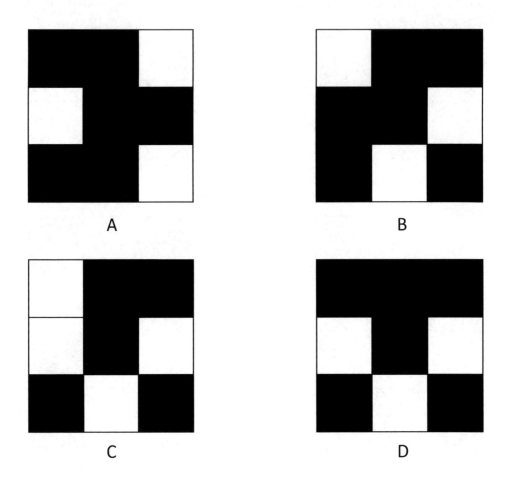

A

B

C

D

Answer

ANSWERS TO CONCENTRATION TESTS – GENERAL CONCENTRATION TESTS

Q1.

1.	1	6.	0	11.	1	16.	0
2.	1	7.	0	12.	0	17.	0
3.	0	8.	0	13.	0	18.	0
4.	0	9.	0	14.	0	19.	0
5.	0	10.	1	15.	1	20.	0

Q2.

1.	4	6.	2	11.	4	16.	4
2.	4	7.	3	12.	3	17.	4
3.	5	8.	0	13.	1	18.	2
4.	3	9.	3	14.	1	19.	1
5.	1	10.	2	15.	1	20.	3

Q3.

1.	4	6.	1	11.	6	16.	4
2.	3	7.	2	12.	2	17.	1
3.	7	8.	3	13.	3	18.	3
4.	3	9.	1	14.	2	19.	2
5.	4	10.	5	15.	4	20.	1

Q4.

1.	1	6.	0	11.	2	16.	2
2.	1	7.	2	12.	3	17.	0
3.	1	8.	1	13.	0	18.	0
4.	1	9.	1	14.	4	19.	1
5.	2	10.	3	15.	1	20.	0

Q5.

1.	5	6.	2	11.	2	16.	1
2.	3	7.	5	12.	3	17.	1
3.	1	8.	1	13.	5	18.	1
4.	2	9.	3	14.	2	19.	2
5.	3	10.	3	15.	2	20.	2

Q6. 52 boxes contain 4 dots.

Q7. 56 boxes contain 4 dots.

Q8. 54 boxes contain 4 dots.

Q9. 56 boxes contain 4 dots.

Q10. 61 boxes contain 4 dots.

Q11. 4

Q12. 6

Q13. P

Q14. 3

Q15. S

Q16. 1

Q17. E

Q18. W

Q19. 7

Q20. D

Q21. C

Q22. A

Q23. D

Q24. C

Q25. B

MECHANICAL COMPREHENSION
TESTS

WHAT ARE MECHANICAL COMPREHENSION TESTS?

Mechanical Comprehension tests have been used for many years as a method of assessing a candidate's ability to perform a specific role. Predominately, they are used in careers which require an ability to work with, or understand, mechanical and technical concepts.

WHAT TO EXPECT?

Mechanical Comprehension tests often comprise of fault diagnosis questions which are used to select personnel for technical roles where they need to be able to find and repair faults in operating systems.

Many Mechanical Comprehension tests require you to concentrate on 'principles' rather than on making calculations, and as such will often include diagrams and pictures as part of the question. For example, you may be shown a diagram of a series of cogs and be asked to work out which way a specific cog is turning if another one rotates either clockwise or anti-clockwise.

WHO TAKES A MECHANICAL COMPREHENSION TEST?

Examples of the type of careers which require this level of aptitude testing include:

- Train Drivers
- Driving careers
- Armed Forces jobs
- Engineering careers
- Emergency services
- Motor Mechanic
- Aircraft Engineer

WHAT IS INCLUDED IN A MECHANICAL COMPREHENSION TEST?

The Mechanical Comprehension test is used to assess mechanical and technical understandings. These types of questions often relate to:

- Gears and Pulleys
- Springs
- Weights
- Levers
- Rotating Objects

The tests are usually multiple-choice in nature and take the format of simple, frequently encountered mechanisms and technical situations. The majority of Mechanical Comprehension tests require a working knowledge of basic mechanical operations and the application of physical laws.

HOW TO PREPARE FOR A MECHANICAL COMPREHENSION TEST?

The only way to prepare for a Mechanical Comprehension test, or any other form of psychometric test, is to practice prior to your assessment. The more you practice, the more competent you will become at successfully completing the questions.

Within this chapter, we have provided you with an array of mechanical and technical question types, in order to better your chances of successfully completing your test.

EXAMPLES OF MECHANICAL COMPREHENSION

Levers and Force

A lever consists of a bar which is balanced on a fixed point, known as the fulcrum.

If you needed to lift the weight, you would need to work out how to calculate the force needed.

Formula:

Force needed = (weight x distance from fulcrum to weight) ÷ distance from fulcrum point where force is being applied.

Example:

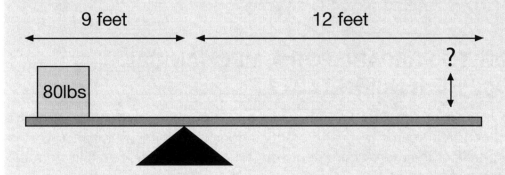

9 feet   12 feet

80lbs

?

- F = (weight x distance from fulcrum to weight) ÷ distance from fulcrum to point where force is being applied.
- F = (80 x 9) ÷ 12
- F = 720 ÷ 12
- F = 60 lbs

Answer:

60 lbs

Pulleys

Single and Double Pulleys

If the pulley is fixed, then the force required is equal to the weight. A simple way to work out how to calculate the force required is by dividing the weight by the number of sections of rope supporting it.

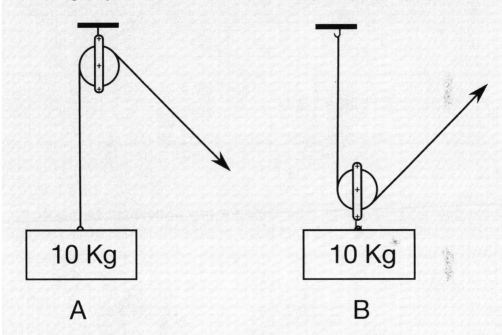

A

B

Diagram A = there is only one section of rope supporting the weight, therefore this can be worked out by = 10 ÷ 1 = 10.

Diagram B = there are two ropes supporting the weight, therefore this can be worked out by: 10 (weight) ÷ 2 (number of ropes supporting the weight) = 5.

Gears

If gears are connected by a chain or belt, then the gears will all move in the same direction.

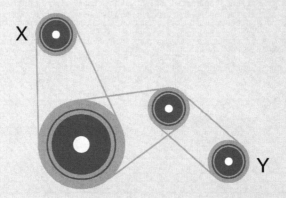

If the gears are touching, then adjacent gears move in the opposite direction. In the example below, X and Y will move in opposite directions.

MECHANICAL COMPREHENSION – TEST SECTION 1

Question 1

In electrical circuits, what does the below diagram represent?

A	B	C	D
Bulb	Battery	Resister	Switch

Question 2

If input effort is 600 ft.lb, what output effort will be produced by a machine with a mechanical advantage of 4?

Answer [   ]

Question 3

Which of the pendulums will swing at the fastest speed?

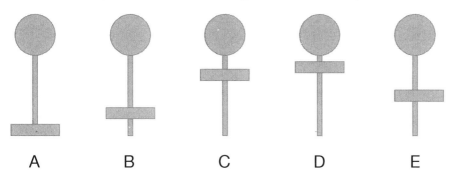

A   B   C   D   E

Answer [   ]

Question 4

At which point(s) should air enter the cylinder in order to force the piston downwards?

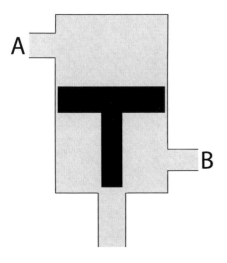

A	B	C
Point A	Point B	Points A and B

Question 5

At what point would the beam balance?

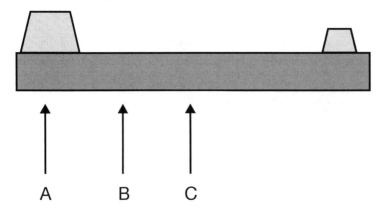

A	B	C
Point A	Point B	Point C

Question 6

How much weight is required to balance the load?

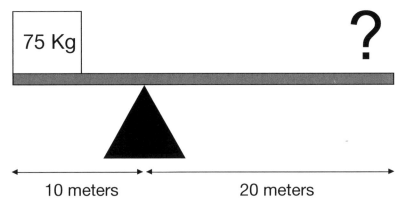

A	B	C	D
37.5 kg	75 kg	125.5 kg	150 kg

Question 7

If the gears in the diagram begin spinning anti-clockwise, what will happen to the spring that is attached to the wall?

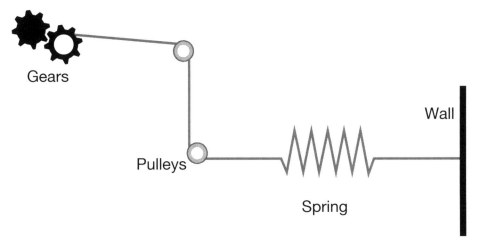

A	B	C	D
The spring will be compressed	The spring will stretch	The spring will touch the gears	Nothing

Question 8

Which tank will not empty?

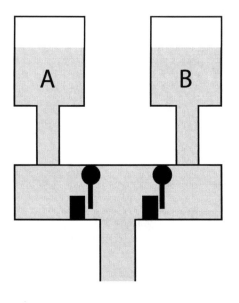

A	B	C
Tank A	Tank B	Both the same

Question 9

Which crane is working under the least tension?

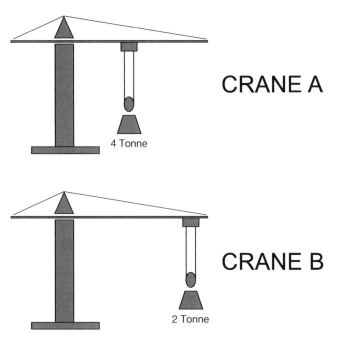

CRANE A

4 Tonne

CRANE B

2 Tonne

A	B	C
Crane A	Crane B	Both the same

Question 10

Which of the following statements will increase the mechanical advantage of this inclined plane?

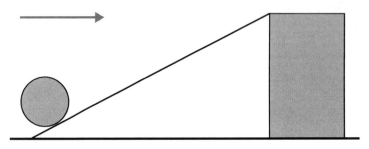

A – Shorten the length of the ramp.

B – Make the ramp longer.

C – Increase the slope of the ramp.

D - Lessen the force acting at the arrow.

Answer

Question 11

If the object on the left side of the scale is 72 ft. away from the balance point, i.e. the fulcrum, and a force is applied 8 ft. from the fulcrum on the right side, what is the mechanical advantage?

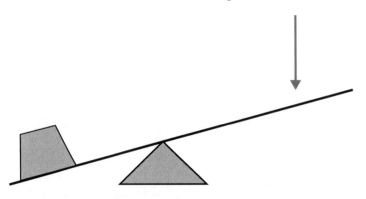

A	B	C	D
9	4.5	18	36

Question 12

Which type of beam can support the greatest load?

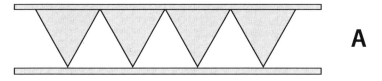 **A**

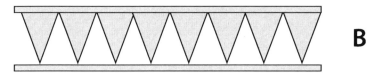 **B**

A	B	C
Beam A	Beam B	Both the same

Question 13

Which cog will make the most number of turns in 30 seconds?

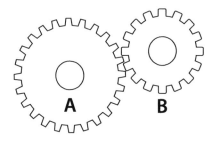

A	B	C
Cog A	Cog B	Both the same

Question 14

At what point would you need to place weight X in order for the scales to balance?

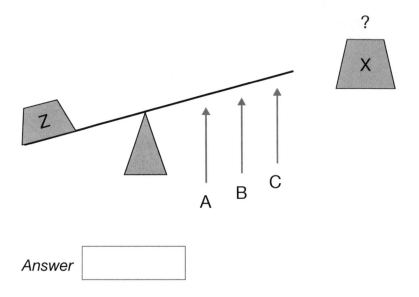

Answer [   ]

Question 15

A force of 15 kg compresses the springs. What will be the total distance that the springs are compressed?

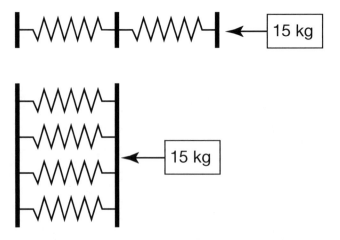

A	B	C	D
2.5 cm	10 cm	7.5 cm	4.5 cm

Question 16

How much force is required to move the following weight?

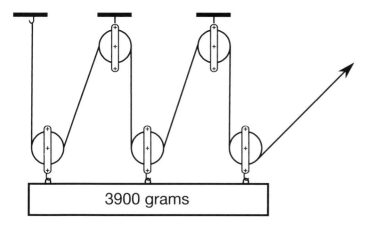

3900 grams

A	B	C	D
65 grams	1950 grams	650 grams	4000 grams

Question 17

Which weight requires the least amount of force?

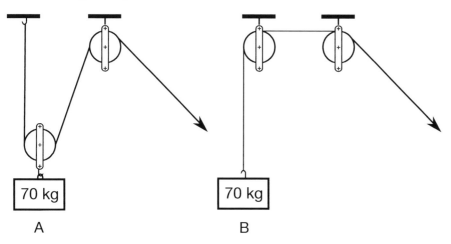

70 kg

A

70 kg

B

A	B	C
Both the same	A	B

Question 18

How many switches need to be closed to light up one bulb?

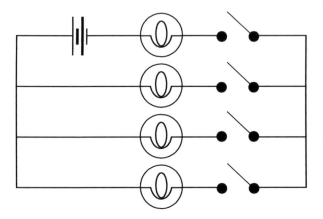

A	B	C	D
1	2	3	4

Question 19

In the diagram, the spring can be stretched 1 inch by a force of 200 pounds. How much force needs to be applied to the object in order to move the object 4.5 inches to the left?

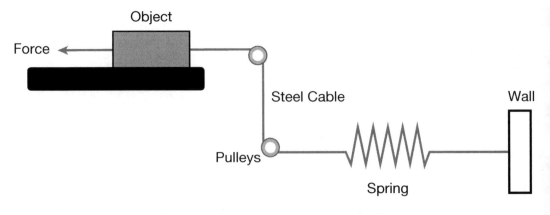

A	B	C	D
900 pounds	450 pounds	800 pounds	90 pounds

Question 20

What would happen if you placed an inflated balloon 15 feet below a water surface?

A – The volume of the balloon would increase.
B – The volume of the balloon would stay the same.
C – The balloon would explode.
D – The volume of the balloon would decrease.

Answer

Question 21

If bar X moves right at a constant speed, how does bar Y move?

A	B	C	D
Right, faster	Right, slower	Right, same	Left, same

Question 22

Which is the most suitable tool for breaking up concrete?

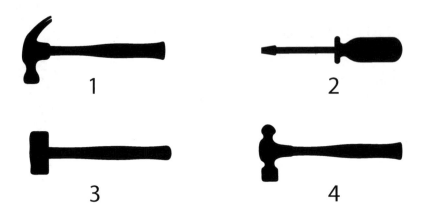

A	B	C	D
1	2	3	4

Question 23

Which hammer is most suitable for general work with metal?

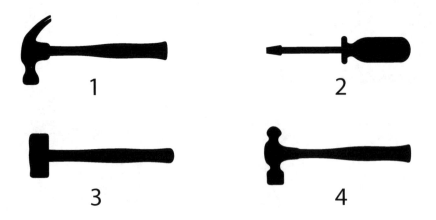

A	B	C	D
1	2	3	4

Question 24

If water was poured in at point Z, which tube would overfill first?

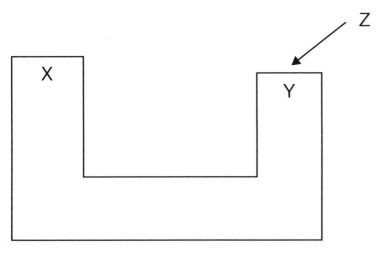

A	B	C
Tube X	Tube Y	Both the same

Question 25

Which of the shelves can carry the heaviest load?

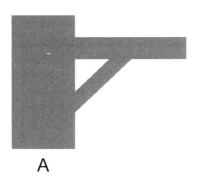

A

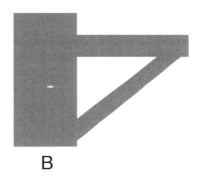

B

A	B	C
Shelf A	Shelf B	Both the same

Question 26

Which rope (A, B or C) would be easiest to pull the mass object over with?

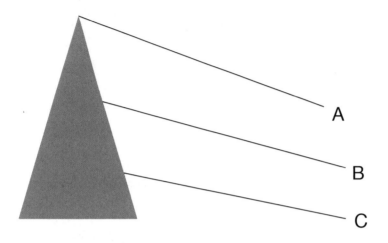

A	B	C	D
Rope A	Rope B	Rope C	Rope B and C

Question 27

At which point will the ball travel at its slowest speed?

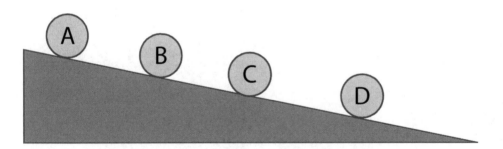

A	B	C	D	E
Ball C	Ball A	Ball D	Ball B	All the same

Question 28

If circle Y rotates anti-clockwise, what way will circle X rotate?

X 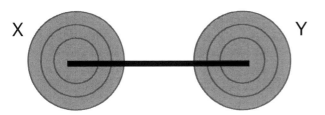 Y

A	B	C
Clockwise	Anti-clockwise	Cannot say

Question 29

In the diagram, two wheels attached by a belt drive have the ratio of 3 : 1. The smaller wheel has a 10cm circumference. How fast would the smaller wheel turn if the larger wheel turned at a rate of 450 rpm?

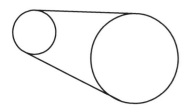

A	B	C	D
1300 rpm	1350 rpm	750 rpm	700 rpm

Question 30

How much force is required to lift the weights?

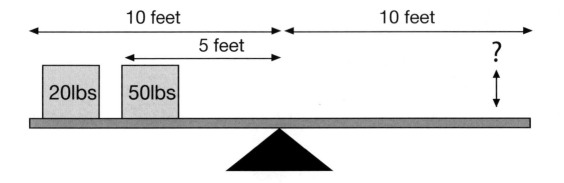

A	B	C	D
20 lbs	70 lbs	35 lbs	45 lbs

ANSWERS TO MECHANICAL COMPREHENSION – TEST SECTION 1

Q1. B = battery

EXPLANATION = the diagram is used to represent a battery.

Q2. A = 2400 ft. lb.

EXPLANATION = 600 x 4 = 2400 ft. lb.

Q3. D

EXPLANATION = the fastest swinging pendulum will be figure D. The position of the rectangle determines how fast the pendulum will swing. It will be at its slowest at Point A. The higher the rectangle, the faster it will swing.

Q4. A = point A

EXPLANATION = for air to be forced downwards, the air needs to enter the cylinder from Point A. If it was to enter from Point B, the air would be forced upwards.

Q5. B = Point B

EXPLANATION = the beam would balance at Point B.

Q6. A = 37.5 kg

EXPLANATION = the distance of the weights from the fulcrum/balance point is double; therefore, the weight required to balance the beam should be halved.

Q7. B = the spring will stretch

EXPLANATION = if the gears moved in an anti-clockwise manner, then the cable connecting everything is going to move left (towards the gears). As a result, the spring will stretch as the cable is being tightened.

Q8. B = Tank B

EXPLANATION = Tank B will not empty because the valve will not permit water to flow past it.

Q9. C = both the same

EXPLANATION = they are both under the same tension. Although the weight lifted by crane A is double that of crane B, the weight is closer to the centre of gravity.

Q10. B = make the ramp longer

EXPLANATION = In order to work out the mechanical advantage of an inclined plane, we must divide the effort of distance by the resistant distance. The ratio of this formula must increase, which means making the distance longer i.e. lengthening the ramp, would increase the mechanical advantage.

Q11. A = 9

EXPLANATION = the effort force where the weight is to be applied (where the arrow is pointing) is equal to the resistance weight of the object on the left side of the scales. To work out the mechanical advantage, you can use the following formula: divide the length of the effort by the length of the resistance. So, $72 \div 8 = 9$. Thus, the mechanical advantage is 9.

Q12 A = Beam A

EXPLANATION = Beam A is the strongest because each triangular section covers a greater surface area.

Q13. B = Cog B

EXPLANATION = the cog with the fewest teeth will make the most number of turns in any given time-frame. Because cog B has fewer teeth, it will complete more turns that cog A.

Q14. A

EXPLANATION = in order for the scales to balance, the weight would need to be positioned at point A.

Q15. C = 7.5 cm

EXPLANATION = in order for the springs to be compressed in parallel with one another, the springs will need to be compressed by half. Therefore, they will be compressed by 7.5 cm.

Q16. C = 650 grams

EXPLANATION = the weight of the object is 3900 grams. There are 6 sections (parts of the rope) supporting the weight. So, you need to divide 3900 by 6 to generate your answer. 3900 ÷ 6 = 650 grams.

Q17. B = A

EXPLANATION = Weight A requires a force equal to 37.5kg, whereas weight B requires a force equal to 70 kilograms.

Q18. B = 2

EXPLANATION = two switches need to be closed in order to light up one bulb. Two switches and one bulb makes up one complete circuit.

Q19. A = 900 pounds

EXPLANATION = 4.5 multiplied by 200 = 900 pounds.

Q20. D = the volume of the balloon would decrease

EXPLANATION = if you were to place a balloon full of air 15 feet under a water surface, the volume of the balloon would decrease. The pressure on the balloon from the water would press inwards, and therefore it would cause the balloon to shrink in size and subsequently decrease the volume of the balloon.

Q21. C = right, same

EXPLANATION = if bar X moves at a constant speed, then Bar Y will move in the same direction, at the same speed. The two large cogs are the same size, as are the two smaller cogs.

Q22. C= 3

EXPLANATION = the most suitable tool to break up concrete would be item number 3 (a sledge hammer).

Q23. D = 4

EXPLANATION = the most suitable hammer to work with metal is item number 4 (a ball-peen hammer).

Q24. B = tube Y

EXPLANATION = If water was being poured from point Z, tube y would overflow first as this is the shorter tube and will therefore overflow first.

Q25. B = shelf B

EXPLANATION = the shelf that is able to carry the most weight is shelf B. The bar underneath, holding the shelf up is positioned better in order to hold more weight. Shelf A has the diagonal bar positioned in the middle, and therefore a lot of weight on the shelf would cause the shelf to collapse on the right side.

Q26. A = Rope A

EXPLANATION = rope A is the best positioned to pull over the mass object. The rope is positioned at the mass' weakest point (the smallest point), and so it would be the easiest place to pull over the object.

Q27. B = Ball A

EXPLANATION = you need to work out which position the ball will be moving at the slowest speed. Note, this question is not asking you about four separate balls, it is asking you about one ball and each stage of the ball being rolled down the slope. So, the slowest point at which the ball will be rolling is point A; point D will be the fastest.

Q28. B = anti-clockwise

EXPLANATION = the straight line running through the centre of both circles indicate that both circles will rotate the same way. Therefore, both circles will be rotating anti-clockwise.

Q29. B = 1350 rpm

EXPLANATION = the large wheel rotates three times slower than the smaller wheel. So, if the larger wheel is rotating at 450 rpm, this means that the smaller wheel must be rotating at a rate three times faster. So, 450 x 3 = 1350 rpm.

Q30. D = 45 lbs

EXPLANATION = $f = (20 \times 10) + (50 \times 5) \div 10$
$f = (200) + (250) \div 10$
$f = 450 \div 10 = 45$ lbs.

MECHANICAL COMPREHENSION – TEST SECTION 2

Question 1

Which weight requires the most force to lift it?

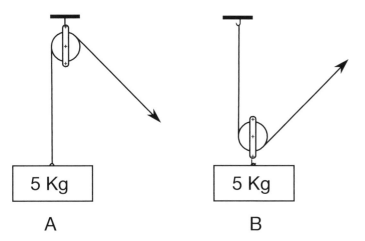

A	B	C
Both the same	A	B

Question 2

How much weight is required to balance point X?

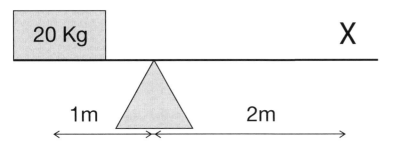

A	B	C	D
5Kg	10Kg	15Kg	20Kg

Question 3

If cog C turns anti-clockwise at a speed of 10rpm, which way and at what speed will cog B turn?

A	B	C	D
10rpm / anti-clockwise	10rpm / clockwise	20 rpm / anti-clockwise	20 rpm / clockwise

Question 4

Which tool would you use to claw nails from wood?

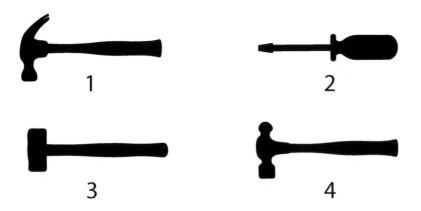

A	B	C	D
1	2	3	4

Question 5

If bulb 2 is removed, which bulbs will illuminate?

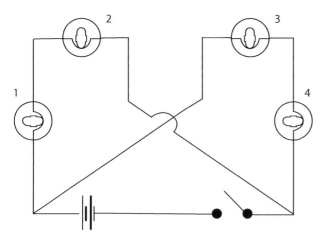

A	B	C	D
1	3	4	None

Question 6

When the switch is closed, how many bulbs will illuminate when bulb 3 is removed?

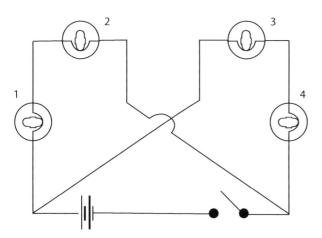

A	B	C	D
None	One	Two	Three

Question 7

If cog B turns anti-clockwise which way will cog A turn?

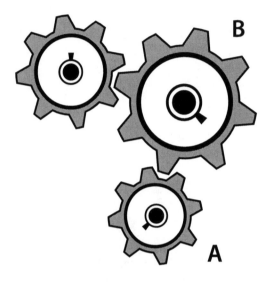

A	B
Clockwise	Anti-clockwise

Question 8

If wheel A is three times the diameter of wheel B, and rotates at 55rpm, what speed will wheel B rotate at?

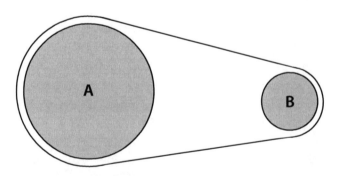

A	B	C
55 rpm	110 rpm	165 rpm

Question 9

How much force is required to lift the 75 kg weight?

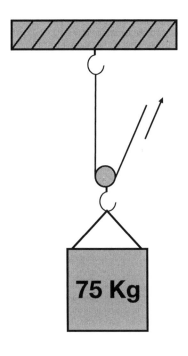

A	B	C	D
15 kg	37.5 kg	75 kg	150 kg

Question 10

A screw has 8 threads per inch. How many full turns are required for the nut to travel 3 inches?

A	B	C	D
8 turns	12 turns	16 turns	24 turns

Question 11

Cog A has 12 teeth and Cog B has 18 teeth. If cog B completes two full turns, how many rotations will Cog A complete?

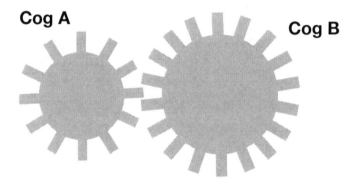

Cog A

Cog B

A	B	C	D
3 rotations	2 rotations	1.5 rotations	1 rotation

Question 12

If Cog 4 turns anti-clockwise, which other cogs will also turn anti-clockwise?

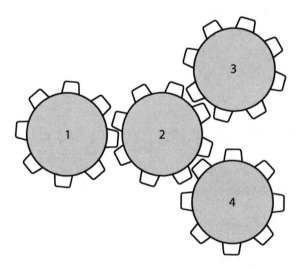

A	B	C	D
Cog 1 only	Cogs 1 and 3	Cog 3 only	Cogs 2 and 3

Question 13

A thick block of wood rests on an even and level, sandpaper surface. What mechanical principle makes it difficult to push this block sideways?

A	B	C	D
Spring force	Gravitational force	Air resistance force	Frictional force

Question 14

When water is poured in to a tank, what happens to the pressure on the surface?

A	B	C
Decreases	Stays the same	Increases

Question 15

The following three HGV's are parked on an incline. Their centre of gravity is identified by a dot. Which of the three HGV's is the most likely to fall over?

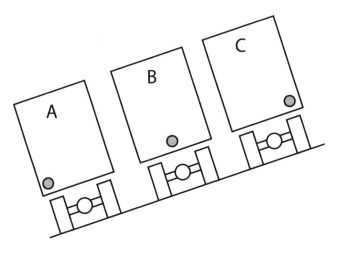

A	B	C
A	B	C

Question 16

Which of the following most resembles a lever?

A	B	C	D
Swing	Car	Elevator	Seesaw

Question 17

In which tube will the water rise the highest?

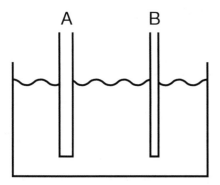

A	B	C	D
Tube A	Tube B	Both the same	Cannot say

Question 18

If the temperature remains constant, what will happen to the volume of trapped gas if the pressure is doubled?

A = the volume it occupies will reduce by 1/3.

B = the volume will double.

C = the volume will reduce by 1/4.

D = the volume will reduce by 1/2.

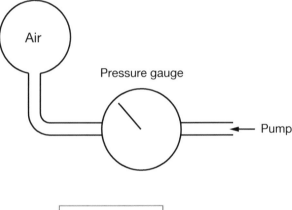

Answer

Question 19

How far would you have to pull the rope up to lift the weight 5 feet?

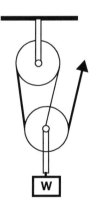

A	B	C	D
5 feet	10 feet	15 feet	30 feet

Question 20

If Cog X turns 40 times, how many times will Cog Y turn?

A	B	C	D
40 turns	80 turns	120 turns	160 turns

Question 21

Which gate is the strongest?

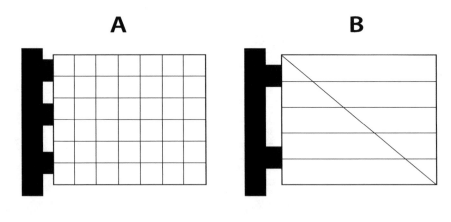

Answer

Question 22

Which of the following pulley systems has a mechanical advantage of 3?

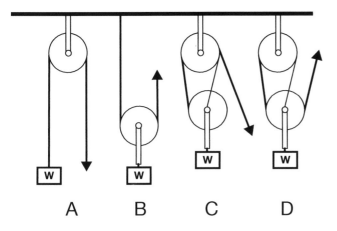

A	B	C	D	E
A and B	C and D	B and D	D	None

Question 23

Which direction should the wind blow in order for the plane to take off with the shortest runway?

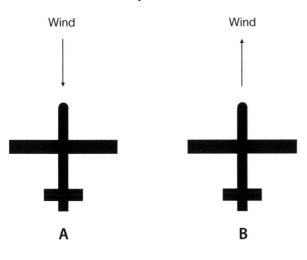

Answer

Question 24

Which wheel will rotate the least number of times in one hour?

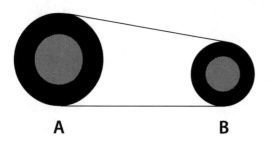

A   B

A	B
Wheel A	Wheel B

Question 25

What shape is the equilibrium?

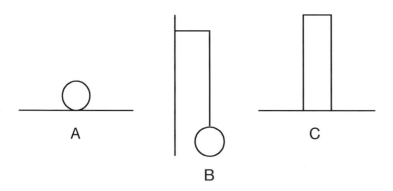

A   C

B

A	B	C	D
Shape A	Shape B	Shape C	All the same

Question 26

If cog C rotates clockwise at a speed of 120 rpm, at what speed and direction will cog A rotate? (rpm = revolutions per minute)

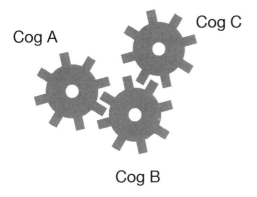

Cog C

Cog A

Cog B

A	B	C	D
120rpm clockwise	120rpm anti-clockwise	40rpm clockwise	40rpm anti-clockwise

Question 27

A cannonball is fired from a cannon horizontally. At the same time you drop a cannon ball of the same weight from the same height. Which will hit the ground first?

A	B	C
Dropped ball	Fired ball	Both the same

Question 28

How much weight in kilograms will need to be added in order to balance the beam?

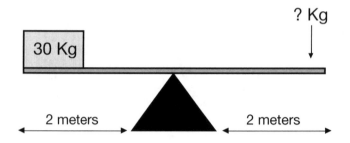

A	B	C	D
10 kg	15 kg	30 kg	60 kg

Question 29

How much weight in kilograms will need to be added in order to balance the beam?

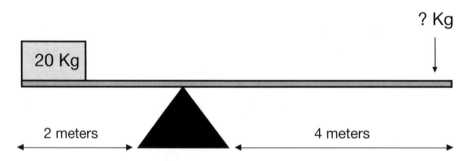

A	B	C	D
10 kg	20 kg	40 kg	80 kg

Question 30

How much weight in kilograms will need to be added in order to balance the beam?

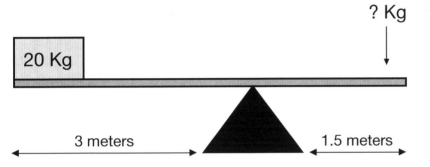

? Kg

20 Kg

3 meters   1.5 meters

A	B	C	D
10 kg	20 kg	30 kg	40 kg

ANSWERS TO MECHANICAL COMPREHENSION – TEST SECTION 2

Q1. B = A

EXPLANATION = If the pulley is fixed, then the force required to lift the weight is the same as the weight, i.e. 5kg. However, when the pulley system is not fixed and it moves with the weight, as is the case with pulley system B, then the weight required to lift it is half the weight. This means that the weight required to lift B is 2.5kg. The answer to the question is therefore answer option B.

Q2. B = 10 kg

EXPLANATION = Point X is twice the distance from the balance point; therefore, half the weight is required. The answer is B, 10Kg.

Q3. B = 10 rpm/clockwise

EXPLANATION = if cog C turns anti-clockwise at a speed of 10rpm, then cog B will rotate at the same speed; but in a clockwise direction.

Q4. A = 1

EXPLANATION = the only tool that you can use from the selection, to claw nails from wood, is hammer A.

Q5. D = none

EXPLANATION = no bulbs would illuminate because the circuit, in its current state, is not working. This is due to the switch being open.

Q6. C = two

EXPLANATION = only two bulbs would illuminate (bulbs 1 and 2). The broken circuit would prevent bulb 4 from illuminating.

Q7. A = clockwise

EXPLANATION = Cog A will turn clockwise.

Q8. C = 165 rpm

EXPLANATION = because wheel A is three times greater in diameter than wheel B, each revolution of A will lead to 3 times the revolution of B. Therefore, if wheel A rotates at 55 rpm, B will rotate at 55 rpm × 3 = 165 rpm.

Q9. B = 37.5 kg

EXPLANATION = this type of pulley system has a mechanical advantage of 2. Therefore, to lift the 75 kg weight will require 75 kg ÷ 2 = 37.5 kg.

Q10. D = 24 turns

EXPLANATION = there are 8 threads per inch. To move the nut 3 inches will require 8 × 3 = 24 turns.

Q11. A = 3 rotations

EXPLANATION = each full turn of cog B will result in 18 teeth ÷ 12 teeth = 1.5 rotations. Two turns of cog B will result in cog A completing 3 rotations.

Q12. B = cogs 1 and 3

EXPLANATION = Cogs 1 and 3 will turn anti-clockwise. Cog 2 is the only cog which will rotate clockwise.

Q13. D = frictional force

EXPLANATION = in this particular case, frictional force is the force that must be overcome in order to slide the object from one side to another.

Q14. B = stays the same

EXPLANATION = the pressure at the surface remains the same, since it has a finite amount of water above it.

Q15. A = A

EXPLANATION = by drawing a vertical line straight down from the centre of gravity, only the line for HGV A reaches the ground outside of its tyres. This makes the HGV unstable.

Q16. D = seesaw

EXPLANATION = a seesaw is the only option which utilises a form of leverage to function.

Q17. B = tube B

EXPLANATION = the force between the water and the glass is greater with the narrower tube, and therefore the water in tube B will rise higher.

Q18. D = the volume will reduce by ½

EXPLANATION = pressure x volume = constant figure.

Q19. C = 15 feet

EXPLANATION = you would need to lift the rope 15 feet in order to lift the weight 5 feet. 5 x 3 (supporting ropes) = 15 feet.

Q20. D = 160 turns

EXPLANATION = Cog X has a total of 20 teeth, whereas cog Y has a total of 5 teeth. Because cog Y has four times fewer teeth than cog X, it will rotate four times for every full rotation of cog X.

Q21. A

EXPLANATION = Gate A is the strongest because there are more strengthening points in the construction of the gate. There are also three supporting hinges as opposed to two on gate B.

Q22. D = D

EXPLANATION = only D has a mechanical advantage of 3, as it has three supporting ropes.

Q23. A

EXPLANATION = in order to take-off with the shortest runway, the aircraft will require a head wind.

Q24. A = wheel A

EXPLANATION = Wheel A is the largest and will therefore rotate the least number of times in any given time-frame.

Q25. D = all the same

EXPLANATION = all three are in the equilibrium state because none of them are moving.

Q26. A = 120 rpm/clockwise

EXPLANATION = Cog A will rotate 120 rpm clockwise. In this particular scenario, each cog has the same number of teeth; therefore, the cogs will rotate at the same speed.

Q27. C = both the same

EXPLANATION = they will both hit the ground at the same time.

Q28. C = 30 kg

EXPLANATION = the distance of the weights from the fulcrum/balance point is identical; therefore, the weight required to balance the beam should be identical.

Q29. A = 10 kg

EXPLANATION = the distance of the weights from the fulcrum/balance point is double; therefore, the weight required to balance the beam should be halved.

Q30. D = 40 kg

EXPLANATION = the distance of the weights from the fulcrum/balance point is halved; therefore, the weight required to balance the beam should be doubled.

CHECKING
TESTS

WHAT ARE CHECKING TESTS?

Checking tests are more commonly used during assessments for careers that require high levels of technical competency. You will normally be required to assess different dials or switches in order to identify where a particular fault lies. Alternatively, you may be required to use 'priority checking tables' to assist you during the analysis stage.

WHAT TO EXPECT

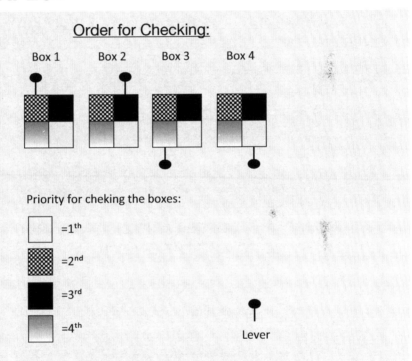

Order for Checking:

Box 1   Box 2   Box 3   Box 4

Priority for cheking the boxes:

= 1th

= 2nd

= 3rd

= 4th

Lever

For these types of questions, it is important to take the time and carefully look at the key you are given.

- For the above example, you will notice that box 4 would need to be checked first. This is because the lever has been placed in a white box (which indicates that it needs to be first priority for checking).

- The next box that would need to be checked is box 1, then box 2, and then box 3.

Answer

4123

Another type of test that you may be asked to complete in regards to Checking tests, are questions based on switches.

In the following question, you have to identify which of the switches is not working. The box on the left side contains four circles, each labelled A, B, C and D. A key to the switches and the function in which they perform is detailed below.

Which switch in the sequence is not working?

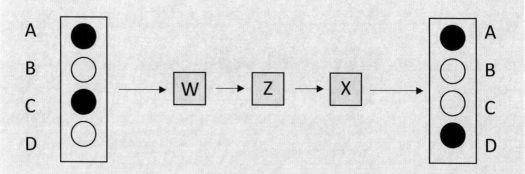

SWITCH   FUNCTION OF THE SWITCH

W   Turns A and C on/off
             i.e. Black to white and vice versa

X   Turns B and D on/off
             i.e. Black to white and vice versa

Y   Turns C and D on/off
             i.e. Black to white and vice versa

Z   Turns A and D on/off
             i.e. Black to white and vice versa

You will notice that the box on the left side contains black circles A and C, and white circled B and D at the start of the sequence. The first switch to operate is 'W', which has the effect of turning circles A and C from black to white, and vice versa. Once switch 'W' operates, the lights on the left will all be white.

The next switch to operate is switch Z, which has the effect of turning circles A and D from black to white and vice versa. Because the circles contained within the box on the left side are all white after the operation of switch W, this now means that circles A and D are black, and circles B and C are white.

You will notice that the box with the four circles located on the right side is now identical to this, which means that the next switch, switch X must be inoperative. If it was working correctly, then the box of circles on the right side would look different. Therefore, the correct answer to the question is Switch X.

CHECKING TESTS – TEST SECTION 1

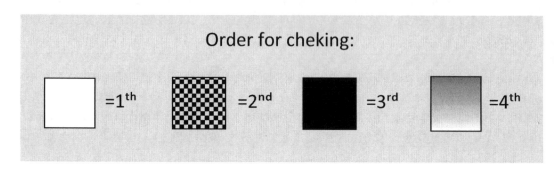

Order for cheking:

=1th =2nd =3rd =4th

For the following ten questions, write down the order in which the boxes should be checked using the 'Order for Checking' sequence above:

Question 1

Box 1   Box 2   Box 3   Box 4

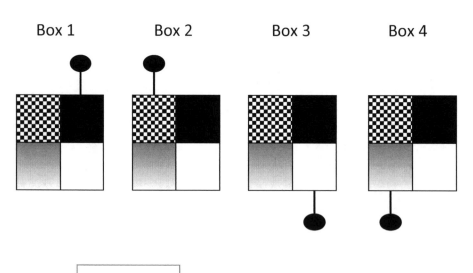

Answer

Question 2

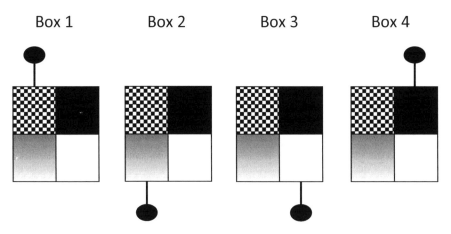

| Box 1 | Box 2 | Box 3 | Box 4 |

Answer

Question 3

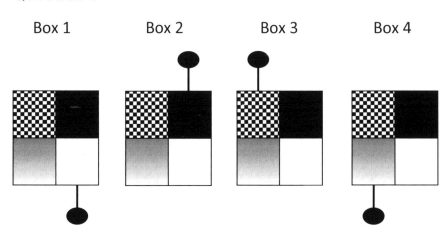

| Box 1 | Box 2 | Box 3 | Box 4 |

Answer

Question 4

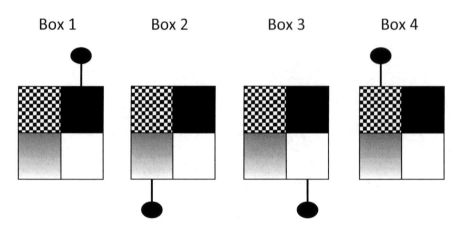

Answer

Question 5

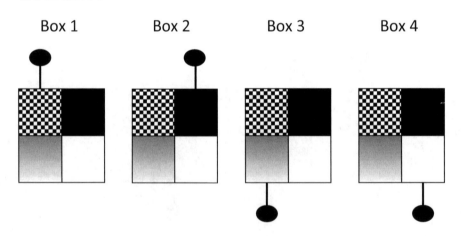

Answer

Question 6

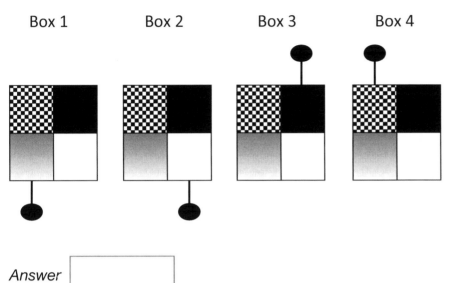

| Box 1 | Box 2 | Box 3 | Box 4 |

Answer

Question 7

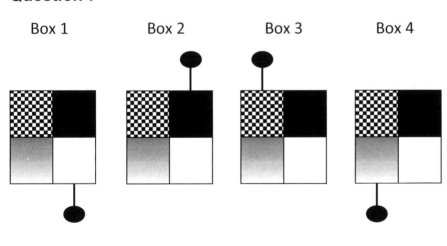

| Box 1 | Box 2 | Box 3 | Box 4 |

Answer

Question 8

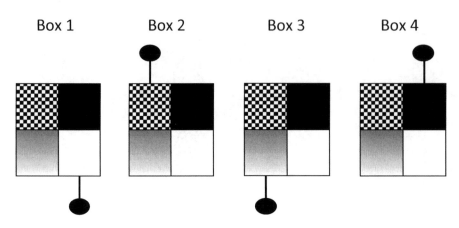

| Box 1 | Box 2 | Box 3 | Box 4 |

Answer [   ]

Question 9

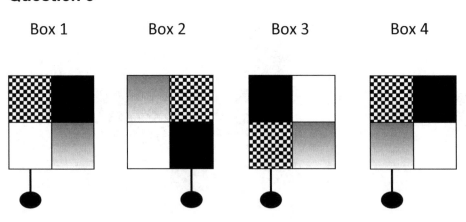

| Box 1 | Box 2 | Box 3 | Box 4 |

Answer [   ]

Question 10

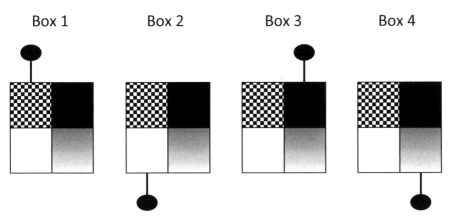

Box 1   Box 2   Box 3   Box 4

Answer

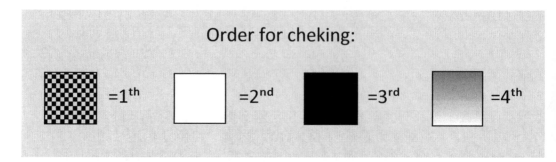

For the following five questions, write down the order in which the boxes should be checked using the 'Order for Checking' sequence above:

Question 11

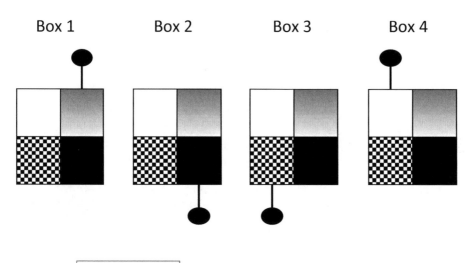

Answer ▢

Question 12

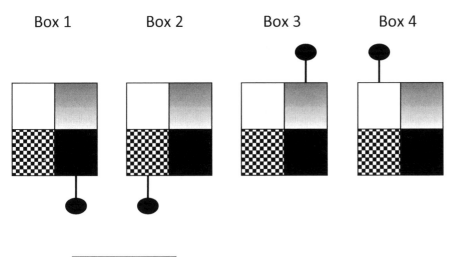

Box 1   Box 2   Box 3   Box 4

Answer

Question 13

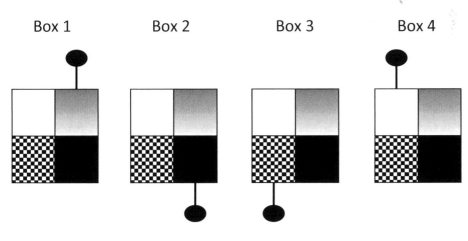

Box 1   Box 2   Box 3   Box 4

Answer

Question 14

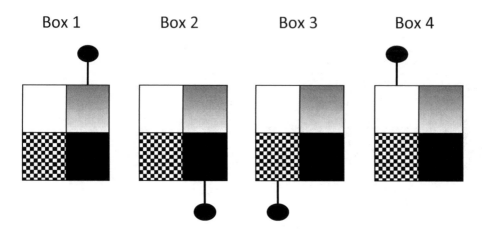

Answer

Question 15

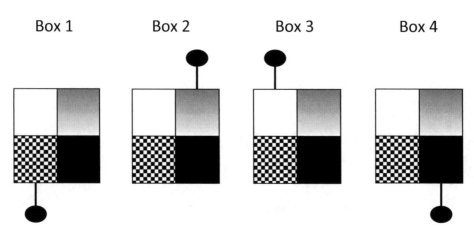

Answer

ANSWERS TO CHECKING TESTS – TEST SECTION 1

Q1. 3214

Q2. 3142

Q3. 1324

Q4. 3412

Q5. 4123

Q6. 2431

Q7. 1324

Q8. 1243

Q9. 1324

Q10. 2134

Q11. 3421

Q12. 2413

Q13. 3421

Q14. 3421

Q15. 1342

CHECKING TESTS – TEST SECTION 2

Question 1

Which switch in the sequence is not working?

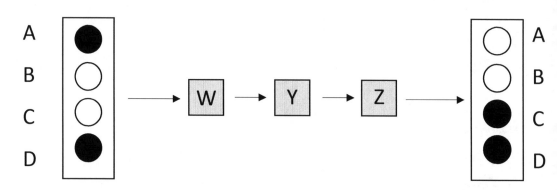

SWITCH   **FUNCTION OF THE SWITCH**

W   Turns A and C on/off
i.e. Black to white and vice versa

Y   Turns C and D on/off
i.e. Black to white and vice versa

Z   Turns A and D on/off
i.e. Black to white and vice versa

Answer _____

Question 2

Which switch in the sequence is not working?

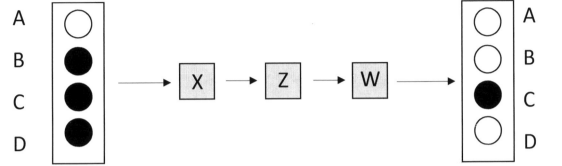

SWITCH   **FUNCTION OF THE SWITCH**

W   Turns A and C on/off
              i.e. Black to white and vice versa

X   Turns B and D on/off
              i.e. Black to white and vice versa

Z   Turns A and D on/off
              i.e. Black to white and vice versa

Answer

Question 3

Which switch in the sequence is not working?

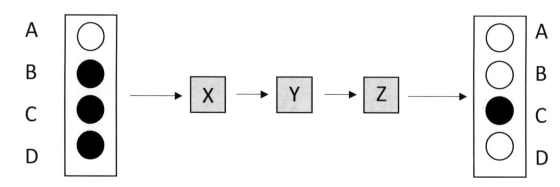

SWITCH   **FUNCTION OF THE SWITCH**

X   Turns B and D on/off
               i.e. Black to white and vice versa
Y   Turns C and D on/off
               i.e. Black to white and vice versa
Z   Turns A and D on/off
               i.e. Black to white and vice versa

Answer

Question 4

Which switch in the sequence is not working?

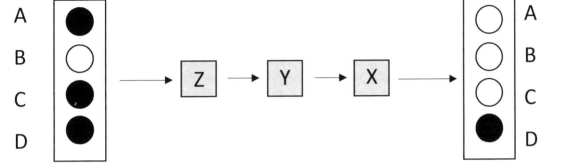

SWITCH   **FUNCTION OF THE SWITCH**

X   Turns B and D on/off
         i.e. Black to white and vice versa
Y   Turns C and D on/off
         i.e. Black to white and vice versa
Z   Turns A and D on/off
         i.e. Black to white and vice versa

Answer

Question 5

Which switch in the sequence is not working?

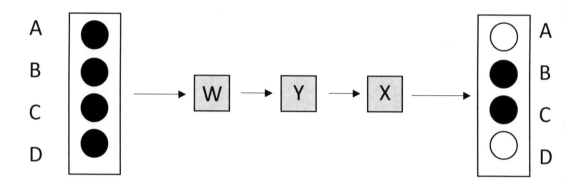

SWITCH   **FUNCTION OF THE SWITCH**

W   Turns A and C on/off
                 i.e. Black to white and vice versa
X   Turns B and D on/off
                 i.e. Black to white and vice versa
Y   Turns C and D on/off
                 i.e. Black to white and vice versa

Answer [   ]

Question 6

Which switch in the sequence is not working?

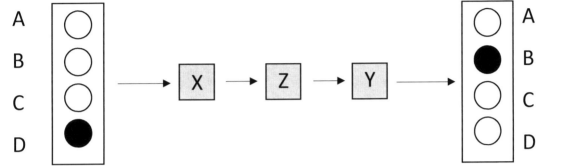

SWITCH **FUNCTION OF THE SWITCH**

X   Turns B and D on/off
           i.e. Black to white and vice versa
Y   Turns C and D on/off
           i.e. Black to white and vice versa
Z   Turns A and D on/off
           i.e. Black to white and vice versa

Answer

Question 7

Which switch in the sequence is not working?

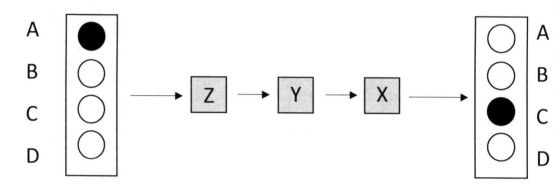

SWITCH   **FUNCTION OF THE SWITCH**

X   Turns B and D on/off
               i.e. Black to white and vice versa
Y   Turns C and D on/off
               i.e. Black to white and vice versa
Z   Turns A and D on/off
               i.e. Black to white and vice versa

Answer [   ]

Question 8

Which switch in the sequence is not working?

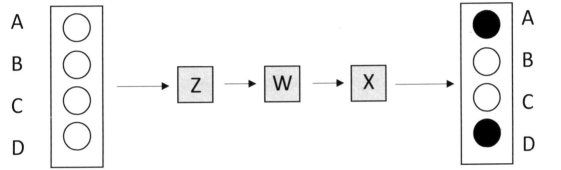

SWITCH   **FUNCTION OF THE SWITCH**

W   Turns A and C on/off
                i.e. Black to white and vice versa

X   Turns B and D on/off
                i.e. Black to white and vice versa

Z   Turns A and D on/off
                i.e. Black to white and vice versa

Answer

Question 9

Which switch in the sequence is not working?

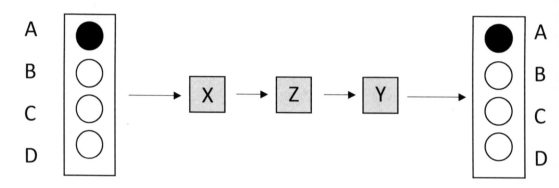

SWITCH **FUNCTION OF THE SWITCH**

X Turns B and D on/off
i.e. Black to white and vice versa

Y Turns C and D on/off
i.e. Black to white and vice versa

Z Turns A and D on/off
i.e. Black to white and vice versa

Answer

Question 10

Which switch in the sequence is not working?

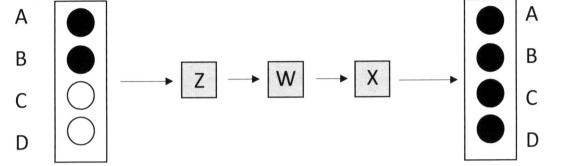

SWITCH   **FUNCTION OF THE SWITCH**

W   Turns A and C on/off
               i.e. Black to white and vice versa
X   Turns B and D on/off
               i.e. Black to white and vice versa
Z   Turns A and D on/off
               i.e. Black to white and vice versa

Answer

Question 11

Which switch in the sequence is not working?

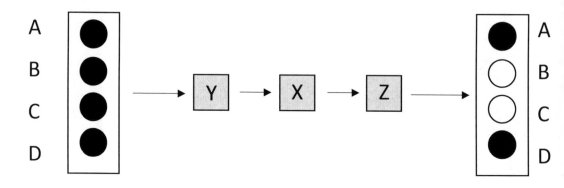

SWITCH **FUNCTION OF THE SWITCH**

X Turns B and D on/off
   i.e. Black to white and vice versa
Y Turns C and D on/off
   i.e. Black to white and vice versa
Z Turns A and D on/off
   i.e. Black to white and vice versa

Answer _____

Question 12

Which switch in the sequence is not working?

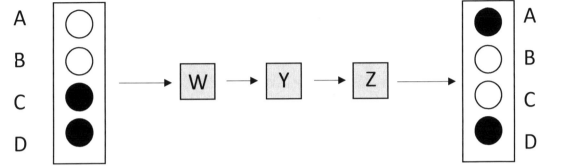

SWITCH	FUNCTION OF THE SWITCH
W	Turns A and C on/off i.e. Black to white and vice versa
Y	Turns C and D on/off i.e. Black to white and vice versa
Z	Turns A and D on/off i.e. Black to white and vice versa

Answer

Question 13

Which switch in the sequence is not working?

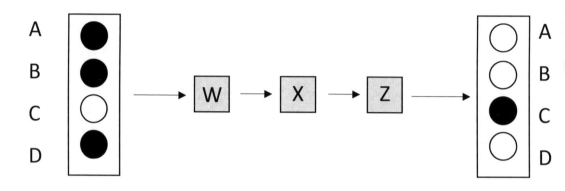

SWITCH **FUNCTION OF THE SWITCH**

W   Turns A and C on/off
             i.e. Black to white and vice versa
X   Turns B and D on/off
             i.e. Black to white and vice versa
Z   Turns A and D on/off
             i.e. Black to white and vice versa

Answer [   ]

Question 14

Which switch in the sequence is not working?

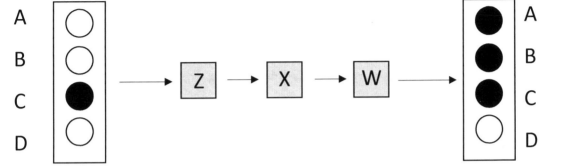

SWITCH **FUNCTION OF THE SWITCH**

W Turns A and C on/off
   i.e. Black to white and vice versa
X Turns B and D on/off
   i.e. Black to white and vice versa
Z Turns A and D on/off
   i.e. Black to white and vice versa

Answer

Question 15

Which switch in the sequence is not working?

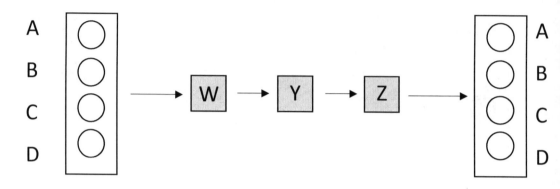

SWITCH **FUNCTION OF THE SWITCH**

W   Turns A and C on/off
        i.e. Black to white and vice versa

Y   Turns C and D on/off
        i.e. Black to white and vice versa

Z   Turns A and D on/off
        i.e. Black to white and vice versa

Answer

ANSWERS TO CHECKING TESTS – TEST SECTION 2

Q1. Switch Y

EXPLANATION = the first switch to operate is 'W', which has the effect of turning circles A and C from black to white, and vice versa. Once switch 'W' operates, circles C and D will be black. **You will notice that the box on the right side is now identical to this, which means the next switch, switch Y, must be inoperative.**

Q2. Switch Z

EXPLANATION = the first switch to operate is 'X', which has the effect of turning circles B and D from black to white, and vice versa. Once switch 'X' operates, circle B changes from black to white, and circle D changes from black to white. (This gives you the image on the right). **You will notice that the box on the right side is now identical to this, which means the next switch, switch Z, must be inoperative.**

Q3. Switch Y

EXPLANATION = the first switch to operate is 'X', which has the effect of turning circles B and D from black to white, and vice versa. Once switch 'X' operates, circle C is the only circle that is black. **You will notice that the box on the right side is now identical to this, which means the next switch, switch Y, must be inoperative.**

Q4. Switch X

EXPLANATION = the first switch to operate is 'Z', which has the effect of turning circles A and D from black to white, and vice versa. Once switch 'Z' operates, only circle C will be black. The next switch to operate is switch Y, which has the effect of turning circles C and D from black to white and vice versa. Once switch Y operates, only circle D will be black. **You will notice that the box on the right side is now identical to this, which means the next switch, switch X, must be inoperative.**

Q5. Switch X

EXPLANATION = the first switch to operate is 'W', which has the effect of turning circles A and C from black to white, and vice versa. Once switch 'W' operates, only circles B and D will be black. The next switch to operate is switch Y, which has the effect of turning circles C and D from black to white, and vice versa. Once switch Y operates, only circles B and C will be black. **You will notice that the box on the right side is now identical to this, which means the next switch, switch X, must be inoperative.**

Q6. Switch Z

EXPLANATION = the first switch to operate is 'X', which has the effect of turning circles B and D from black to white, and vice versa. Once switch 'X' operates, only circle B will be black. **You will notice that the box on the right side is now identical to this, which means the next switch, switch Z, must me inoperative.**

Q7. Switch X

EXPLANATION = the first switch to operate is 'Z', which has the effect of turning circles A and D from black to white, and vice versa. Once switch 'Z' operates, only circle D will be black. The next switch to operate is switch 'Y', which has the effect of turning circles C and D from black to white, and vice versa. Once switch 'Y' operates, only circle C will be black. **You will notice that the box on the right side is now identical to this, which means the next switch, switch X, must be inoperative.**

Q8. Switch W

EXPLANATION = the first switch to operate is 'Z', which has the effect of turning circles A and D from black to white, and vice versa. Once switch 'Z' operates, only circles A and D will be black. **You will notice that the box on the right side is now identical to this, which means the next switch, switch W, must be inoperative.**

Q9. Switch X

EXPLANATION = the first switch to operate is 'X', which has the effect of turning circles B and D from black to white, and vice versa. You will notice that the start of the sequence has only circle A that is black; and this is identical to the end of the sequence, whereby only circle A is black. **This means that the first switch in the sequence, switch X, must be inoperative.**

Q10. Switch X

EXPLANATION = the first switch to operate is 'Z', which has the effect of turning circles A and D from black to white, and vice versa. Once switch 'Z' operates, only circles B and D will be black. The next switch to operate is 'W', which has the effect of turning circles A and C from black to white, and vice versa. Once switch 'W' operates, all of the circles will be black. **You will notice that the box on the right side is now identical to this, which means the next switch, switch X, must be inoperative.**

Q11. Switch Z

EXPLANATION = the first switch to operate is 'Y', which has the effect of turning circles C and D from black to white, and vice versa. Once switch 'Y' operates, only circles A and B will be black. The next switch to operate is 'X', which has the effect of turning circles B and D from black to white, and vice versa. Once switch 'X' operates, only circles A and D will be black. **You will notice that the box on the right side is now identical to this, which means the next switch, switch Z, must be inoperative.**

Q12. Switch Y

EXPLANATION = the first switch to operate is 'W', which has the effect of turning circles A and C from black to white, and vice versa. Once switch 'W' operates, only circles A and D will be black. **You will notice that the box on the right side is now identical to this, which means the next switch, switch Y, must be inoperative.**

Q13. Switch Z

EXPLANATION = the first switch to operate is 'W', which has the effect of turning circles A and C from black to white, and vice versa. Once switch 'W' operates, only circles B, C and D will be black. The next switch to operate is 'X', which has the effect of turning circles B and D from black to white, and vice versa. Once switch 'X' operates, only circle C will be black. **You will notice that the box on the right side is now identical to this, which means the next switch, switch Z, must be inoperative.**

Q14. Switch W

EXPLANATION = the first switch to operate is 'Z', which has the effect of turning circles A and D from black to white, and vice versa. Once switch 'Z' operates, only circles A, C and D will be black. The next switch to operate is 'X', which has the effect of turning circles B and D from black to white, and vice versa. Once switch 'X' operates, circles A, B and C will be black. **You will notice that the box on the right side is now identical to this, which means the next switch, switch W, must be inoperative.**

Q15. Switch W

EXPLANATION = the first switch to operate is 'W', which has the effect of turning circles A and C from black to white, and vice versa. You will notice that the start of the sequence contains zero black circles, and this is the same for the end of the sequence. **This means that the first switch in the sequence, switch W, must be inoperative.**

A FEW
FINAL WORDS...

You have now reached the end of your Psychometric testing guide. We have no doubt that you will feel more competent in a variety of different testing formats. We hope you have found this guide an invaluable insight into the different types of psychometric testing that you could face during job selection processes.

For any psychometric test, there are a few things to remember to help you perform at your best...

REMEMBER – THE THREE P'S!

1. **Preparation.** This may seem relatively obvious, but you will be surprised by how many people fail psychometric testing because they lacked preparation and knowledge regarding their test. You want to do your utmost to ensure the best possible chance of succeeding. Be sure to conduct as much preparation prior to your assessment, to ensure you are 100% prepared to complete the test successfully. Not only will practising guarantee improved scores, but it will also take some of the pressure off leading up to that all important test. Like anything, the more you practice, the more likely you are to succeed.

2. **Perseverance.** Everybody comes across times whereby they are setback or find obstacles in the way of their goals. The important thing to remember when this happens, is to use those setbacks and obstacles as a way of progressing. If you fail at something, consider 'why' you have failed. This will allow you to improve and enhance your performance for next time.

3. **Performance.** Your performance will determine whether or not you are likely to succeed. Attributes that are often associated with performance are **self-belief**, **motivation** and **commitment**. Self-belief is important for anything you do in life. It allows you to recognise your own abilities and skills and believe that you can do well. Believing that you can do well is half the battle! Being fully motivated and committed is often difficult for some people, but we can assure you that, nothing is gained without hard work and determination. If you want to succeed, you will need to put in that extra time and hard work.